The New Generation Z in Asia

THE CHANGING CONTEXT OF MANAGING PEOPLE

Series Editor: Professor Emma Parry, Cranfield School of Management

The New Generation Z in Asia: Dynamics, Differences, Digitalisation

EDITED BY

ELODIE GENTINA
IESEG School of Management, France

EMMA PARRY
Cranfield School of Management, United Kingdom

emerald
PUBLISHING

United Kingdom – North America – Japan – India – Malaysia – China

Emerald Publishing Limited
Howard House, Wagon Lane, Bingley BD16 1WA, UK

First edition 2020

Reprints and permissions service
Contact: permissions@emeraldinsight.com

British Library Cataloguing in Publication Data
A catalogue record for this book is available from the British Library

ISBN: 978-1-80043-221-5 (Print)
ISBN: 978-1-80043-220-8 (Online)
ISBN: 978-1-80043-222-2 (Epub)
ISBN: 978-1-80043-223-9 (Pbk.)

INVESTOR IN PEOPLE

Contents

Dedication

Many researchers, teachers, and students who are part of the international scientific community probably once came across the name of Christian Scholz. As a university professor from Saarbrücken, Germany, his oeuvre covered various disciplines in social science, such as business-related human resource management, information management, and media management, conflating it with psychological, historical, and sociological references. Since 2014, when he started his topical journey with a seminal book (Wiley, 2014), he was one of the first international researchers profoundly focussing on the 'Generation Z', its characteristics, qualities, attitudes, preferences, and expectations towards employers and society. This focus on Generation Z directed his attention to Southeast Asia and its young generation ready to shape the future.

Through this book, I pay tribute to Christian Scholz who passed away 4 October 2019 at the age of 66. It would have never been written without the expertise and effort of Christian. In 2017, he brought together various researchers and young academics in a conference in Bangkok to discuss the particularities of the Generation Z in Asia. In his research, Christian pursued the idea that there is globally more than one type of Generation Z and that the cross-cultural differences could be identified. Based on our mutual interest, I made friends with Christian, and we both decided to bring our knowledge together in the first book on Generation Z in Asia. I would have very much loved to finalise it and celebrate its release together with him.

Christian Scholz was a researcher of great intellectual originality and his deep knowledge of Generation Z around the world – his research trips on this topic took him across Europe, America, Africa, and Asia that were reflected in further international publications, among them 'Generation Z in Europe' (Emerald, 2019) – made him a respected researcher in our academic community. Beyond that, he published far more than 20 scientific books and more than 670 journal articles.

In addition to his scientific competence which characterised him, to his great intellectual curiosity and to his immense and remarkable scholarliness, he was very sympathetic, friendly, pleasant, and generous. The academic community will always remember Christian Scholz with honour and gratitude.

Today, I dedicate this work to you, Christian!

Elodie Gentina

About the Contributors

Editors

Elodie Gentina is an Associate Professor of Marketing at IESEG School of Management in France. Her principal research interests lie in Generation Z and consumer behaviour/management. She is the author of two books on Generation Z (Dunod). She has published many articles on Generation Z in *Journal of Business Research*, *Journal of Business Ethics*, *Information and Management*, and *Computers and Education*. She regularly presents papers at international conferences, including Europe, United States, and Asia-Pacific. She is also the CEO E&G Consulting Group, specialising in Generation Z (Management). She acts as a consultant to numerous companies on management, Human Resource issues.

Emma Parry is a Professor of Human Resource Management and Head of the Changing World of Work Group at Cranfield School of Management in the United Kingdom. Her research interests focus on the impact of the changing context on work, the workplace, and the workforce, specifically the influence of national context, changing workforce demographics, and technological advancement. She has published several books and numerous peer reviewed articles in these areas, including several that focus on generational diversity. She is a Fellow of the British Academy of Management, an Academic Fellow of the Chartered Institute of Personnel and Development, and an Honorary Fellow of the Institute for Employment Studies, as well as a Visiting Fellow at Westminster Business School.

Chapter Authors

Muhamad Irfan Agia is a Consumer Psychologist who holds a Master's Degree in Economic and Consumer Psychology from Leiden University, Netherlands. He applies insights from psychology and behavioural economy to better understand consumer behaviour, decision-making, and behaviour change.

Nisreen Ameen is a Lecturer in Marketing at Royal Holloway, University of London. Her research interests include digital marketing, human–computer interaction, consumer behaviour, artificial intelligence enabled customers service, security and ethics of retailers use of consumers' data, digital education, and e-business and technology adoption.

Amitabh Anand is an Assistant Professor at SKEMA Business School, Université Côte d'Azur, France. His research interests are in human behaviour in a multidisciplinary context and discovering new ways to perform scientific reviews and has won several awards in research. Furthermore, his works are published in leading management journals and he is also part of the editorial advisory/review board of *Management Decision* and *Employee Relations.*

Adilla Anggraeni is currently a Faculty Member of Binus Business School, Bina Nusantara University International Undergraduate Programme. She received her doctoral degree from the University of Indonesia. Her research interests include consumer behaviour, retail management, tourism marketing, and luxury branding. She has published several articles in *International Journal of Business and Information Management, Pertanika Social Science,* as well as *International Journal of Online Marketing.*

Ryan Brading is an Assistant Professor at the College of Management, National Sun Yat-sen University, Kaohsiung, Taiwan. During his PhD research in the Ideology of Discourse Analysis Programme, University of Essex, England, he was trained as a political scientist. He also learned business management skills during his postgraduate studies at Royal Holloway, University of London. His publications and research interests are about populist practices, student movements, youth's apolitical attitude distrust of traditional party politics, and ambitions.

Shaheema Hameed is an Assistant Professor (Management), Banasthali Vidyapith, India. Her doctoral research focussed on the managerial competencies of the Generation Z. She has presented her research work in various national and international forums. Her areas of specialisation are human resource management, organisational behaviour, and business communication.

Zahrotur Rusyda Hinduan or Rosie is an Associate Professor at the Faculty of Psychology Universitas Padjadjaran, Bandung, West Java, Indonesia. She received her PhD degree from the Department of Work and Social Psychology, Maastricht University, The Netherlands. Her research areas focus on the behaviours of young people in work and health settings as well as the behavioural intervention. She has also demonstrated history of working in the higher education management.

Jiyoung Hwang is an Associate Professor of Marketing at Bryan School of Business and Economics, University of North Carolina at Greensboro, United States. She holds her PhD in Retailing and Consumer Studies from Ohio State University and MS in International Retailing from Michigan State University. Her research interests include the impact of cross-cultural consumer behaviours and global branding. She has published articles in *European Journal of Marketing, Journal of Business Research, Journal of Small Business Management,* and *Journal of Services Marketing,* among others. She also wrote a book, *The Future of Retail Business: How Technology Has Reshaped Consumption.*

Ahmad Jamal is a Reader in Marketing and Strategy, and the Deputy Head of Section, Learning, and Teaching (Marketing) at Cardiff University Business School, United Kingdom. His research interests include exploring the interplay among culture, ethnicity and consumption in offline, and online digital contexts. His work has appeared in scholarly journals such as *Journal of Business Research*, *European Journal of Marketing*, or *Information Systems Frontiers*. He is the co-author for *Routledge Companion to Ethnic Marketing*. He has presented his work at many international conferences across the world.

Yunus Kalender is an undergraduate student in the Department of Business Administration, TOBB University of Economics and Technology, Ankara, Turkey. He is continuing his education with specialisation on marketing and consumer behaviour. He intends to pursue his academic career in the same field. At the same time, he engages in assisting business projects by collecting and analysing data and guiding start-up firms build their marketing and branding plans. His main research interests include the interaction between and among consumers and markets. For instance, he is working on a research project on how consumers build romantic relationships or develop relationship habits by utilising consumption objects and services available on the market.

Ghazala Khan, PhD, is a Lecturer at Monash University Malaysia. She has over 23 years in tertiary education in Malaysia. She has won numerous teaching awards including the Best Lecturer Award for School of Business under the Monash University Student Association. Her research interests lie in Islamic marketing, consumer socialisation, and pedagogy. She has presented her work at numerous international conferences and published in international refereed journals, such as *Journal of Islamic Marketing and International Journal of Business and Globalisation*.

Vimala Kunchamboo, PhD, is a Lecturer at Monash University Malaysia in the Marketing Department. Her research interest focusses on consumer behaviour and marketing, specifically on areas related to sustainable consumption and self-identity. She has research manuscripts published in some of the top marketing journals and conferences such as *Journal of Business Research* and *The Association of Consumer Research*.

Meera Mathur is a Professor (Management) at MLS University, Udaipur, India. She has a vast teaching and research experience of over 20 years. Her research papers have been presented at various conferences and seminars and are published in reputed national and international journals. Her research interests are human resource management, consumer behaviour, and environmental sustainability.

Hoa Phuong Nguyen is a Lecturer in the Department of Publication and Distribution, Hanoi University of Culture, Vietnam. She has completed her Master in Management in University of Technology in Vietnam and has over 18 years of teaching experience. Her specialisation is applied mathematics and business strategy. She is active in consulting and training for various businesses in the nation. Her research area concerns market analyses and pricing methods for technology products in Vietnam. She has co-authored several ministry-funded applied research projects and book chapters for local university's press.

Linh Hoang Nguyen is a Lecturer at Hanoi Open University, Faculty of Tourism, Vietnam. He has completed his Master in Management at IESEG School of Management and is currently pursuing his PhD degree in University of Lille, France. His doctoral dissertation addresses advertising efficiency in smartphone. His research interest lies in the behaviours of Vietnamese consumers in a modern context, especially in digital communication and green consumption. He has published in various international academic journals and presented his work at several international conferences, such as Young Consumers, OMEE, Macro Marketing Conference, and CERR.

Mototaka Sakashita is a Professor of Marketing at Graduate School of Business Administration, Keio University and Keio Business School, Japan. He obtained his PhD from Kobe University (Japan) in 2004 and worked at Sophia University (Japan) as an Assistant Professor from 2004 to 2007. He has been a Faculty Member at Keio University since 2007. He was a Research Fellow of the Retail Analytics Council at Northwestern University from 2015 to 2018, and has been a research affiliate of the Spiegel Digital & Database Research Center at Northwestern University since 2018. He serves as an editorial board of International Journal of Marketing & Distribution since 2019. His research interests include consumer behaviour, retail management, brand management, and integrated marketing communications.

Berna Tarı-Kasnakoğlu is an Associate Professor of Marketing at TOBB University of Economics and Technology, Ankara, Turkey. She is a Consumer Behaviour Researcher in Turkey. She obtained her PhD degree in Marketing from Bilkent University, where she focussed on the (medical) consumption of aesthetic surgery and qualitative research methodologies. Her research interests particularly focus on patient–consumer behaviour, co-creation, and service relationships.

Fandy Tjiptono is currently a Senior Lecturer at the School of Marketing and International Business, Victoria University of Wellington (VUW), New Zealand. Prior to joining VUW, he was an Academic Staff at Monash University Malaysia. His main research interest is consumer behaviour and marketing practices in Southeast Asia. His research has been published in several reputable journals such as *Journal of Business Ethics*, *European Journal of Marketing*, and *Journal of Retailing and Consumer Services*, among others.

Meltem Türe is a Senior Lecturer in Marketing at Royal Holloway, University of London, United Kingdom. She received her PhD in Marketing from Bilkent University in Turkey. Her research interests involve sustainability and waste, value, ethical consumption, and ideology. She has published her work in journals such as *Journal of Consumer Research, Journal of Business Research, Consumption Markets & Culture,* and *Marketing Theory* as well as in edited book chapters. She has been teaching marketing courses including marketing principles, consumer behaviour, ethical marketing, research writing, and marketing research at undergraduate and graduate levels.

Ying Wang is an Assistant Professor of Economics at the School of International Economics and Trade at Jiangxi University of Finance and Economics, Nanchang, China. Her research focusses on culture and trade. Her work has appeared in prestigious academic journals in China, such as *Journal of International Trade and Contemporary Finance and Economics.* She also has published a monograph titled *Research on the Cultural Trade Policy of China.*

Zhiyong Yang is a Professor of Marketing and Department Head of the Department of Marketing, Entrepreneurship, Sustainable Tourism and Hospitality at the University of North Carolina Greensboro. His research focusses on consumer decision-making. His work has appeared in over 30 journals, including the *Journal of Marketing, Journal of Consumer Research,* and *Journal of the Academy of Marketing Science.* His research has been funded by Statistics Canada, FQRSC Canada, and NSF China. He serves on the guest editorship and the editorial review boards of several reputed journals. He also received competitive research awards from Harvard Center for Risk Analysis, the University of Texas-Arlington, and Cardiff University.

Ewe Soo Yeong is a Lecturer at Monash University Malaysia. Her specialties lie in consumer psychology and experimental research methods. Her current research interest is in consumer decision making, specifically irrational behaviour in decision making. Her other areas of research interest include information processing and message framing. Her multidisciplinary training in economics, finance and marketing is particularly useful when solving research problems. Her work has been published in respected journals such as *Marketing Intelligence and Planning* and *Journal of Behavioral Finance.*

Melannie Zhan is a Part-Time Lecturer. She received her PhD in Communication and MSocSc in Media Management at Hong Kong Baptist University. Her research areas mainly lie in the field of advertising, health communication, and strategic marketing communication. In particular, she examines the message framing effects, health communication campaigns, and motivational effectiveness relating to self-regulation. Her research publications are in *PR* magazine (Germany) and *International Journal of Human Movement and Sports Sciences.* Before she joined academia, she worked in the advertising profession in Hong Kong for more than six years.

Generations Z in Asia: Foreword

Around 18 months ago I had the privilege of contributing both a chapter (on Generation Z in the UK), and the foreword, to a book on Generations Z in Europe, edited by Christian Scholz and Anne Renning. This book provided a useful and unique analysis of the characteristics of the younger generation in different European countries. For some time, I have been complaining about the tendency for both scholars and practitioners to take a universal approach to generations and to assume that the characteristics of generations are the same regardless of the country in which the generations that an author is discussing are based. It was therefore a delight to be part of a book that took a contextual approach to studying the characteristics of a particular generation. It was because of this experience that I jumped at the chance to co-edit this current text – on Generations Z in Asia – and to include this within my book series on *The Changing Context of Managing People*.

It is important to note, of course, that accepting this request was also tinged with sadness – a co-editor for this text was only needed because Professor Christian Scholz – who both conceptualised and started work on this text had been taken seriously ill, and later passed away. Having worked with Christian on the previous text, I feel compelled to recognise his passion for this topic and the enthusiasm that both got this manuscript moving and brought the first text to fruition. This book undoubtedly belongs to Christian (along with Elodie Gentina) –I see myself therefore as no more than a caretaker in seeing this book to its completion.

My personal involvement in editing this text – and the memory of Christian – means of course that I am particularly delighted to be able to introduce this new book as part of the series. The continent of Asia becomes increasingly dominant in the world landscape in relation to its economic growth, population size and growing influence on aspects such as technologies and fashion. With this in mind, it is important that we understand the characteristics of the Asian people both as consumers and employees. And yet, research in this area is still limited. In relation to generational differences, scholars have historically drawn on western models of generational groups with very few researchers exploring the attitudes and expectations of different age cohorts in Asia in particular. Not only does this book address that need, but it also goes one step further by considering the values and preferences of the younger generation in different countries and regions of Asia to examine the similarities and differences between those of different nationalities. Given the rich historical and cultural landscape within Asia, alongside differences in religion, economic climate and tradition, this provides a fascinating discussion of Generation Z in different Asian countries and the factors that have driven their values and expectations. I hope that you will enjoy this text as much as I have enjoyed editing and reading it.

Emma Parry
Series Editor

Part I

Generation Z in Asia: A Research Agenda

Chapter 1

Generation Z in Asia: A Research Agenda

Elodie Gentina

Abstract

Generation Z, including individuals born from the mid-1990s to the late 2000s, is said to be different from other generations before. Generation Z is said to be the generation of digital natives, with multiple identities; a worried and creative generation who value collaborative consumption; and a generation looking forward. The authors present here tentative observations of Generation Z in Asia using theoretical approaches and scientific backgrounds: the authors show how socialisation theory (parents and peer group) and technology (relationship with smartphones) offer meaningful perspectives to understand Generation Z behaviours in Asia. Finally, the authors ask some key questions about dealing with Generation Z in Asia in the field of smartphone use, consumer behaviour (shopping orientation), collaborative consumption (sharing), and work context.

Keywords: Generation Z; digital natives, Asia; consumers; workers; research

Introduction

For several years, Millennials, digital natives, and other names for 'Generation Y' have been the focus of academic research (e.g. Business Administration, Behavioural Management, Sociology, Psychology, etc.) and even more of practitioners in companies, politicians, teachers, parents, and of course of the media. However, over the past few years, a new generation slowly has moved into focus: Generation Z, including individuals born from the mid-1990s to the late 2000s. This generation of digital natives has grown up in a digital, technology-saturated world. We cannot understand Generation Z without understanding the context in which they have grown up. Then we can examine their characteristics, their behaviour as consumers, and their behaviour at work.

The New Generation Z in Asia: Dynamics, Differences, Digitalisation
The Changing Context of Managing People, 3–19
doi:10.1108/978-1-80043-220-820201002

Worldwide, young people from 'Generation Z' are characterised by similar consumption practices with respect to clothing, music, and media use, pointing to the evidence of a 'global youth culture'. This presumed uniformity, however, might be inaccurate. Recent research suggests that 'Generation Z' adapts global consumption practices and meanings to fit local contexts (Kjeldgaard & Askegaard, 2006). Consistent with this finding is a handful of cross-cultural studies that reports significant differences in consumer behaviour between highly individualistic cultures (e.g. Western cultures) and strongly collectivist cultures (e.g. Eastern cultures). This leaves open questions: How does the Generation Z look in other regions of the world? Are there specific patterns? Unique questions? Global questions? Much remains unknown, in particular about the behaviours of Generation Z especially in Asia.

The Concept of Generation

The concept of generation is a cross-disciplinary concept with different meanings, linked to age, genealogy or the filiation, and historical period. We focus here on the definition of generation proposed by Attias-Donfut (1988) in Sociology which relies on four different meanings:

1. generation in the demographic sense, gathering all people belonging to the same age range;
2. generation in the genealogical and family sense, making the distinction between the older generation (e.g. parents and grandparents) and younger generation (children) with a normalised hierarchical relation of the domination of the former over the latter;
3. generation in the historical sense, as the length of time required to renew individuals in public life, estimated as the time needed for a child to become independent and integrated in public life (estimated at 30 years on average);
4. generation in the socio-cognitive or sociological sense, gathering a group of individuals born in the same time period, during which they have shared unique events created by their common age situation within history (referring to generational cohort). For instance, Baby Boomers had the Vietnam War. *Millennials* had 9/11 and the financial crisis. For *Generation Z*, their life-altering world event might be the *Coronavirus* crisis, and the accompanying slew of school closings, quarantines, and high unemployment rates.

There exist different generational cohorts 'whose members are linked to each other through shared life experiences during their formative years, including macroeconomic conditions' (Pekerti & Arli, 2017, p. 390):

- Baby Boomers born approximately between 1950 and 1964.
- Generation X born approximately between 1965 and 1979.
- Generation Y born approximately between 1984 and 1988.
- Generation Z or digital natives born after 1995.

Prior studies in consumer behaviour refer to generational cohorts to explain similarities related to their consumption behaviours inside the same age cohort and differences between different age cohorts (Pekerti & Denni, 2017). For instance, consumers in younger Generation Y are more impulsive (Hsiao & Chang, 2007) and are more permissive of questionable consumer behaviours (Freestone & Mitchell, 2004). Other studies in the management have shown some differences between age cohorts concerning their working relationships. For instance, members of Generation X are more intrinsic in their work motivation than Generation Y. Generation Z is more realistic than Generations Y and Z with regard to perceiving ethicality of work situation (Boyd, 2010).

Given that sharing life experiences related to consumption behaviour and working relationships is concerned, we naturally favour generation in its socio-cognitive or sociological sense. However, we do not focus on this exclusive sociological dimension of generation here, we also take into consideration the genealogical/family and historical perspectives present in socio-cognitive and historical approaches of generation.

Characteristics of Generation Z

A Generation of Digital Natives

The new generation of digital natives, who were born around the end of the first decade, can be considered as a new breed of digital citizens. They have unprecedented access to technology. Unlike Generation X or Y, who are 'digital immigrants', Generation Z gathers the first true digital natives who have abandoned traditional computers for mobile devices. Members of Generation Z do not need to familiarise themselves with technology by comparing it to something else. On the contrary, they propose new ways of thinking about how technology can be effectively used. Generation Z perceives the world through different eyes: what is a novelty for digital immigrants is something ordinary, for digital natives as it is an integral part of their lives. For instance, 55% of parents estimate that their children under the age of 12 are more technologically knowledgeable than themselves (Dingli & Seychell, 2015).

A survey by Project Tomorrow (tomorrow.org) found that Generation Z is digitally literate, connected, experiential, social, and demanding of instant gratification. A 2017 Pew Research Center report showed that 92% of American teens go online daily and 91% of them are connected to the Internet through mobile devices. By age 20, these young adults will have spent around 20,000 hours online exploring their place and identity in the world. Many adolescents consider smartphones as integral parts of their lives and can hardly imagine living without them (Roberts, Yala, & Manolis, 2014). For example, in South Korea (the country with the highest smartphone penetration rate worldwide), almost 75% of tweens (aged between 10 and 15) spend more than 5 hours per day using a smartphone (Roberts et al., 2014). Adolescents spend on average more than 3 hours per day on their smartphone, suggesting that smartphone addiction among adolescents is a prevalent problem among members of Generation Z (Gentina & Delécluse,

2018). Smartphone addiction is 'the excessive use of smartphones in a way that is difficult to control' (Gökçearslan, Mumcu, Haşlaman, & Çevik., 2016, p. 640). More specifically, nomophobia, defined as a fear of having to go without mobile devices (Roberts et al., 2014), is emerging as a common phenomenon among Generation Z.

Generation Z loves their online audience but also value their anonymity. They know how to manage their digital privacy because they have grown up with a keen understanding of the line between public and private in online settings, and, thus, preserve their privacy. This can explain why Generation Z has less interest in Facebook, preferring social media. Generation Z can more easily keep their interactions restricted to their intimate friends or present a carefully curated image. Generation Z tries to keep communication private, and, thus, prefers private social networks such as Snapchat.

A Generation with Multiple Identities

Members of Generation Z express themselves through their personal characteristics, appearance, clothes, hobbies, and interests. At the same time, members of Generation Z, who spend most of their time online, express themselves in the real world while also extending and complementing their offline social life by using the digital environment. Thus, they manage their identity online and offline.

The way of expressing oneself is the main difference between Generation Z (digital natives) and Generation Y (digital immigrants). Digital natives are able to change many aspects of their personal identities much quicker and easier than it was before, thanks to online applications or online social networks (e.g. Facebook, My Space, Snapchat). They create their identity online thanks to a new profile in a social network, where they present themselves in a way that could be strikingly different from the way they present or express themselves in real space. Thus, members of Generation Z usually change aspects of their personal and social identities almost constantly and experiment with multiple identities online thanks to their profile pictures and avatars (as they change their clothes or hairstyle).

Friendships are important in Generation Z's lives. Adolescence is marked by transformational intrapersonal changes in identity and increased need to belong to a peer group (Baumeister & Leary, 1995). If digital immigrants (Generation Y) still prefer to make friends in person, Generation Z (digital natives) is open for friendship with people from around the world, thanks to their constant access to online social networks. Members of Generation Z flocked to social networks such as Facebook and Twitter to continue their social interactions with people who are already a part of their extended social network (Ellison, 2007). Facebook provides opportunities for young people to make new friends (Madge, Meek, Wellens, & Hooley, 2009). Moreover, Twitter attracts Generation Z who is interested in engaging in short conversations with other teens to receive and share information with others, a way to develop more social interactions (Kwon, Park, & Kim, 2014).

Another major shift between Generation Z and other generations (Generations Y, X, and Baby Boomers) is related to the method of watching television. Among

American adults, 59% of them cite cable or satellite as their primary method of watching television, according to a 2017 Pew Research study. On the contrary, the majority of Generation Z use their smartphone as their primary medium to watch videos. In a recent Business Insider survey (2018) conducted among 104 teens nationwide, only 2% of Generation Z said that cable was their most-used choice for video content. Nearly a third said YouTube was their most-used source for video content, and 62% said streaming including Netflix or Hulu. They watch YouTube as a niche for hobby-driven content, such as beauty or cooking show.

A Worried Generation

A generation is 'an identifiable group that shares birth years, age, location, and significant life events at critical developmental stages' (Smola & Sutton 2002: 364). Members of a generation share a history and common experiences, and this collective consciousness creates their worldview. Each generation is shaped by national and international events that take place during their formative years, when their identity and world views are still in flux. Throughout the world, the younger generation has grown up with the War on Terror, the spread of violent jihadism and terrorism. The Coronavirus pandemic might be a watershed moment in the lives of Generation Z. According to survey of US teenagers (ages 13–17) from Common Sense Media taken in March–April 2020, 63% are worried about the effect that COVID-19 has on their family's ability to make a living or earn money and 42% feel 'more lonely than usual'. Members of Generation Z have grown up in a world that hasn't always made them feel secure. Thus, they are pessimistic about the future – and overall seem unhappy with the state of the world that they have inherited. Overall, 37% of young people think the world is getting worse, compared to 20% who think it is getting better (39% think neither) (Broadbent, Gougoulis, Lui, Pota, & Simons, 2017). In March 2020, a Pew Research Center survey showed that half of young people from Generation Z (ages 18–23) reported that they or someone in their household had lost a job or taken a cut in pay because of the outbreak.

   Their greatest sources of anxiety, experienced by around half of Generation Z throughout the world, were the age-old concerns of money and school. Despite media focus on the issue, the pressures of social media were only seen by 10% of young people as one of their main sources of anxiety. There is some variation in the level of happiness depending on cultures. The highest happiness levels tend to be in developing countries such as Indonesia (90%), Nigeria (78%), and India (72%), and the lowest happiness levels are in advanced economies such as France (57%), Australia (56%), and the United Kingdom (57%) (Broadbent et al., 2017).

A Creative Generation

Members of Generation Z seek to make, collaborate, and co-create, as they want control and preference settings (Saettler, 2014). They apply their innate talent with new technologies and social media to launch new businesses and participate in the creation of new products that appeal to their peers and others. Online social

networks function not only as socialising channels but also as means to participate in co-creation processes. Generation Z want to collaborate, interact, create,
and share their ideas on social media platforms. According to Gurtner and Soyez
(2016, p. 101), 'young consumers can be described as "agents of changes" and
thus more open to innovative technologies'. As the most connected, educated,
and sophisticated generation in history, they don't just represent the future, they
are creating it (Kingston, 2014).

Growing up in the midst of a recession makes Generation Z less likely to believe
in the availability and security of good jobs. Instead, they are more focussed on
creating opportunities for themselves. They exhibit strongly innovative, entrepreneurial, and independent spirits, and 40% of Generation Z claim that they plan to
invent something that will change the world (Seemiller, 2016). They place a lot of
emphasis on being resourceful and entrepreneurial: 72% of high school students
and 65% of college students want to start their own business (Gentina & Delécluse, 2018). Not only is Generation Z a group of consumers, but they are also
the next generation of business owners. Generation Z will start businesses and the
peer-to-peer (P2P) economy will continue expanding.

A Generation Who Values Collaborative Consumption

Generation Z is often defined as a specific and unique class of materialistic consumers. Their materialistic values – and modern young consumers (adolescents, children) may be among 'the most brand-oriented, consumer-involved, and materialistic
generation in history' (Schor, 2004, p. 13) – are primarily determined during their
adolescent years, especially if they have sufficient material resources to achieve a specific, positive social identity through their consumption. Yet in contrast with these
seemingly widespread concerns about Generation Z's materialism, we revisit the very
fundamental question about the extent to which Generation Z should be considered
materialistic consumers, in the conventional sense of the term. Generation Z values experience more than material goods and aims not mainly to possess items but
rather to exchange them. More specifically, the Coronavirus pandemic is likely to
change Generation Z's perspective, because it has caused Generation Z to re-think
how they spend their money and what their financial goals are. Generation Z seeks
consumption-based, alternative means, such as exchanging and sharing practices.

Besides possessions (sharing tangibles), sharing intangibles such as sharing
online enables new sharing possibilities. Sharing with others online includes
open-source code writing; sharing information on Internet bulletin boards (BBs)
and chat rooms; publishing blogs (Weblogs), vlogs (video logs), and Web sites;
contributing to collaborative online games; participating in P2P file sharing,
maintaining listservs; and responding to e-mail requests. Those who make use
of these online resources are a part of Internet sharing. Generation Z is the first
digital native generation who is impacting the current P2P economy. According
to Nielsen (2018), among 68% of global respondents who rent products from others in shared communities, 35% are Generation Z consumers.

The sharing economy is the result of living through the financial crisis and economic slump, when the concept of ownership could feel fleeting. Collaborative

consumption is often associated with the sharing economy and takes place in organised systems, in which participants conduct sharing activities in the form of renting, lending, trading, bartering, and swapping goods and services, etc. (Bardhi & Eckhardt, 2012; Belk, 2014). The main motives behind Generation Z's engagement in sharing practices are to satisfy their need of community belonging and cost savings.

A Generation Looking Forward

Contrary to the myth of a self-absorbed generation, young people across the globe have a strong commitment to their world: 67% say that making a wider contribution to society (beyond looking after oneself and one's family and friends) is important.

Generation Z feels the weight of environmental issues, with 66% saying that climate change makes them fearful for the future. Generation Z constitutes a large citizen group, with the potential to exert a powerful collective drive towards environmental protections in society (Lee, 2008). Supporters of environmental protection tend to be young and the majority of members of Generation Z believe that their own actions are significant for environmental protections, such as reducing car travel, decreasing hot water use, and sorting household waste (Gentina & Muratore, 2012).

Another concern for Generation Z is the possibility of having access to a good education. Two-thirds of young people (69%) are fearful of the future because of the continued lack of education for some children.

Moreover, because Generation Z grew up as true digital natives, 84% of young people overall across the world cite technological advancements (e.g. in medicine, renewable energy, and computing) as a factor in making them feel hopeful for the future. Other sources of hope, including 'more peaceful values among the young generation' and 'the global spread of democracy and human rights', achieved lower scores (74% and 69%, respectively). Young people place less faith in these trends for the future (Broadbent et al., 2017).

Members of Generation Z overwhelmingly think that their values are influenced by traditional sources: their parents first (89%) followed by friends (78%), teachers (70%), and then celebrities (30%) and politicians (17%) (Broadbent et al., 2017).

Tentative Observations of Generation Z in Asia

Parents and the Peer Group: Important Socialisation Agents in Asia

The Protected Role of Parents. Parent–child interactions play a critical role in children's consumer socialisation (Yang & Laroche, 2011). Two dimensions characterise parental messages: socio-orientation versus concept-orientation. Socio-oriented messages promote conformity of the child to parental control, whereas concept-oriented messages encourage children to develop their own ideas and promote an open exchange of ideas in parent–child relationships. Family communication patterns vary across cultures. Typically, parents from individualistic cultures (e.g. United States, United Kingdom) promote independence, self-reliance, and assertiveness in their children, by encouraging their children to be self-expressive, and, thus, tend to be more concept-oriented in their communication with their children. In contrast, Asiatic parents from collectivist cultures value dependence, self-discipline, obedience to rules, and adult authority, and, thus, tend to be more socio-oriented in their communication with their children (Rose, Bush, & Kahle, 1998). Collectivist values are at the centre of children's socialisation in Asiatic culture. For instance, in China, the Confucian value, filial piety is particularly related to Chinese parent–child communication. The notion of filial piety dictates that children obey their parents without question. In Japan, mothers encourage consideration for others, strong family attachments, and the desire to please the family (Hess, Keiko, Hiroshi, & Gary, 1980). 'Doi (1962, p. 132) believes "amae" – a highly interdependent and indulgent relationship that encourages dependence on others – is the key to understanding relationships between Japanese parents and their children' (Rose, 1999, p. 806). Japanese parents foster respect for parental authority and obedience to seniors (Sakashita & Kimura, 2011). In India, parents maintain a high level of control over their children. Although some differences exist among social strata, Indians value tradition, conformity, and strong family ties (Singh & Smith, 2001). In general, parents from Asiatic and collectivist cultures consider Generation Z consumers as too immature to make their own decisions and exert control over their attempts at influence (Rose, Dalakas, & Kropp, 2003).

One under-researched issue is: How members of Generation Z actually influence their parents' consumer behaviours in Asia? More importantly, from a theoretical perspective, what processes lead young people in Asia to affect their parents' consumption behaviours, and what strategies do they use?

One facet of socialisation involves learning how to become a competent agent of influence through the use of sophisticated influence strategies (John, 1999). Literature suggests that these strategies can be classified into two categories: unilateral and bilateral strategies (Bao, Fern, & Sheng, 2007). The former is one-sided, whereas the latter is bidirectional and dynamic (Cowan & Avants, 1988). Typical unilateral strategies refer to direct request, persuasion, and playing on emotions while typical bilateral strategies include bargaining, reasoning, and coalition (Bao et al., 2007). How do these two types of influence strategies and parental styles differ in Asia?

The Normative Influence of the Peer Group.   While young people are generally susceptible to peer influence, it would be useful to analyse how the nature of such interpersonal influence differs across East Asia through South Asia, Southeast Asia to Western Asia. The measure of susceptibility to peer influence relies on Bearden, Netemeyer, and Teel's (1989) scale, which comprises two dimensions. The first, *normative influence,* is defined as 'the need to enhance one's image with significant others or to conform to the expectations of others regarding purchase decisions'. The second, *informative influence*, refers to the 'tendency to learn about products or brands by observing and/or seeking information from others' (Bearden et al., 1989, p. 474). Do young people from Generation Z prefer to use specific sources of influence, normative versus. informative, and are there some differences depending on the country in Asia?

The Impact of Technology on Asiatic Digital Natives

Digital natives around the world have a lot in common: hyper connectivity, constant attachment to their smartphone, a connection with digital influencers, and the ability to easily learn new technologies. However, are digital natives completely homogenous in Asia?

The rise of the penetration of mobile phones in Asia drives widespread Internet connectivity, and transforms consumer behaviour. In 2014, Asia had 3.3 billion mobile phone subscriptions, or nearly one for every man, woman, and child. By 2019, the region will have almost 4.3 billion mobile subscriptions, or 117 for every 100 people (Asia's Digital Disruption, 2015). Asia maintains and outperforms the rest of the world with regards to the Internet or mobile phone usage. On the Internet population ranking, Japan (94%), South Korea (92%), and Taiwan (88%) are the leading localities, according to the Youth Mobility Index (YMI, Asia, 2018). Although South Korea and Taiwan fall behind Japan in the area of Internet usage, the highest percentage of digital natives was found in South Korea (7%) and Taiwan (10.3%).

Smartphones come to the fore once more when Snapchatters are asked to select the device they consider to be their most important Internet access point: 51% of Asiatic people say smartphones are the most important device for using the Internet, compared to 38% of people from North America and 43% of people from Europe.

Nearly one billion individuals across Asia are now active users of social media. There are some differences of the type of online social network across different countries. Snapchatters in the Western regions of North America and Europe tend to be much more engaged with Snapchat than their counterparts in the Asia Pacific. To take an example, 62% of Snapchatters in North America report engaging with Snapchat at least once a day, compared to less than a quarter among those in Asia Pacific. Moreover, although Facebook is still the most popular platform in the world, specific platforms are important especially in China where Facebook is blocked. In China, the most successful platforms are messaging apps rather than the broadcasting format. For instance, WeChat (86%) is the dominant force in China, with microblogging platform Sina Weibo (67%), video service Youku (64%), and Qzone (63%) in the next tier of services (Global Web Index, 2018). Line in Japan, and Kakao in Korea.

Moreover, live video broadcast is a huge business in Asia. Of total Internet users in China, half of them uses live streaming apps. In Japan, Thailand, and Korea, users watch 300–500 min of live streaming content per month.

Questions Dealing with Generation Z in Asia

Smartphones as Part of Life in Asia

Beyond describing the different uses of online social networks in Asia, a key question is to examine Asiatic cultural differences in the motivations that lead Generation Z to use online social networks and their smartphones. Are there similarities or differences in such motivations related to the use of online social networks across Asiatic cultures? Understanding these mechanisms and their differences in Asia is of crucial importance for socially responsible marketers who aim to connect with Generation Z consumers in Asia, and for policy makers who aim to protect young people from the long-term negative effects of smartphone dependency. How do marketers and policy-makers tailor their messages and communication strategies to fit the different motivations that underlie the use of online social networks and smartphone?

Smartphones are central to many societies but they have been integrated into Asian cultures in many ways: 'there is the obligatory "food porn" photograph at the beginning of any meal; in Japan it is an entire subculture with its own name – keitai culture' (Chen, 2015, https://www.bbc.com/news/world-asia-33130567). Moreover, there is a clear difference between Western and Eastern cultures when it comes to education. For instance, in China, young people and their parents are looking for high-quality education and understand the importance of education. In some Asiatic societies where young students are hard workers, the smartphone is their only connection to friends. How do different forms of education as well as parental styles in Asia affect smartphone use?

Addiction to smartphone usage is a common problem among Generation Z worldwide. It manifests itself in the excessive usage of their phones. Given the emergence of the global smartphone teen market, the need to understand smartphone addiction and the mechanisms underlying smartphone addiction among Generation Z is also salient from a cross-cultural perspective (Wang, Sigerson, & Cheng, 2019).

But are all of Generation Z addicted to their smartphone? Does Generation Z in Asia prefer online or offline methods, and why? Asia tends to be a global collectivist culture in which people usually consider the need of the group (families, friends) and feel more connected to the group. Because nomophobia is the degree of an individual's anxiety at not being able to communicate with the group by losing connectedness (Yildirim & Correia, 2015), recent research hypothesises that individuals living in a collectivist culture (such as Asia) would have more nomophobic tendencies (Arpaci, Yardimci Cetin, & Turetken, 2015). For instance, Arpaci (2017) makes the distinction between horizontal collectivism versus vertical collectivism (emphasising hierarchy) and has shown that nomophobia is significant only in vertical collectivistic cultures, but not in horizontal collectivistic (emphasising equality) cultures. Moreover, Hofstede (2003) argued that countries with low power distance but high uncertainty avoidance (such as Japan) tend to adopt advanced technologies more quickly. Therefore, the theoretical cultural dimension theory developed by Hofstede (2001) may have interesting implications for the way in which Asiatic Generation Z uses interactive technologies.

Shopping Behaviours and Consumer Decision Making in Asia

Research to date has often assumed the similarity of Generation Z in their shopping behaviours (e.g. Tully, 1994). However, little is known about cross-cultural differences in consumer decision making styles and shopping behaviour across cultures. Several motives of shopping are socially and culturally anchored. Moreover, fundamental differences in parental socialisation philosophies that exist between Eastern and Western cultures may impact Generation Z's decision-making styles. It is widely believed that Asiatic parents exhibit a high level of control over their children, are protective, and alert their children to always try to 'do things right'.

However, it is important to note that the traditional Asiatic family system, which values children's dependence on the family and the unquestioned acceptance of parental authority, can be questioned today. For instance, China is a collectivist culture with high-power distance (Hofstede, 2001), which explains that Chinese parents have strict control over the kinds of products their children can or cannot buy. But today modern Chinese parents also allow their children more freedom in choice of brands of the permissible products.

Are there different shopping orientations (utilitarian vs. hedonic) across Asiatic cultures? Does Asiatic Generation Z place more importance on price and performance attributes (utilitarian orientation) or on emotional image attributes (hedonic orientation) when making purchase decisions?

From Purchasing to Sharing: Generation Z and Collaborative Consumption in Asia

The concept of consumer sharing is attracting the attention of both researchers and practitioners given the growth of the sharing economy (Gansky, 2010). Most of research on sharing has focussed primarily on individual consumers in single and individualistic national contexts e.g. the United States (Bardhi & Eckhardt, 2012; Lamberton & Rose, 2012), Canada (Scaraboto, 2015), New Zealand (Ozanne & Ozanne, 2011), France (Gentina & Fosse-Gomez, 2012), and England (Tinson & Nuttall, 2007). However, a few studies have examined sharing practices in families in collectivistic and Asiatic cultures (Gentina, Hogg, & Sakashita, 2017; Gentina, Huarn, & Sakashita, 2018).

Statistics have shown that among those who are willing to participate in a shared economy, almost half in Asia Pacific (49%) and Middle East/Africa (45%) are Generation Z, compared with 28% in Latin America, 18% in North America, and 17% in Europe (Nielsen's Global Sharing Economies Report, 2013). Questions that could be asked about this include:

- How do contemporary consumers in Asia draw distinctions between sharing, lending/borrowing, gift giving, and commodity exchange? How do these distinctions differ across cultural, economic, and political systems in Asia?
- What does Generation Z share in Asia: tangible goods or intangibles such as experiences? What are the new forms of sharing in Asia? With whom do members of Generation Z share (family or outside the family)?
- How do sharing practices differ across different family structures and Asiatic cultures in which different emphases on extended family, differing gender roles, alternative notions of gendered spaces, and different degrees of collectivism are common (Belk, 2010)?

- What are the psychological and social mechanisms that explain such cross-cultural differences in sharing practices?
- What can be done to encourage prosocial sharing of rides, cars, durables, toys, and other resources that are now used wastefully?

Prior research has shown that the practices of sharing are much more intense in collectivistic cultures which value social links and consideration of others, than in individualistic countries, which emphasise individual assertiveness (Belk, 2007). For instance, this positive view of interdependence is demonstrated through the intense experiences of sharing rituals in China, as seen in high preference for group travels, beverage sharing (Gongfu tea ceremony), and others. Both the Chinese national culture and their religion stress sharing practices: Buddhism emphasises 'dana', or generous sharing; and Confucianism 'shi', or giving, as an antidote to consumerism. Shi (giving) can be linked up with different nouns, including giving goods (*shi shan*) and giving medicine (*shi-yi*), but much more often with giving teaching/education (*shi jiao*). The result is not only less materialism but also more community. Sharing is viewed as a prescribed norm in China with the concept of '*zhanguang*' (meaning 'share the light') (Belk, 2007; Gentina, Tang, & Gu, 2017).

Sharing is also viewed as a prescribed norm in Japan (Gentina et al., 2017), which values social links and consideration of others. The sense of a 'we identity' governed by the perspective of *'being part of a cohesive whole, whether it be (that of) a family, clan, tribe, or nation'* (Belk, 1984, p. 754) is demonstrated through the intense experiences of sharing rituals, such as the communal bath house *(Sentō* and *onsen*), the tea ceremony (*Sado* or way of tea), and the spring cherry blossom festival where families and friends share food and drink to celebrate the start of spring (*Hanami*).

What is the nature of sharing in Asia? Does sharing refer to an other-oriented, an act of 'generosity', which is regarded as positive, productive, and enjoyable leisure activity? Or instead, does sharing refer to an egoistic act, turned towards individuals themselves, rather than altruistic?

The concept of 'self' is a fundamental assumption shared within a culture, which may help understand the other-oriented vs. self-centred nature of consumer behaviour (Tynan, McKechnie, & Chhuon, 2010). In a collectivist culture, the sense of self is governed by the perspective of 'being part of cohesive whole, whether it be (that of) a family, clan, tribe, or nation' (Belk, 1984, p. 754).

Future Generation Z at Work Across Asia

What is the relationship of Generation Z in Asia to work and to management? What are their expectations from a company? How should managers respond to these expectations?

ADECCO (2014) conducted a survey among 948 Generation Z across Asia, comprising respondents from China, Hong Kong, Japan, Korea, Malaysia, Singapore, Taiwan, Thailand, and Vietnam. The survey assessed Generation Z's ambitions, their employment preferences, their attitudes to the workplace, and how optimistic they are about the future – in work and in life. Interesting cultural differences were underlined. For instance, in South East Asia, members of Generation Z seem more confident than younger people in China and North Asia about how the educational system will prepare them for the workplace.

Social media is also a relevant criterion in shaping their choices for employment: 26% of Asiatic members of Generation Z state that they plan to use social media to seek advice on career. The leads to the following questions:

What motivates Generation Z in Asia at work? Are there different sources of motivation depending on the different national cultures in Asia? Concerning the sources of motivations, more than 50% of members of Generation Z in Asia are ready to choose a first job with a lower salary to get better training and have experience. They seem to prefer to work in an interesting environment for their first employment.

Moreover, why is Asiatic Generation Z talent more likely to pursue entrepreneurship? May be due to the fact that technology is so malleable in a sense that creates the opportunity for customised experience, members of Generation Z step away from traditional and defined roles. According to ADECCO (2014), 30% of Generation Z in Asia state that they would like to start their own business. They will start their own business as a start-up rather than taking over an existing business such as family company.

How is optimism versus pessimism shaping Generation Z in Asia? With Asia being the world's growth region, Asiatic young people tend to be optimistic and think that they will be better off than their parents, contrary to the European Generation Z who are rather pessimistic. In which sector of activity does Generation Z in Asia want to work? It appears that Asiatic Generation Z shows no interest in traditional industries (manufacturing) but prefers to work in service industries (advertising, marketing, consulting, media, hospitality, arts, sports, and entertainment). If at all, for which countries does this hold true? And what could be the consequences?

Conclusion

We know quite a lot about global patterns of Generation Z. We have a few assumptions about Generation Z in Asia, but many questions. Given the relevance of Asia as a whole and the countries behind it, these questions need answers. However, Asia is no homogeneous area. Therefore, it makes no sense to go at least at this point for generalisable conclusions: We have to understand each country in its individuality, with the drivers behind the development of the Generation Z in its countries, with its norms and values, with its behaviour, both as consumer and at work.

This book is one of the first to provide a detailed examination of this generation within Asia, comparing the Asiatic Generation Z in relation to country and culture-specific drivers based on interdisciplinary and international scientific research. It presents a generation born with digitalisation and mobile technology, who have grown up through COVID-19 and climate change. We do not talk about the Generation Z in Asia in the singular, because beyond the similarities between young people in Asia, we identify striking differences. As a result, we prefer to use the plural and talk about Generations Z in Asia. The objective of the book is to give the reader a chance to understand Generation Z across Asia. This includes societal and managerial feelings, goals, concerns, and behaviour of a vast continent that stretches from East Asia through South Asia, Southeast Asia to Western Asia.

The books is structured in 11 country-specific chapters stretching from East Asia through South Asia, Southeast Asia to Western Asia: China, Hong Kong, Japan, and Taiwan (East China); India and Pakistan (South Asia); Indonesia, Vietnam, and Malaysia (Southeast Asia); and Turkey and UAE (Western-Asia). All country-specific chapters follow the same structure, with every chapter giving us analyses of native researchers from across Asia. The book starts by contextualising the research: demographics; industry structure; economic growth; identity (preservation of local differences, regional integration); general values and norms (economic growth and values); socialisation (parents, peers, school); and public policy. Second, the book describes the main characteristics of Generation Z: description (size, behaviour, values, dreams, fears, political attitude); social media life (digital revolution, the role of influencers, web 2.0/3.0/4.0, community, online social networks, smartphone, Internet); ethics; and public policy (standard of what is right or wrong, what is considered as ethical for Gen Z) and special features (for instance 'maker scene'). Third, it describes members of Generation Z as consumers using a range of theoretical approaches and scientific backgrounds: e.g. shopping behaviours (retail, at the mall/online, how the web changes shopping behaviour); buying, having, being (materialism, relations with brands, brand loyalty/products vs. sharing, collaborative consumption). Fifth, it presents Generation Z at work, focussing on both their expectations (work–life blending, vision of the work place of the future, loyalty) and their behaviours within companies (communication, digitalisation, relationships with the team, authority/leadership, intrapreneurship/entrepreneurship). The last section gives some managerial implications so that readers understand how to deal with Generation Z in marketing and in management, telling readers how to deal with Generation Z as future consumers and workers in Asia.

References

ADECCO. (2014). Generation Z – The next generation of workers in Asia. *An Adecco Asia Research Study & White Paper*, Quarter 2.

Arpaci, I. (2017). Culture and nomophobia: The role of vertical versus horizontal collectivism in predicting nomophobia. *Information Development, 35*(2), 1–11.

Arpaci I, Yardimci, C. Y., & Turetken, O. (2015). A cross-cultural analysis of smartphone adoption by Canadian and Turkish organizations. *Journal of Global Information Technology Management, 18*(3), 214–238.

Asia's Digital Disruption. (2015). Infograph: How technology has changed Asia's consumer behavior. Retrieved from https://www.marketing-interactive.com/infograph-technology-changes-consumer-behaviour/

Attias-Donfut, C. (1988). *Sociologie des générations: l'empreinte du temps*. Paris : Presses Universitaires de France.

Bao, Y., Fern, E. F., & Sheng, S. (2007). Parental style and adolescents in family consumption decisions: An integrative approach. *Journal of Business Research, 60*(7), 672–680.

Bardhi, F., & Eckhardt, G. M. (2012). Access-based consumption: The case of car sharing. *Journal of Consumer Research, 39*(4), 881–898.

Baumeister, R. F., & Leary, M. R. (1995). The need to belong: Desire for interpersonal attachments as a fundamental human motivation. *Psychological Bulletin, 117*(3), 497–527.

Bearden, W. O., Netemeyer, R. G., & Teel, J. T. (1989). Measurement of consumer susceptibility to interpersonal influence. *Journal of Consumer Research, 1*(4), 473–481.

Belk, R. (2014). You are what you can access: Sharing and collaborative consumption online. *Journal of Business Research, 67*(8), 1595–1600.

Belk, R. W. (1984). Cultural and historical differences in concepts of self and their effects on attitudes toward having and giving. In T. C. Kinnear (Ed.), *Advances in consumer research* (Vol. 11, pp. 754–763). Provo, UT: Association for Consumer Research.

Belk, R. W. (2007). Why not share rather than own? *The ANNALS of the American Academy of Political and Social Science, 611*(1), 126–140.

Belk, R. W. (2010). Sharing. *Journal of Consumer Research, 36*(5), 715–734.

Boyd, D. (2010). Ethical determinants for generations X and Y. *Journal of Business Ethics, 93*, 465–469.

Broadbent, E., Gougoulis, J., Lui, N., Pota, V., & Simons, J. (2017, January). *Generation Z: Global citizenship survey*. London: Varkey Foundation. Retrieved from https://www.varkeyfoundation.org/sites/default/files/Global%20Young%20People%20Report%20(digital)%20NEW%20(1).pdf. Accessed on March, 15, 2018.

Business Insider Survey. (2018). Gen Zs never watch TV, are stressed about Snapchat, and are concerned that technology has ruined their mental health—Here's what it's REALLY like to be a teen in 2018. Retrieved from https://www.businessinsider.fr/us/teens-gen-z-generation-z-what-teens-are-like-2018-6

Chen, H. (2015). Asia's smartphone addiction. *BBC News*, Singapore. Retrieved from https://www.bbc.com/news/world-asia-33130567

Common Sense Media – SurveyMonkey Poll. (2020). How teens are coping and connecting in the time of the Coronavirus. Retrieved from https://www.commonsensemedia.org/sites/default/files/uploads/pdfs/2020_surveymonkey-key-findings-toplines-teens-and-coronavirus.pdf

Cowan, G., & Avants, K. (1988). Children's influence strategies: Structure, sex differences, and bilateral mother–child influence. *Child Development, 59*(5), 1303–1313.

Dingli, A., & Seychell, D. (2015). *The new digital natives. Cutting the chord*. Princeton, NJ: Princeton University Press.

Doi, T. (1962). Amae: A key concept for understanding Japanese personality structure. In J. Smith & R. K. Beardsley (Eds.), *Publications in anthropology* (pp. 132–139). New York, NY: Viking Fund Publications.

Ellison, N. B. (2007). Social network sites: Definition, history, and scholarship. *Journal of Computer Mediated Communication, 13*(1), 210–230.

Freestone, O., & Mitchell, V. W. (2004). Generation Y attitudes towards e-ethics and Internet-related misbehaviours. *Journal of Business Ethics, 54*(2), 121-128.

Gansky, L. (2010). *The Mesh: Why the future of business is sharing*. New York, NY: Penguin Group.

Gentina, E., & Delécluse, M. E. (2018). *La Génération Z: Des Z Consommateurs aux Z Collaborateurs* [*Generation Z: From Z consumers to Z co-Workers*]. Paris: Dunod (in French).

Gentina, E., & Fosse-Gomez, M. H. (2012). Shall we share our clothes? Understanding clothing exchanges with friends during adolescence. In K. Diehl & C. Yoon (Eds.), *Advances in consumer research* (Vol. 43, pp. 181–185). Duluth, MN: Association for Consumer Research.

Gentina, E., Hogg, M. K., & Sakashita, M. (2017). Identity (re)construction through sharing: A study of mother and teenage daughter dyads in France and Japan. *Journal of Retailing and Consumer Services, 37*, 67–77.

Gentina, E., Huaran, K. H., & Sakashita, M. (2018). A social comparison theory approach to mothers' and daughters' clothing co-consumption behaviors: A cross-cultural study in France and Japan. *Journal of Business Research, 89*, 361–370.

Gentina, E., & Muratore, I. (2012). The process of ecological resocialization by teenagers. *Journal of Consumer Behaviour, 11*(2), 162–169.

Gentina, E., Tang, T. L. P., & Gu, X. (2017). Does bad company corrupt good morals? Social bonding and academic cheating among French and Chinese teens. *Journal of Business Ethics, 146*(43), 639–667.

Global Web Index. (2018). Millennials. Examining the attitudes and digital behaviors of Internet users aged 21–34.

Gökçearslan, Ş., Mumcu, F. K., Haşlaman, T., & Çevik, Y. D. (2016). Modelling smartphone addiction: The role of smartphone usage, self-regulation, general self-efficacy and cyberloafing in university students. *Computers in Human Behavior, 63*, 639–649.

Gurtner, S., & Soyez, K. (2016.) How to catch the generation Y: Identifying consumers of ecological innovations among youngsters. *Technological Forecasting & Social Change, 106*, 101–107.

Hess, R. D., Keiko, K., Hiroshi, A., & Gary, G. P. (1980, December). Maternal expectations for mastery of developmental tasks in Japan and the United States. *International Journal of Psychology, 15*, 259–271.

Hofstede, G. (2001). *Culture's consequences: Comparing values, behaviors, institutions, and organizations across nations.* Thousand Oaks, CA: Sage.

Hsiao, C.-H., & Chang, W.-L. (2007). The relationship between money attitude and compulsive buying among Taiwan's Generation X and Y. *Journal of Accounting, Finance and Management Strategy, 3*(2), 95–114.

John, D. R. (1999). Consumer socialisation of children: A retrospective look at twenty-five years of research. *Journal of Consumer Research, 26*(3), 183–213.

Kingston, A. (2014). Get ready for Generation Z. Retrived from: http://www.macleans.ca/society/life/get-ready-for-generation-z/

Kjeldgaard, D., & Askegaard S. (2006). The glocalization of youth culture: The global youth segment as structures of common differences. *Journal of Consumer Research, 33*(2), 231–247.

Kwon, S. J., Park, E., & Kim, K. J. (2014). What drives successful social networking services? A comparative analysis of user acceptance of Facebook and Twitter. *The Social Science Journal, 51*, 534–544.

Lamberton, C. P., & Rose, R. L. (2012). When is ours better than mine? A framework for understanding and altering participation in commercial sharing systems. *Journal of Marketing, 76*(4), 109–125.

Lee, K. (2008). Factors promoting effective environmental communication to adolescents: A study of Hong Kong. *China Media Research, 4*(3), 28–96.

Nielsen's Global Sharing Economies Report. (2013). Retrieved from http://www.collaboriamo.org/media/2014/06/global-share-community-report-may-2014.pdf

Madge, C., Meek, J., Wellens, J., & Hooley, T. (2009). Facebook, social integration and informal learning at University: It is more for socialising and talking to friends about work than for actually doing work. *Learning, Media and Technology, 34*(2), 141–155.

Ozanne, L. K., & Ozanne, J. L. (2011). A child's right to play: The social construction of civic virtues in toy libraries. *Journal of Public Policy and Marketing, 30*(2), 263–276.

Pekerti, A. A., & Denni, D. (2017). Do cultural and generational cohorts matter to ideologies and consumer ethics? A comparative study of Australians, Indonesians, and Indonesian Migrants in Australia. *Journal of Business Ethics, 143*, 387–404.

Pew Research Center. (2017). About 6 in 10 young adults in U.S. primarily use online streaming to watch TV. Retrieved from http://www.pewresearch.org/fact-tank/2017/09/13/about-6-in-10-young-adults-in-u-s-primarily-use-online-streaming-to-watch-tv/

Pew Research Center. (2020). On the cusp of adulthood and facing an uncertain future: What we know about Gen Z so far. Retrieved from https://www.pewsocialtrends.org/essay/on-the-cusp-of-adulthood-and-facing-an-uncertain-future-what-we-know-about-gen-z-so-far/

Roberts, J., Yaya, L., & Manolis, C. (2014). The invisible addiction: Cell-phone activities and addiction among male and female college students. *Journal of Behavioral Addictions*, *3*(4), 254–265.

Rose, G. M. (1999). Consumer socialization, parental style, and developmental timetables in the United States and Japan. *Journal of Marketing*, *63*(3), 105-119.

Rose, G. M., Bush, V. D., & Kahle, L. R. (1998). The influence of family communication patterns on parental reactions towards advertising: A cross-national examination. *Journal of Advertising*, *27*(4), 71–85.

Rose, G. M., Dalakas, V., & Kropp, F. (2003). Consumer socialisation and parental style across cultures: Findings from Australia, Greece and India. *Journal of Consumer Psychology*, *13*(4), 366–376.

Saettler, M. (2014). How to target Gen Z, the new consumer on the block, via mobile. Retrived from http://www.mobilemarketer.com/cms/news/research/18316.html

Sakashita, M., & Kimura J. (2011). Daughter as mother's extended self. In A. Bradshaw, C. Hackley, P. Maclaran (Eds.), *European Advances in Consumer Research* (Vol. 9, pp. 283–289). Duluth, MN: Association for Consumer Research.

Scaraboto, D. (2015, June). Selling, sharing, and everything in between: The hybrid economies of collaborative networks. *Journal of Consumer Research*, *42*, 152–176.

Schor, J. B. (2014). *Born to buy: The commercialized child and the new consumer cult*. New YorK, NY: Simon and Schuster.

Seemiller, C. (2016). Three identities of the Generation Z Era: The inventor. Retrieved from: https://www.linkedin.com/pulse/3-identities-generation-z-era-inventor-corey-seemiller-phd

Singh, V., & Smith, P. (2001). India gets by. *New York Times Upfront*, *133*, 14–17.

Smola, K., & Sutton, C. D. (2002). Generatv for the New Millenium. *Journal of Organizational Behavior*, *23*(4), 363–382.

Tinson, J., & Nuttall, P. (2007). Insider trading? Exploring familial intra-generational borrowing and sharing. *The Marketing Review*, *7*(2), 185–200.

Tully, S. (1994). Teens: The most global market of all. *Fortune*, May 16, 34–41.

Tynan, C., McKechnie, S., & Chhuon, C. (2010). Co-creating value for luxury brands. *Journal of Business Research*, *63*(11), 1156–1163.

Wang, H. Y., Sigerson, L., & Cheng, C. (2019). Digital nativity and information technology addiction: Age cohort versus individual difference approaches. *Computers in Human Behavior*, *90*, 1–9.

Yang, Z., & Laroche, M. (2011). Parental responsiveness and adolescent susceptibility to peer influence: A cross-cultural investigation. *Journal of Business Research*, *64*, 979–987.

Yildirim, C., & Correia, A. P. (2015). Exploring the dimensions of nomophobia: Development and validation of a self-reported questionnaire. *Computers in Human Behavior*, 49, 130-137.

Youth Mobility Asia. (2018). The Digital Natives' Republic of Asia Dakki Kong, Feb 15, 2018 YMI Blog.

Part II

What the Experts Tell Us About East Asia

Chapter 2

Generation Z in China: Implications for Global Brands

Zhiyong Yang, Ying Wang and Jiyoung Hwang

Abstract

Generation Z makes up 20% of China's population, and accounts for the highest share of household spend at 13% (vs. 3% for the United Kingdom and 4% for the United States). To advance marketers' understanding about this group of consumers and capitalise on China's booming market, this chapter uses rich statistics and information to show that China's Generation Z has distinct behaviour patterns, which can be attributed to the unique background in which they grew up: (1) rigidity of social stratification, (2) abundance of materialism, (3) digital era, (4) limited (vs. extended) family, and (5) heavy schoolwork. Growing up in such a background, Generation Z's lifestyle and consumption-related attitudes and behaviour are distinct from their predecessors. The chapter presents specific actions that marketers can take when targeting this distinct group of consumers in China, along with useful guidelines to HR managers for hiring them.

Keywords: Generation Z; China; consumption; materialism; digitalisation; social commerce

Introduction to China

Since the reform and open-door policy in 1978, China's economy has been growing rapidly. According to China National Bureau of Statistics (2019), China's Gross Domestic Product (GDP) growth rate averaged 14.74% in 1978–2018, which was faster than any other Asian countries and was three times as much as the world average during that time period. China has become the second largest economy since 2010. But as per the latest World Bank growth stage classification criteria, China is still at the middle-income stage and considered to be a middle-income developing country, due to its per capita income (Fantom & Serajuddin,

The New Generation Z in Asia: Dynamics, Differences, Digitalisation
The Changing Context of Managing People, 23–37
Copyright © 2020 by Emerald Publishing Limited
doi:10.1108/978-1-80043-220-820201005

2016). Specifically, China had 1.405 billion people in 2017, accounting for 18.82% of the world's total population; its per capita GDP was $8,643, 80.56% of the world's average. According to the World Bank WDI database (2018), China's per capita income is only 14.52% of that of the United States, 22.48% of that of Japan, and 28.91% of that of South Korea.

China's economic growth is associated with the evolution of values. From the late-1970s to 1980s, the advancement of reform and social progress drove Chinese people to demand equal rights, pay attention to self-consciousness, and advocate human dignity (Yang, 1998). In the 1990s, deepening the reform of the system and speeding up the construction of a socialist market economy became two major themes to promote China's social development, and strengthened young people's sense of competition and self-improvement (Yang & Kou, 2018).

China joined the WTO in 2001, and started to take advantage of economic globalisation, which in the meantime, increased people's awareness of rights and responsibilities, competitive consciousness and the spirit of contract (Pu & Yang, 2018). The parents of Generation Z were young at that time. According to Yang and Kou (2018), the youth (i.e. parents of Generation Z) in this era desalinated their ideals and beliefs, emphasised pragmatism, and no longer bemoaned the loss of ideals, but strove to participate in the distribution of wealth. They had diversified values, emphasising speed, novelty, individuality, and self-promotion (Yang & Kou, 2018). All these values have exerted profound influences on Generation Z's lifestyle and consumption-related attitudes and behaviour.

Basics of Generation Z in China

Generation Z accounts for 30% of the global population and about 20% of the population in China (Bo, 2019). As shown below, there are five aspects of the unique background in which they grew up, which explain why their lifestyle and consumption-related attitudes and behaviour are distinct from their predecessors.

Five Aspects of the Background in Which Generation Z Grew Up

The background in which China's Generation Z grew up contains the following five aspects that are unique to this population. First, they grew up in an era where the mobility of social rank became rigid. The elasticity coefficient of intergenerational income of Chinese residents is 0.4514, much higher than the average of other countries (Xin, 2018). This shows that the income level of Chinese descendants is largely determined by that of their parents. It has now become more difficult for those on the bottom rungs of the economic ladder to move upwards and easier for those on the top rungs to stay there (Chen & Cowell, 2015).

Second, Generation Z grew up with good material wellbeing. In 2000, the disposable income of urban households in China was RMB6,280, 4.16 times than that of 1990 (National Bureau of Statistics of China, 2001). In 2018, the per capita disposable income of Chinese residents was RMB28,228 (urban: RMB39,251; rural: RMB14,617; National Bureau of Statistics of China, 2001). A big portion of spending is on children's education. In 2000, the per capita expenditure on education, culture, and entertainment of urban residents accounted for 12.56% of the total expenditure on per capita consumption, 3.38% higher than that in 1990 (National Bureau of Statistics of China, 2001).

Third, they grew up in a digital era. The number of Internet users in China reached 772 million in December 2017, with the penetration rate of 55.8%, which exceeded the global average (51.7%) by 4.1%. Also, 70% of Generation Z in China begins using the Internet in primary and secondary schools, and 61.7% browses the Internet every day (Zhang, 2018). The Internet provides a platform to satisfy their needs for novelty and self-expression, through uploading and sharing dynamic information, interacting with others, and engaging in online services (Zhang, 2018).

Fourth, most Generation Zers lived in small families with 3–4 people, quite different from their predecessors who usually lived in extended families. The shrinking size of the family, along with the good education of the parents, promotes changes in family relations, with family members being more likely to treat each other equally. The percentage of parents of Generation Z who are willing to listen to their child's opinion in 2015 was 9.7% higher than that 10 years ago; also, 30.9% of China's Generation Z often talk to their parents about their innermost thoughts and feelings, an increase of 5.5% compared with Generation Y (Zhang, Sun, & Zhao, 2017).

Fifth, the burden of schoolwork is heavy for Generation Z. Since the mid-1980s, a 'competition mechanism' has been introduced into secondary education, which increases competition consciousness among teachers and students in China (Zhao, 2011). Because of that, schools usually keep students in classes for long hours, assign large amounts of homework, and organise countless mock exams (Zhao, Selman, & Haste, 2015). Primary school students in China spend an average of 8.1 hours and the junior-high school students spend an average of 11 hours at school (Zhang et al., 2017). During the working day, primary school students spend 1.7 hours on their homework, and junior school students spend 3 hours. Over weekends, the average time that primary-school and junior-high-school students spend on homework is 2.8 hours and 4.3 hours, respectively (Zhang et al., 2017). As the only child in most of the families, Generation Z shoulders the responsibilities and hopes from six adults, including father, mother, and four grandparents (Yang & Laroche, 2011).

Social Media

Because of the unique characteristics associated with their growth, Generation Z almost grew up on small screens, being surrounded by mobile phones, social media, and the Internet, resulting in their access to information mainly from their fingertips. As the mobile-only generation, China's Generation Zers spend many hours on social media such as WeChat, QQ, and Weibo. In the meantime, the potential problems of screen addiction have also emerged, with nearly 60% of Generation Z in China having mobile phone dependence, 31.0% spending more than 5 hours a day on a small screen (Zhang, 2018), and 66% using smartphones for social purposes (Useit, 2016).

Their social media consumption can be characterised by the following: earlier contact with the network; more open and pluralistic network mentality; stronger autonomous expression of network opinions; more subdivided network of social relations; higher dependence on the Internet; and stronger demand for intelligent devices (Zhang, 2018). Interestingly, China's Generation Zers are willing to buy memberships of social video platforms as they consider copyright more important, which is newer recognition than previous generations (People's Daily Online, 2019). Sharing their daily life and experiences through social media is an essential part of their communication. Getting 'likes' among the followers is indispensable for them, otherwise 'face' is lost (Doctoroff, 2019). At the same time, Generation Zers appear to be cautious about their communications via social media, as they are 'more responsible for what they say and do online than people born during the 1980s' (Gu, 2017).

Despite the freedoms that China's Generation Z enjoyed in the Internet, the socialisation goals of the Chinese culture have not been shaped much. According to Laroche, Yang, Kim, and Richard (2007), despite the influence from Western cultures and the Internet, Chinese cultural traditions are so firmly entrenched that the core values will unlikely see rapid changes, such as those concerning respect for authorities and parents. Children nowadays are still expected to return home for Chinese New Year to pay respect to their parents, with more than three billion train trips being taken in February 2018 alone (Doctoroff, 2019).

Generation Z as Consumers in China

Generation Zers have emerged as promising consumers receiving increasing attention from both practitioners and academics, especially in China. They account for the highest share of household spending at 13%, compared to only 3% for the United Kingdom and 4% for the United States. Also, they spend more in the categories of technology (e.g. mobile phones, media subscriptions) and clothing compared to their Western counterparts. Next, we discuss their consumption attitudes and behaviour in more details.

General Consumption Attitudes of China's Generation Z

Due to the unique aspects accompanying their growth, China's Generation Z has some unique patterns of consumption attitudes and behaviour. RTG Consulting conducted research with 5,000 Chinese consumers and 45 industry experts in 2017 and found some distinctive traits of China's Generation Z: they pursue enjoyment of everyday life; meaning of life; are open-minded for other cultures; and seek global trends (Marc-Olivier, 2017). According to Bloomberg (2019), China's Generation Z is more optimistic than their peers elsewhere in the world (41% vs. 26%). Also, they believe that their life is better than the life of previous generations such as Generation X (28% vs. 24%). In addition, their lifestyles are liberated by Internet-fuelled connectivity (Doctoroff, 2019). They have distinct personalities, pursue fashion, and are keen on various forms of cultural entertainment, such as network video games, comics and animation, and honourable person CS (Airui, 2018). Their expenditures for leisure and recreation increased significantly, especially on games, live broadcasting, music, sports, fitness, and travel (Cui, 2018). According to the Research Report on the Upgrading of Offline Entertainment Consumption (2018), the proportion of cultural entertainment consumption of China's Generation Z has exceeded 24.5%, higher than that of the post-80 and post-70 generations.

With respect to brand loyalty, Generation Zers in China pay great attention to brands, but their brand loyalty is low. Compared with 10 years ago, Generation Z's loyalty to brands has dropped by 7% in China (Aomei Group, 2016). With respect to their preference for local brands, while Tencent Social Ads (2018) showed that they prefer domestic brands, Marc-Olivier (2017) showed that, compared to older generations, Generation Z in China does not have strong preferences for local brands.

Spending Power and Decision Style

As the only child at home, China's Generation Zers are generally spoiled while being pushed to the extreme in academic excellence. They get more pocket money from their parents than Generation Yers, having RMB600 per month (Sequoia Capital, 2018). Generation Z's savings in the first-tier cities in China reached RMB2,890 per person, higher than in other cities, with 80% of Generation Zers having clear deposit goals, especially girls in shopping and tourism-related purposes (Sequoia Capital, 2018).

Generation Zers pursue high-quality goods and diversification, centring on 'looking cool' (Gu, 2017). In making product choices, they seek friends' recommendations and look at online reviews through such digital channels as WeChat, microblog, tremor, live broadcasting, and Douyin (Cui, 2018). But they are also assertive and do not blindly accept external influences. According to a recent survey by Wang (2018), 66% of Generation Zers in China made many decisions by themselves. Categories that highlight their own tastes – such as mobile phones and clothing – have become their main purchases (Mei, 2018). Huawei, Apple, and Xiaomi are their top three favourite smartphone brands (Penguin Think Tank, 2018).

Important Factors for Generation Z's Shopping in China

Convenience, efficiencies, and social interactions are important drivers of their shopping (Pan, 2017). According to China's Generation Z Pictures (2018), more than 85% of them are accustomed to online payment, such as Alipay and WeChat Pay, due to convenience. Also, fast delivery from online retailers is now another key to Generation Zers' shopping. They prefer the delivery within 2 hours, half-a-day, or the same-day, but are not satisfied with next-day delivery (Zhang, 2017). To them, fast delivery is a basic expectation, rather than a benefit.

In research on online experiences among China's Generation Zers, Ye, Barreda, Okumus, and Nusair (2019) found that interactivity and brand experience are less important in their brand choices. Social interaction becomes paramount to increase their trust in online vendors, future visit intention, and purchase intention at Taobao. Aesthetic design becomes another important factor to satisfy their need for uniqueness. Filier and Lin (2017), for instance, investigated important factors that enhance their repurchase intention of smartphones, and found that along with other factors (i.e. perceived quality, brand popularity, subjective norm, and cultural influence), design appeal has significant impact on their repurchase intention. When being asked about the most important factor that drives their mobile phone choices, 35% of China's Generation Zers indicated appearance of the phone as their top choice (camera: 30%; GPS: 20%; and quality: 10%; Sohu, 2018).

Peer Groups and Influencers

A unique point of influencers is that China's Generation Zers have high dependence on online opinion leaders (网红) or key opinion leaders (KOLs) when making shopping decisions. The range of China's KOLs is much broader than that of Western influencers, including video bloggers, socialites, and columnists popular on social media platforms. In 2016, the value of China's KOL economy was estimated about $8.6 billion (Yang, 2019).

China's Generation Zers proactively reach a web celebrity who they perceive similar to themselves. That's why it is common to see web celebrities having millions of followers in China. China's Generation Zers often create a phantom for a KOL and spend lots of money on the products or services endorsed by that KOL. According to Hong Kong's South China Morning Post (2019), China's online opinion leaders turned fans into sales, creating an industry of nearly $9 billion. For example, Dayi Zhang, an Internet blogger, created his own clothing and beauty brands in Taobao and gained RMB170 million on Singles Day in 2017 alone. A recent study by Accenture showed that more than 70% of China's Generation Zers prefer buying goods directly through social media, while the global average is 44%. As more platforms are emerging, their influence is expected to grow (Yang, 2019). According to Chan, Leung Ng, and Luk (2013), the degree of being attractive, funny, and expressive of celebrity is the important factors for Generation Z's brand recall.

Digital Payment and Shopping Channels

As an Internet Maven, 10% of Generation Zers purchase online and 64% visit online websites every day (Doctoroff, 2019). Online shopping, especially through mobile phones, is their first way to think about daily shopping, as they are the mobile-only generation (Gu, 2017). When having shopping needs, their first reaction is to pick up their mobile phones to check the price, style, and online reviews before placing an order (Cui, 2018). Taobao is their first choice, with 26% of China's Generation Z visiting Taobao every week (Liang, 2017).

Compared with 10 years ago, Generation Z's willingness to pay in cash has dropped by 18% (Aomei Group, 2016). About 80% of Generation Zers in China use WeChat or Alipay as the primary means of payment for shopping, which includes grocery items, books, games, and music (Lei, Jiang, & Lu, 2018). According to research conducted by Accenture on Generation Z in 13 countries, 70% of

China's Generation Zers prefer purchasing products through social media, which was far more than the 44% of their counterparts in other countries (WARC, 2017).

Luxury Brands Preferred

China is the second largest market for luxury consumption after the United States, with Millennials and Generation Zers being the top two groups of luxury shoppers in China (Halo, 2017). Generation Zers in China spend 15.0% of household income on luxury, whereas their counterparts in the United States and in the United Kingdom only spend less than 4.0% of household income (Bloomberg, 2019). Before turning 21 years old, China's Generation Zers on average spend more than $7,000 on luxury products (Halo, 2017). Family is a major financial source for them, allowing them to make impulse purchases, seek for self-expressions and uniqueness, and prefer luxury brands (Shu-Lan et al., 2017).

Interestingly, China's Generation Zers do not go to companies' official websites to buy luxury items; instead, they prefer purchasing them through social media sites. WeChat mini programmes are more popular than renowned Western luxury e-retailers such as Yoox/Net-A-Porter and the perception of similar taste to their own is an important motivator for luxury brand choice (Zheng, 2018). In general, China's Generation Z considers self-expression and fashion trend more important than showing-off through luxury brands, which lead them to favour such brands as Supreme, Kenzo, Stussy, and Bape, since these fashion brands carry the profound cultural and historical background to convey the intrinsic value of the one who uses it (Wang, Jin, & Yang, 2020; Zhang & Sun, 2016).

Sharing Economy

Global sharing economy has reached $8 trillion in 2017 (Microbusiness, 2017). The sharing economy in China is also growing rapidly, reshaping business and consumer lifestyles. The contribution of the sharing economy to China's GDP is expected to grow from 3% to 10% by 2020 (Lo, 2017). Notably, China-based ride-sharing company Didi defeated Uber and became the prominent market leader in China. Also, bicycle-sharing companies such as Ofo and Mobike have emerged as major sharing economy companies in China. Besides ride/bike sharing, many start-ups and Internet giants – including Tencent, Alibaba, and Baidu – have also contributed to the rise of the sharing economy in China.

Sharing economy services are mainly ordered through smartphones. As a mobile-only generation, China's Generation Zers are well grounded for sharing and renting, instead of buying (Lo, 2017). Moreover, China's Generation Zers – especially those living in the first-tier cities such as Beijing, Shanghai, and Guangzhou – are in more competitive environments because of rising house prices and the labour market than are Millennials who have already settled down (Biondi, 2019). Thus, to achieve their goal of being stylish without financial hassles, the sharing economy has emerged as a cost-effective alternative for them. For example, fashion rental platforms such as YCloset and Ms Paris with seven million members have become very popular among China's Generation Zers (Biondi, 2019).

China's Generation Z at Work

Characteristics of China's Generation Z Employees

Since 2018, Generation Z in China has been entering the workforce (Romann & Ho, 2018). According to the 2018 Talent Q report, China's Generation Z has its own characteristics in understanding and choosing the workplace, especially in four respects (Heyi, 2018). First, China's Generation Zers have active and inno- vative thinking styles, and strong personal judgment. According to McDonald's White Paper on Generation Z's Professional View in China, 97% of their Genera- tion Z employees are confident in their teamwork skills, capabilities of learning new things, interpersonal communications, and creativity.

Second, China's Generation Zers care about work–life balance. While pursu- ing the interest of work, work is mainly driven by interest. They do not work overtime for pure earnings, but pay special attention to the sense of work and personal experience (Zhu, 2018). Only when they consider the task is valuable, are they willing to work overtime. In the meantime, multitasking is a natural part of their life, because they get used to switching between multiple smartphone apps, and from tasks to tasks. Most of these employees have good living conditions, tend to be 'deeply Internet-enabled', and expect many tedious processes to be automated (Romann & Ho, 2018).

Third, China's Generation Zers feel that an equal and fair atmosphere in the organisation is very important. They are not afraid of challenging authority and do not like to obey some organisational rules. Although they have low loyalty to the enterprise, they value the spirit of contract and teamwork. They respect com- petent leaders, and value the ability and personal charm of their superiors more than power. As Generation Zers in China enter the workforce, they are increas- ingly choosing non-traditional careers that suit better their desired lifestyle than a traditional 9–5 job (Romann & Ho, 2018).

Finally, China's Generation Zers have a broader view of the world. As the liv- ing condition of this generation has improved, their foreign exchange and learn- ing are more extensive than earlier generations. Many of Generation Zers have seen the world since childhood, with a good understanding of the differences between China and foreign countries. They can view, analyse, and solve prob- lems from multiple perspectives, and actively accept and conscientiously abide by internationally prevailing practices and norms, and become a genuine 'interna- tionalisation' generation (Cai, 2017).

The Work Environment of Generation Z

There are mainly three differences between Generation Z and other genera- tional employees in the work environment. First, China's Generation Zers have a broader range of career choices. When considering career choices, they do not just look at China, but also other countries, including Europe and North Amer- ica. Second, the new generation of employees in China are more competitive than their predecessors. Good education, training, and international experience make them no longer as fond of the 'iron rice bowl' as the other generations. Third, they have a higher degree of marketisation and will not suffer from 'job choice phobia' like employees in the 1970s and 1980s.

Since Generation Z employees have the advantages of wider career choice, stronger employment competitiveness, and a higher degree of marketisation, does this mean that they have longer career planning, firmer career aspirations, and stronger career psychology? This is not the case, due to some constraints from both the readiness of the employees themselves, and the work environment. The work environment in China is unique in several aspects. Corporate hierarchies are rigid in China and confrontations with superiors are avoided. Relationships (*Guanxi*) are still crucial for success as is physical appearance (Doctoroff, 2019). Partly because of these challenges, China's Generation Zers seem not to be enthusiastic in the traditionally 'hot positions' such as government positions, banking, and engineering careers. Instead, they are interested in becoming Internet celebrities (e.g. KOL), along with new career paths such as data scientist and UX (User eXperience) designers. Self-employment appears to be a second dream for them in order to pursue flexibility (Zheng, 2018).

While China's Generation Z is under increasing pressure for employment, in many cases, they are not fully aware of what they want. Furthermore, the current curriculum in higher education 'still focuses on students' learning, rather than aiming to satisfy social needs, causing the discrepancy between universities' talent cultivating and the social demand' (Ni, 2017; p. 880). Also, being the only child, China's Generation Z is under the substantial impact of family for their job options, but the ways of thinking are different and so is the value pursued. As such, social pressure, tertiary education, family influences, and individual factors may generate some difficulties in these young generations' job search (Ni, 2017). As an alternative, Generation Zers appear to prefer taking a gap year instead of going directly into the job market to search for more opportunities for a job they like or to prepare for future studies (Qi, 2017).

How to Deal with Generation Z in China

Approaches to Targeting Generation Z in China

Approaches in Marketing.   The distinctive characteristics of China's Generation Z bring brand inspiration to enterprises. The first is to focus on brand connotation and conviction. Having a world-wide known brand name does not guarantee success when reaching Generation Z; foreign companies need to have a deeper understanding about their desires and the 'hooking points'. Considering Generation Zers' high attention and low loyalty to brands, marketers need to seize the 'first moment of truth', and establish the person–brand relationship. Marketers are advised to give a reason-brand connotation, brand inheritance, and brand spirit to China's Generation Zers, so that they can stay with the brand. For this generation, the hollow preaching lacks conviction. What China's Generation Zers need are objective facts, accurate data, and their own analysis and judgment. Only by constantly letting this generation better understand themselves and build their self-confidence, can a brand have a stronger and longer vitality (Mei, 2018).

One of the important approaches is to integrate target consumers' identity into brand communications. As mentioned earlier, Generation Z in China is looking for stylish and personalised offerings. So, devising brand messages that resonate the identity is likely to attract their attention and increase brand loyalty. Taking Goodenough Clothing, a Chinese fashion wear brand, as an example, scarcity is one of the approaches it takes. New models are launched frequently, and new products are available every week, but only 10–60 pieces per model are produced, sometimes even limited to particular stores. This enhances the purchase intention of China's Generation Z.

Another approach is to emphasise experience and create content that stimulates person–brand interactions. China's young consumers expect digital experiences from offline stores, rather than just preferring online shopping (Pan, 2017). Thus, although China's Generation Z has mobile-based lifestyles, marketers should be cautious about focussing only online. To effectively target China's Generation Z, providing seamless, omnichannel experiences is crucial. Take StayReal as an example. It combined coffee with fashion brands and generated interesting stores that integrated clothing, coffee, and music, to convey a way of life to Generation Z. It became very popular among China's Generation Zers, as it projects that shopping and leisure are the same thing as life itself; stores are not only stores but also social or living places. These all allow China's Generation Z to have a better brand experience, thus, driving sales. By doing so, their high expectation of convenience, efficiency, mobile, and omnichannel experience is satisfied by the brand experiences offered by companies.

A third approach is to dig into consumers' area of interest. The life of Generation Z in China is relatively monotonous, due to them growing-up as the only child in the family. To make communication more interesting, brands can use game-based strategies and mechanisms, as well as cute language and expressions. Brands can choose some special social issues to build an interactive platform, increasing people's sense of social participation and brand awareness. Take New Balance as an example, it has published several kinds of micro-film advertisements, such as 'My predecessor is excellent', 'Watching Watson attack Shylock', and 'Late Night Canteen'. Themes are also selected from the hot topics at that time. Down-to-earth materials, impressive copywriting, delicate video plots, and interactive contents need to be integrated together to elicit emotional attachment from China's Generation Z towards the brands.

A fourth approach is to facilitate family decision making. Laroche et al. (2007) suggested that brands should allocate more budget to parents in China, because they play dominant roles in family purchases. However, unlike the parents in the past, the parents of Generation Z tend to respect their children's opinions when they buy goods for the household. In the choice of high-tech products, for example, more and more Chinese parents listen to the suggestions of their children. Therefore, high-tech brands should not ignore interaction with children. What is more, Generation Z is the digital and Internet generation. Information search and purchase may occur at any time. Faced with the situation of Generation Z using fragmented time to search and their possible purchase demand, marketers need to lay down their purchase channels as far as possible.

Approaches in Human Resource Management

China's Generation Z employees are quite different from other generations in personality, needs, growth, concerns, and interests. According to McDonald's White Paper on Generation Z's Professional View in 2018, China's Generation Z generally believes that work is a necessity for growth, and more than 95% of respondents are willing to make extra efforts to do a good job. In terms of career choice, the most important factors are team atmosphere, learning opportunities, and training systems. China's Generation Z employees desire an egalitarian relationship with their bosses and a flat organisational culture. They attach importance to personal growth opportunities, have a strong sense of purpose, and aspire to succeed.

Therefore, it is important for HR managers to adjust management approaches to fit the identity of these employees and generate a sense of belongingness. For example, Generation Z is accustomed to doing everything digitally, so they expect to be able to communicate instantly (Romman & Ho, 2018). Thus, leaders should have participatory communication, and timely feedback with Generation Z employees.

Also, it may not be wise to issue important notices before holidays. If there is a real requirement of timeliness, it is necessary to communicate and explain to Generation Z employees in advance. In a study of over 600,000 micro-blogs of more than 2,000 Generation Z employees in China, 48% of their topics were on weight loss, 23% complaining of minor ailments, 15% on dietary health, and 8% on physical exercise (Chuangyeshuoshi, 2016). It can be seen that Generation Z in China attaches great importance to health, and is eager to hear about how the organisation promotes the health and safety of workers – including emotional safety (Romman & Ho, 2018).

Finally, according to Heyi's Talent Q Report (2018), Generation Z employees in China are more willing to follow leaders who can find their strengths. They want a leader who is the soul of a team, who gathers people, encourages and inspires them, gives them goals and directions, and leads them forward. In addition, caring for subordinates, affinity, communicating actively, listening to subordinates' opinions, paying attention to subordinates' training and counselling, and matching resources are also important aspects of the ideal leadership in their eyes.

Communication Strategies

China's Generation Zers engage with friends through both online and offline channels. We would like to follow Doctoroff's (2019) suggestion to propose four ways to communicate with this group of consumers. The first approach is to dramatise 'the now', that is, offering a platform for them to capture the moments they value about and make an innovative story associated with such moments and distribute to the mini groups in social media. Tiktok represents a great example in this regard. It provides a platform that empowers everyone to be a creator directly from their smartphones, and encourages users to share their passion and creative expression through videos, which has gained a great success among China's Generation Z.

A second approach is to provide brand experiences that develop affinity and mash up with older generations. Xianyu (闲鱼), Alibaba's second-hand app, is for mash-ups across different generations. It now purports to facilitate daily sales of 200,000 used products. The platform seeks to distinguish itself from Taobao by pitching itself as a social as well as commercial experience. In November 2018, Tencent's tech news site cited an unnamed insider, saying that Xianyu was so successful that it would be spun off into its own business unit and become a next money-generator for the company.

A third approach is to use innovative viral marketing messages. Mobile viral marketing is an effective and indispensable approach for China's Generation Z. As shown in Yang, Liu, and Zhou (2012), mobile messages targeting Generation Z should be entertaining, useful, and relevant; in the meantime, a key factor that leads to success is to contain self-involved values for easier viral effects. Also, when celebrity endorsement is concerned, it is advised that popularity, good image, and celebrity-brand image congruity are crucial for China's Generation Z (Chan, Ng, & Luk, 2013).

A final approach is to set up mechanisms to reduce risks in purchases when targeting them. China's Generation Z proactively seeks information from friends, family, and online celebrities. They also often compare online and offline options. Part of the reason is to minimise the potential risks in their purchases. Therefore, it is important for marketers to use such strategies as testimonials, online reviews, a friendly return policy, and a without-hassle return process to facilitate their decisions.

Conclusions

To advance marketers' understanding about Generation Z in China and capitalise on China's booming market, this chapter uses rich statistics and information to show that China's Generation Zers have a unique set of lifestyle and consumption-related attitudes that are distinct from their predecessors, including seeking one-off, limited edition products; willingness to put in extra effort to support brands that adhere to high ethical standards; being susceptible to the influence of friends, family, and celebrities; and so on. Armed with this information, the chapter presents specific guidelines that marketers can follow when targeting this distinct group of consumers in China, along with suggestions to HR managers with respect to hiring China's Generation Z.

References

Airui. (2018). Retrieved from: https://mp.weixin.qq.com/s/6p-l_R5ZMUWP6e6zqove3w

Aomei Group. (2016). Research report on post-00s population. *China Chain Store*, *4*, 82–84.

Biondi, A. (2019). China's sharing economy comes to fashion. Vogue. Retrieved from https://www.voguebusiness.com/consumers/china-sharing-economy-rental-fashion-second-hand. Accessed on March 28.

Bloomberg. (2019). China's generation Z teens spend more and worry less than you do. https://www.bloomberg.com/news/articles/2019-01-23/china-s-gen-z-teenagers-spend-more-and-worry-less-than-you-do

Bo, X. (2019, January 30). China's Generation Z outshines global peers in boosting consumption: report. http://www.xinhuanet.com/english/2019-01/30/c_137787306.htm

Cai, N. (2017). Management details of new generation eEmployees_Difficulties, countermeasures and enlightenment of post-90s and post-00s Management. *Tsinghua Business Review, 4*, 58–63.

Chan, K., Leung Ng, Y., & Luk, E. K. (2013). Impact of celebrity endorsement in advertising on brand image among Chinese adolescents. *Young Consumers, 14*, 167–179.

Chen, Yi & Cowell, F.A. (2015). Mobility in China. *Review of Income and Wealth, 63*(2), 203–218.

China National Bureau of Statistics. (2019). *China Statistical Yearbook.* Beijing: China Statistics Press.

Chuangyeshuoshi. (2016). Retrieved from https://www.jianshu.com/p/9e972d43fc26

Cui, R. (2018). Analysis of China's post-00s consumption. *National Circulation Economy*, 10–11.

Doctoroff, T. (2019). China's post 95 generations: New dreams, new doubts. Retrieved from https://iaaglobal.org/leadership/chinas-post-95-generation-new-dreams-new-doubts. Accessed on January 8.

Fantom, N., & Serajuddin, U. (2016). The World Bank's classification of countries by income. World Bank Group, January, Policy research working paper 7528.

Gu, Y. (2017). Entertainment age for all: The generations after 90s and 00s leading individual consumption. *China's Strategic Emerging Industries, 9*, 25–27.

Halo, V. (2017, December 13). Chinese millenials and Gen Z to drive luxury sales by 2021. *Retail in Asia.* https://retailinasia.com/headline/chinas-millenials-and-gen-z-to-drive-luxury-sales-by-2021/

Heyi. (2018). Retrieved from http://k.sina.com.cn/article_6360531723_17b1e030b00100cfal.html

Laroche, M., Yang, Z., Kim, C., & Richard, M.-O. (2007). How culture matters in children's purchase influence: A multi-level investigation. *Journal of the Academy of Marketing Science, 35*(1), 113–126.

Lei, Q., Jiang, X., & Lu, Q. (2018). *Survey on Generation Z: Over 80% using digital pay. Southern Morning News.* Retrieved from http://dy.163.com/v2/article/detail/DR8N9LPT05129E3H.html

Liang, B. (2017). Research on Internet behavior of post-00s based on Taobao. *Western Leather, 5*, 68–70.

Lo, W. (2017). Management theories and business models. *Fung Business Intelligence.* Retrieved from https://www.fbicgroup.com/sites/default/files/Business_Innovation_inChina_p4.pdf

Marc-Olivier, A. (2017). What Adidas and Dior are doing to win over China's Gen Z. Retrieved from https://www.linkedin.com/pulse/what-adidas-dior-doing-win-over-chinas-gen-z-arnold-marc-olivier/. Accessed on August 1.

Mei, Z. (2018). Consumption trends and responses of the Gen Zers: Speaking for yourself. *Business School, 9*, 93.

Microbusiness. (2017). The $8trillion sharing economy is now. Retrieved from https://www.macrobusiness.com.au/2017/11/8trillion-sharing-economy-now/, Accessed on November 9.

National Bureau of Statistics of China. (2001). China Statistical Yearbook. China Statistics Press, Beijing, China.

Ni, X. (2017). Exploring causes and countermeasures of the employment difficulties for college graduates in the new era. In *7th International conference on education and management (ICEM 2017)* (Vol. 53, pp. 879–882). The Netherlands: Atlantis Press.

Pan, Y. (2017). Weibo has more influence over China's Gen Z consumers than WeChat. *Jing Daily.* Retrieved from https://jingdaily.com/chinas-gen-z-prefers-to-shop-on-weibo-to-wechat/. Accessed on August 30.

Penguin Think Tank. (2018). Research report on post-00s and post-05s. Penguin Think Tank, September, China. https://www.sohu.com/a/311742419_99957719

Pu, Q. & Yang, C. (2018). The evolution course of youth thought in the 40 years of reform and opening-up and the experience and enlightenment of ideological education. *Research on Chinese Youth, 4,* 20–27.

Qi, X. (2017, June 7). China's post-95s generation of university graduates are not quite ready to become adults. *Global Times.* http://www.globaltimes.cn/content/1050464.shtml

Romann, A., & Ho, D. (2018). Gen Z looks to the future. *China Daily.* Retrieved from https://www.chinadailyhk.com/articles/89/94/204/1540798406474.html. Accessed on October 29.

Sequoia Capital. (2018). The study of entertainment activities of generation Z. Retrieved from http://www.cioall.com/uploads/f2018110511561678424.pdf

Shu-Lan, L. I. U., Zhang, L. F., & Mu-Chen, D. O. N. G. (2017). A study of the post-95s college students' consumption status through social surveys. *DEStech Transactions on Social Science, Education and Human Science.* DOI: 10.12783/dtssehs/icesd2017/11679

Sohu. (2018). Retrieved from https://www.sohu.com/a/233998671_100098499

Tencent Social Ads. (2018). Tencent research report on post-00s. Tencent Social Ads, June, China. https://new.qq.com/omn/20180706/20180706A01FXF.html

Useit. (2016). Generation Z's smart phone usage and app usage. Retrieved from https://www.useit.com.cn/thread-12845-1-1.html

Wang, D. (2018). Only "commodity + content + service" can impress "post-00s". *Su Ning Easy Buy (HangZhou), 4,* 23–25.

Wang, L., Jin, M., & Yang, Z. (2020). Regulatory focus and consumption of counterfeit luxury goods: Roles of functional theories of attitudes and perceived similarity. *Journal of Business Research, 107,* 50–61.

World Bank WDI database. (2018). Retrieved from https://databank.worldbank.org/reports.aspx?source=worlddevelopment-indicators

Xin, M. (2018). Study on intergenerational income rank mobility and its influencing factors in China. Master thesis, Shandong University, Jinan.

Yang, H., Liu, H., & Zhou, L. (2012). Predicting young Chinese consumers' mobile viral attitudes, intents and behavior. *Asia Pacific Journal of Marketing and Logistics, 24,* 59–77.

Yang, J., & Kou, Q. (2018). The change and evolution of youth values in the past 40 years of reform and opening-up. *Chinese Youth Social Sciences, 37*(4), 15–22.

Yang, X. (1998). Theme variation in fluctuation: Tracking and evaluating the values of Chinese youth since the reform and opening-up. *Contemporary Youth Studies, 4.*

Yang, X. (2015). The app usage of Generation Z in China. Retrieved from http://www.chanpin100.com/article/24727

Yang, Y. (2019, March 14). How China's online opinion leaders – or KOLs convert fans to sales, creating a nearly US 9 billion industry. South China Morning Post. https://www.scmp.com/tech/big-tech/article/3001599/how-chinas-kolsconvert-fans-sales-creating-nearly-us9-billion.

Yang, Z., & Laroche, M. (2011). Parental responsiveness and adolescent susceptibility to peer influence: A cross-cultural investigation. *Journal of Business Research, 64*(9), 979–987.

Ye, B. H., Barreda, A. A., Okumus, F., & Nusair, K. (2019). Website interactivity and brand development of online travel agencies in China: The moderating role of age. *Journal of Business, 99,* 382–389.

Zhang, B. (2018). Research on the characteristics of internet users of the generations after 90s and 00s. *Think Tank Era, 9,* 251–252.

Zhang, M. (2017). Gen Z are driving China's consumer trend with impulse buying and instant gratification. *South China Morning Post*. Retrieved from https://www.scmp.com/business/china-business/article/2108141/gen-z-are-driving-chinas-consumer-trend-impulse-buying-and. Accessed on August 24.

Zhang, M., & Sun, H. (2016). Research on chao brand marketing strategy based on the psychological appeal of generation z consumers. *Modern Decoration (Theory)*, 5, 290–291.

Zhang, X., Sun, H., & Zhao, X. (2017). From "post-90s" to "post-00s": A survey report on the development of children and adolescents in China. *Research on Chinese Youth*, 2, 98–107.

Zhao, X. (2011). Development under stress: The culture of academic competition and adolescent friendship participation in China's secondary school. Unpublished dissertation. Harvard Graduate School of Education, Cambridge, MA.

Zhao, X., Selman, R. L., & Haste, H. (2015). Academic stress in Chinese schools and a proposed preventive intervention program. *Cogent Education*, 2, 100–477.

Zheng, R. (2018). A look at China's fickle but affluent Gen-Z consumers. *Jing Daily*. Retrieved from https://jingdaily.com/china-affluent-gen-z-agility/. Accessed on December 5.

Zhu, G. (2018). Intergenerational characteristics, performance and incentive strategies of post-90s employees. *Leadership Science*, 11, 57–58.

Chapter 3

Generation Z in Hong Kong: Simple While Multi-tasking

Melannie Zhan

Abstract

Hong Kong is a significant market with a strong economy, unique geography, and ongoing trade activities in the Asia Pacific region. This city keeps changing after the sovereignty returned to China 1997. Facing this historical change, how do Generation Z adopt these changes? This chapter draws a comprehensive picture of the context for Generation Z in Hong Kong, including political issues, their communication with families and peers, their opinions on consumption, and their preferences in relation to jobs. Instead of saying that 'they are too young', we try to understand more about this generation and its specific characteristic

Keywords: Generation Z; Hong Kong; identity; politics; work; consumption

Introduction to Hong Kong: Hongkongers versus Chinese

Hong Kong Special Administrative Region of the People's Republic of China (HKSAR), Hong Kong for short, is a cosmopolitan metropolis where old traditions blend perfectly with Western culture and post-modern trends. According to the statistics released by the Census and Statistics Department (2019a), the provisional estimate of the Hong Kong population is 7.5 million, including 3.4 million males and 4.0 million females (mid-2018). The population in Hong Kong is ageing. The largest generation is the Baby Boomers (55–75-year-olds) that occupy 25.5% of the total population. Generation Z (0–24-year-olds) including the people aged under 9 years is at 21.3% (Table 1). Generation Z is unique as the first generation to not have experienced the British Government.

The New Generation Z in Asia: Dynamics, Differences, Digitalisation
The Changing Context of Managing People, 39–53
doi:10.1108/978-1-80043-220-820201006

Table 1.   Hong Kong Age Breakdown (Mid-2018) (Census and Statistics Department, 2019b).

Age Group	Male ('000)	Female ('000)	Both Sexes ('000)	Both Sexes (% of the Total Population)
0–9	303.6	282.6	586.2	7.8
10–24	508.8	496.9	1,005.7	13.5
25–39	691.2	968.5	1,659.7	22.2
40–54	735.2	1,003.9	1,739.1	23.3
55–74	929.8	970.9	1,900.7	25.5
75–84	173.6	191.7	365.3	4.9
> = 85	68.1	126.2	194.3	2.6
All age groups	3,410.3	4,040.7	7451.0	100

Hong Kong is one of the most densely populated places in the world. In the range of 1,104 square kilometres, the population density is approximately 7,100 people per kilometre. With the limited natural resources and crowded land, Hong Kong is one of the major financial centres of the Asia-Pacific region. Hong Kong's economy is characterised by free trade, low taxation, and minimum government intervention, with strong links to mainland China and the rest of the Asia-Pacific region. In 2018, GDP in Hong Kong reached US$48,958,000 (HKTDC Research, 2019). Hong Kong is the world's seventh largest exporter of merchandise trade and the world's 15th largest exporter of commercial services in 2017, according to the World Trade Organisation. Financial services, tourism, trading and logistics, and professional and producer services are four traditionally critical industries in Hong Kong (Census and Statistics Department, 2018a), which generate a value of HK$1,367.5 billion in 2016 (Table 2).

As a special administrative region of the People's Republic of China, Hong Kong is allowed a high degree of autonomy as enshrined in the Basic Law, the constitutional document governing the political, judicial, and economic frame-work of Hong Kong as well as guaranteeing its capitalistic way of life under the 'one country, two systems' principle, which is in effect for 50 years. However, Hong Kong is facing a slew of intractable and inter-linked problems. Extremely high housing prices have left many unable to afford even a tiny apartment in this city of 7.4 million people, a problem exacerbated by money surging in from the mainland. Meanwhile, bitter political divisions over the relationship with Beijing have left the government incapable of tackling such socio-economic challenges. The conflicts between politics and economics have caused a series of controversies.

More and more of the younger generation actively join the social debates. The growing sense of youth frustration in Hong Kong is often attributed to the high cost of living and Beijing's deepening crackdown, which also leads to public attention on self-identity. The public opinion program from The University of

Table 2. Value of the Four Key Industries (Census and Statistics Department, 2018a).

Industry	Value Added at Current Prices (2016), HK$Mn
1. *Financial services*	429,100 (17.7%)
(a) Banking	270,200
(b) Insurance and other financial services	158,900
2. *Tourism*	112,400 (4.7%)
(a) Inbound tourism	89,600
(b) Outbound tourism	22,900
3. *Trading and logistics*	523,100 (21.6%)
(a) Trading	446,300
(b) Logistics	76,800
4. *Professional services and other producer*	302,900 (12.5%)
(a) Professional services	118,100
(b) Other producer services	184,800

Hong Kong has been undertaking a longitudinal tracking survey about people's ethnic identity in Hong Kong. This survey on ethnic identity reflects people's political attitudes and underlying cultural values. The latest survey found that 52.9% of interviewees described their ethnic identity as 'Hongkongers', 23.5% of interviewees described their ethnic identity as 'Hongkongers in China', 12.3% of interviewees described their ethnic identity as 'Chinese in Hong Kong', and only 10.8% of interviewees described their ethnic identity as 'Chinese' (HKU POP Site, 2019a, 2019b). 'Hongkongers' and 'Chinese' can be considered as 'strong and pure identities' (Chung & Tai, 2012). The notion of 'Hongkongers' recognises that people as Hongkongers can be entitled to more freedom, including freedom of expression, and visa-free access or visa-on-arrival for the Hong Kong Special Administrative Region (HKSAR) to enjoy 166 countries and territories. The 'Chinese' identity refers to the fact that people who are Chinese might not be entitled to as much freedom as Hongkongers because of the developing legislation. The 'Hongkongers' and 'Chinese' categories usually refer to political differences.

On the other hand, 'Hongkongers in China' and 'Chinese in Hong Kong' are the other categories which can be combined to mean 'mixed or ambivalent identities' (Chung & Tai, 2012). Technically, 'Hongkongers in China', meaning 'ethnically Hongkongers living in China', implies a stronger sense of 'Hongkongers' identity, while 'Chinese in Hong Kong', meaning 'ethnically Chinese living in Hong Kong', implies a stronger sense of 'Chinese'. For the people who find it difficult to define or to make a definite choice on ethnic identity, 'Hongkongers in China' and 'Chinese in Hong Kong' could be a solution.

Table 3. Age Range of 'Proud of Becoming a National Citizen of China' and 'Appraisal of the Central Government's Policies on Hong Kong' (17–20/06/2019) (HKU POP Site, 2019).

Date of Survey: 17–20/06/2019		18–29	30–49	50 or Above
Proud of becoming a national citizen of China	Yes	8.4% (14)	18.7% (66)	37.5% (186)
	No	89.8% (150)	77.4% (257)	60% (297)
	Don't know / hard to say	1.8% (3)	2.7% (9)	2.6% (13)
	Total	100% (167)	100% (332)	100% (496)
Appraisal of the Central Government's policies on Hong Kong	Positive	8.5% (14)	17.2% (57)	32.2% (160)
	Half-half	15.2% (25)	23.2% (77)	18.5% (92)
	Negative	71.5% (118)	56.9% (189)	43.9% (218)
	Don't know / hard to say	4.8% (8)	3% (10)	5.4% (27)
	Total	100% (165)	100% (332)	100% (497)

Looking at empirical data, 76.4% of interviewees identified themselves as 'Hongkongers' in a broad sense (i.e. either as 'Hongkongers' or 'Hongkongers in China'), and 23.1% of interviewees identified themselves as 'Chinese' in a broad sense (i.e. either as 'Chinese' or 'Chinese in Hong Kong').

In a survey conducted after the two rallies against the extradition bill, the strength rating of the 'Hongkongers' identity reached a record high since 1997, while the strength rating of the 'Chinese' identity reached a record low since 1997. The 18–29-year-olds expressed their strong negative attitude to the item: 'proud of becoming a national citizen of China' and 'appraisal of the Central Government's policies on Hong Kong' (Table 3).

The results clearly show that the Hong Kong public struggles in relation to their ethnic identities. Such conflicts are especially evident among the younger generation. The proportion of 18–29 year olds who describe their ethnic identity as 'broadly' Chinese has dropped from 9.5% to 6.9% from July to December 2018 to January to June 2019 (HKU Pop, 2019a). Over the same period, the proportion of that same age group describing their broad identity as 'HongKonger' has jumped from 88.8% to 92.5% (HKU Pop, 2019b). More and more people are trying to protect the Hong Kong lifestyle and independence through presenting their ethnic identities.

Basics of Generation Z in Hong Kong: Social Media Lovers

What do We Know?

According to the report from the Hong Kong Census and Statistics Department (Census and Statistics Department, 2019b), Generation Z in Hong Kong (born in 1995–2010) has about one million people, accounting for 13.5% of the total population, including 508,800 males and 496,900 females.

Hong Kong is divided into three main areas named Hong Kong Island, Kowloon, and New Territories. There are a total of 18 districts in the three areas. Generation Z is not evenly distributed across the 18 districts: more than half of young people (56.4%) live in the New Territories in 2011 (Social Sciences Research Centre, The University of Hong Kong, 2015). In contrast, the youth population in Hong Kong Island was declining. In 2018, the total number of people in the labour force was 3,979,000 in Hong Kong (Census and Statistics Department, 2018b).

The Importance of Social Media

Generation Z has a positive attitude towards social media usage. The Chinese University of Hong Kong conducted a telephone survey of 829 respondents including 50.5% males and 29.5% females aged from 15 to 29 in 2016 to examine the technographic profile of the younger generation in Hong Kong. The findings demonstrated that most of the younger generation in Hong Kong spent 4–5 hours online daily and 1–2 hours on Facebook (Centre for Youth Studies Hong Kong Institute of Asia-Pacific Studies, 2017). Facebook is the most frequently used social media platform (67.7%), followed by WhatsApp (14.4%), Instagram (12.2%), and WeChat (3.4%). Notably, Instagram was far more popular among youths aged 15–19 (Table 4).

More than half of respondents (53.6%) spent 2–5 hours online daily (Centre for Youth Studies Hong Kong Institute of Asia-Pacific Studies, 2017). Among various social media activities, the most common one was to 'browse friends' status' (24.1%), followed by 'browse public affairs news' (20.9%), 'instant messaging' (11.6%), and 'browse living and lifestyle information' (10.1%) (Table 5). Based on Table 6, the top three social media activities can be categorised as social communication, seeking news, and entertainment.

Despite the fact that the younger generation in Hong Kong enjoys social media a lot, they still trust the information sourced from traditional media.

Table 4.   Social Media Most Frequently Used by Youth in Hong Kong (Centre for Youth Studies Hong Kong Institute of Asia-Pacific Studies, 2017).

Social Media	Age 15–19 (%)	Age 20–24 (%)	Age 25–29 (%)
Facebook	54.2	74.8	72.5
Instagram	29.2	9.0	2.0
WhatsApp	10.6	12.9	17.4
WeChat	3.4	1.1	5.7
Sina Weibo	0.4	0.4	1.0
Twitter	0.4	0.0	0.3

Nearly half of the respondents obtained public affairs information on social media (46.4%), television (21.7%), websites (15.5%), newspaper/magazines (13.1%), and radio (2.8%) (Centre for Youth Studies Hong Kong Institute of Asia-Pacific Studies, 2017).

The Relevance of Politics

The young generation is more and more concerned about political issues in Hong Kong. The above study also tested the younger generation's attitude towards government. Two-thirds of the respondents were dissatisfied with the government's performance, with 33.6% being 'quite dissatisfied', 32.1% 'dissatisfied', and 29.8% indicating 'half and a half'. The trust rate was low. Nearly two-thirds of the

Table 5.   Most Frequent Social Media Activities by Youth in Hong Kong (Centre for Youth Studies Hong Kong Institute of Asia-Pacific Studies, 2017).

Social Media Activities	%
Browse friends' status	24.1
Browse public affairs news	20.9
Instant messaging	11.6
Browse information about living/lifestyle	10.1
Share others' posts	6.6
Press 'Like' or other emotional buttons	6.6
Watch video	3.9
Browse information on entertainment	3.8
Browse comments	3.2
Update personal status	3.5

Table 6.   Top Online Shopping Categories for Hong Kong Consumers (G0-Globe, 2018).

Online Shopping Category	Percentage
Clothing / accessories	41.7
Airlines	36.7
Travel	36.2
Hotels	36.0
Home appliances / electronic products	30.2
Online games	29.3

respondents distrusted the Hong Kong government. Compared with the 15–19 year age group, the 20–24, and 25–29 year age groups showed a higher level of negative attitudes towards the Hong Kong government (Centre for Youth Studies Hong Kong Institute of Asia-Pacific Studies, 2017). In general, respondents had a negative attitude towards the Hong Kong government. The result matches the youth's struggles with Hong Kong identity. Due to such a negative attitude, the rate of tolerance of political radicals was low.

The younger generation is active in political pacification both online and offline. They are free to express their own opinions and standpoints. About 75.2% of respondents had participated in political activities online. To 'post or share political/public affairs information or comment online' was the most common activity, with 25.1% of the respondents indicating participation 'once or twice', 21.9% saying 'several times', and 12.3% indicating 'often'. '"Like" or join any online group about politics or public affairs' were the second most common (24.1% 'once or twice', 16.1% 'several times', and 16.1% 'often') (Centre for Youth Studies Hong Kong Institute of Asia-Pacific Studies, 2017). By contrast, 'create an online group for politics or public affairs' was the least common, with 96.1% of youth reporting that they had no experience with that activity.

Meanwhile, the younger generation also participated in offline political activities. About 5.6% participated in offline activities. 'Take part in an offline march or demonstration' was the most common, with 21.3%, 6.1%, and 0.9% of respondents reporting that they had participated 'once or twice,' 'several times', and 'often', respectively. The least common activity was to 'contact a legislator or government official for public affairs in person, by phone, or by letter', with 93.6% of the respondents indicating that they had never done that (Centre for Youth Studies Hong Kong Institute of Asia-Pacific Studies, 2017).

Members of Generation Z as Consumers in Hong Kong: Living in the High-end Consumption Market

Consumption in Hong Kong is characterised by a cramped living environment and a keen interest in luxury brands. As a result of cramped living environments, large family gatherings tend to be held in restaurants, and friends are usually received outside the home. As resources are limited people turn to the material interests of the family instead of class-based activities, and more people have started to distrust the government and politics. As capital income is high, Hong Kong people remain materialistic in their minds and their personal values.

The younger generation also reflects such personal values. A university study interviewed more than 2,400 teenagers from 20 schools in Hong Kong in 2017 (Elizabeth, 2017) and found that Hong Kong teenagers can be materialistic, self-centred, and distrustful of the government. Thirty per cent of interviewees said that they agreed that making money was more important than other things, 19% of them agreed that money buys respect and more than 45% of them considered that 'making money is more important than other things' and 'money buys respect' were widely accepted by their peers as well (Elizabeth, 2017). This suggests that 'cash' is the only thing on their minds.

The growth of social media in the younger generation's life has already changed their values. Many luxury brands consider Hong Kong as a big potential market in the Asia-Pacific region and spend lots of advertising spending in the Hong Kong market to maintain their brand awareness. In the first 6 months in 2015, seven luxury brands including Hermes, Burberry, Cartier, Chanel, Christian Dior, Louis Vuitton, and Prada spent a total of 444 million Hong Kong dollars on advertising (admanGo, 2015). The huge advertising spending in Hong Kong has no doubt built up a shopping heaven to Hong Kong. The young generation is unable to escape such a luxury shopping atmosphere through social media. About 93% of shoppers intend to maintain or increase spending on luxury goods in the next 5 years (Yang, 2018), which also suggests that young shoppers will be the main consumption power in the future. Millennial and Generation Z shoppers spend more time on luxury information searches than before. 89% of shoppers aged 18–34 spend up to 3 weeks researching a luxury purchase (Yang, 2018). What's more, shopping is becoming more and more frequent due to the environment of fast fashion and overnight style sensations. The same study demonstrated that 52% of the shoppers aged 18–34 years shop for premium purchases once every 3 months, while just 41% of shoppers aged 35 or above did the same.

Generation Z in Hong Kong is poor at money management. Some of them start to face financial problems at an early age. A majority of respondents (people aged 18–64) including Generation Z were living with a surplus (76%) or a break-even (17%) financial status (Education Centre Investor, 2014). Respondents with a monthly household income below HK$20,000 (about US$2,500) were more likely to live with a deficit (Education Centre Investor, 2014). Among them, 77% of people aged from 18 to 29 have a surplus, 17% of them are break-even, and 6% of them have a deficit. People aged below 30 are happy-go-lucky shoppers, and occupy 35% of the general public in Hong Kong (Education Centre Investor, 2014). Generation Z is in this group as well, who generally lack clear life goals and are subject to influences from peer groups and hedonistic temptations. As they tend to have fewer family responsibilities, they are poor at controlling expenses and spend a bigger proportion (27%) of their income on entertainment or leisure expenses, compared with the general population (21%) (Education Centre Investor, 2014).

The economic market tries hard to persuade Generation Z to buy luxury products through credit cards and personal loan services. The younger generation aged 15-35 in Hong Kong has significant credit card debt, according to a survey from the Public Opinion Program of the University of Hong Kong in August 2015 (Ejinsight, 2015). Respondents had 2.5 credit cards each on an average, especially the younger generation in their 20s who had an average monthly income of HK$18,000 (US$2,200). They charged an average of HK$8,200 (US$1,000) a month to their credit cards, which was about 45% of their monthly income (Ejinsight, 2015).

It seems that the younger generation in Hong Kong considers shopping as one of their biggest entertainments, and shows an overly optimistic attitude in relation to their abilities to pay debts. In Hong Kong, it is easy to apply for a credit card. Many banks set up street booths. People dropping by can use their ID number and telephone number to apply for a credit card easily. The aggressive marketing of credit cards and personal loans to the younger generation has become controversial. Young consumers might fall into debt because of insufficient financial resources.

Nielsen (2017) found that online commerce represents a channel that brands need to pay attention to. Online shopping is not new: 7.5 million Hong Kong consumers spend more than 24 hours a week on the Internet; 88% of consumers in Hong Kong made at least one purchase online in the last 3 months, and 4 in 10 online consumers in Hong Kong have made purchases via their mobile devices in the last 3 months. Therefore, it represents a notable facet of the overall consumer experience; especially for Generation Z who enjoys it a lot. Consumers aged from 20 to 29 are identified as important online shoppers (Nielsen, 2017).

The top three online shopping categories for Hong Kong consumers are clothes/accessories, Airlines, and travel (Table 6). Compared with other generations, Generation Z travel more frequently than the other generations. Airlines travels and hotels share a significant portion of all categories. One-third of college students (age 20) have already travelled in more than 15 countries in their 20s.

Generation Z at Work in Hong Kong

About 40.2% of the labour force is aged from 15 to 24, just behind the age group from 25 to 44 (86.2%) and 45 to 64 (69.3%) (Census and Statistics Department, 2018c). As the majority of the population in the 15–19 age group is studying, the rate of labour force activity is lower than the other age groups. Labour force participants include those who are employed or who are looking for work. The expansion of opportunities for higher education in Hong Kong in recent years has led more young people to continue their studies. According to the Census and Statistics Department, the size of the labour force from March to May 2019 was 3,983,200, and the employment rate was 97.1% (Census and Statistics Department: The Government of the Hong Kong Special Administrative Region, 2013).

In the Hong Kong monthly digest of statistics report, the younger generation aged 15–24 constituted a notable share of part-time employees. They accounted for 20.4% of part-time employees in 2017, compared to only 6.3% of the full-time employed (Census and Statistics Department: The Government of the Hong Kong Special Administrative Region, 2018). Even in the age of high prices and high rents, young entrepreneurs in Hong Kong have emerged. Two Facebook websites for cheap travel information set up after the 90s attracted 280,000 likes in 2 years and a monthly income of 14.16 USD. According to a survey conducted by the Chinese University of Hong Kong Entrepreneurship Research Centre and Google (CUHK, 2015), young entrepreneurs believe that social support such as workspace and funds is increasing, and they are optimistic about the prospects for entrepreneurship.

Work–life balance is an essential factor when choosing a job for Generation Z. According to the JobsDB report in The Standard (March, 2019a, 2019b), 20% of 6,000 survey respondents put salary and overall compensation as the top priority, followed by the work–life balance with the number of 13.1% (Cindy, 2019). It is worth noting that 13.6% of the respondents are Generation Z, who, aged between 18 and 23, perceived work–life balance as a vital factor when choosing a job. Generation Z is less worried about obtaining a full-time or long-term job agreement, but instead is more open to accepting part-time jobs or being freelancers. Only 27.1% of young people consider a permanent job as crucial (Cindy, 2019). Furthermore, 32.7% of respondents think it is essential to find a job without overtime.

Families in Hong Kong encourage the younger generation to take a part-time job in order to gain pocket money (Chan, 2010). Therefore, most of Generation Z start to have a part-time job when entering into college. These part-time jobs include helpers on the campus; convenience store cashiers; store retailers; or others. Depending on their course arrangements, some young people have more than one part-time job at the same time. Generation Z in Hong Kong, therefore, gets used to having multiple careers from college. This might be the reason why most of Generation Z prefer to take part-time jobs: in contrast to full-time jobs, part-time jobs usually have no strict requirements in relation to employees' number of jobs. Some of Generation Z while studying in secondary school have started a business on Instagram or worked as YouTubers, for instance, selling items such as snacks that they brought back from their family trip in Japan or other Asian countries.

Despite the debate between government and Generation Z, the Hong Kong government tries to open more job opportunities to the younger generation to build up communication paths. In recent years, the Hong Kong government has been working on e-government services and has recruited the younger generation to join the system. An online discussion forum called the 'Public Affairs Forum' has been launched and keeps recruiting more young people. Furthermore, the government has also hired some communication officers and technological officers to set up their Facebook, Instagram, and WeChat accounts to maintain dialogue with the younger generation. As a result, Generation Z in Hong Kong also tries to build communication paths with the government through these job opportunities.

How to Deal with Generation Z in Hong Kong: Multi-tasking and Multi-generation

As Consumers

Despite the fact that Generation Z in Hong Kong has a positive attitude to high-end products, they are not loyal towards brands (Tofu gear, 2018). Growing up in a rapidly developing society, Generation Z is used to adopting new things, as well as new brands. Generation Z in Hong Kong, therefore, seems to be more open to switching brands. Except for the brand's popularity, they also look for quick fulfilment. Quick fulfilment includes same-day delivery, excellent after-sale-service, and a comfortable online or offline shopping experience (Tofu gear, 2018). When faced with such selective consumers in Generation Z, marketers should be aware that they might only have one shot at selling to them. Forty per cent of consumers from Generation Z abandon their relationship with brands after just one negative experience (Tofu gear, 2018). Thus, marketers should be careful when dealing with Generation Z.

First, as Generation Z relies heavily on peer influence, marketers should try to amplify the impacts of peer recommendations. For instance, marketers should try to encourage people to share their comments online. Second, marketers should use more celebrity endorsements, Key Opinion Leaders (KOL), or influencers. Several studies have proved that celebrity endorsement has a positive impact on brand awareness, attitudes towards brands, and has implications on brand fans (Chan, Leung, & Luk, 2013). Because of the popularity of influencer marketing, Generation Z in Hong Kong relies on KOL or influencers' recommendations heavily. Third, based on the frequent activities on social media of Generation Z, marketers should always remember to advertise on social media platforms.

As Employees

Hong Kong employers are facing a problem in dealing with Generation Z. Randstad, a recruitment and HR consultancy, surveyed Hong Kong employees in 2015 and found that 62% of the respondents thought that Generation Z was proficient in technology. Sixty-six per cent of employees believe that Generation Z was proficient in technology and can drive innovation in the workplace. Furthermore, the survey (Ranstad, 2015) also found that 75% of respondents believed that Generation Z paid more attention to work–life balance than the other generations. Local companies might not value such working attitudes, as most employers in Hong Kong are happy to see their employees stay late in the office. However, Generation Z pays more attention to work–life balance and usually tries to finish work on time, at 6 o'clock in the evening. They are reluctant to trade their private time for work time. A report on the employment status of Hong Kong's tertiary students in 2018 (JobsDB, 2019a, 2019b) showed that 14% of 553 local graduates and undergraduates were not willing to work overtime and 72% of them were only willing to work a maximum of 6 hours of overtime a week. JobsDB reported that this number has been rising since 2016. That's might be the reason why 'flexible working hours' are the most attractive working benefits selected by the fresh Generation Z graduates (21%). 'Early leave on festival day' and 'early leave on Friday (at least once a month)' were endorsed by 14% and 12%, respectively (JobsDB, 2019a, 2019b). These numbers demonstrate how much Generation Z is concerned with work–life balance. Thus, it is suggested that companies should consider planning their Human Resources strategy from the direction of the diversified workforce. Although some enterprises in Hong Kong have implemented the '4+1' working week (4 days working in the office and 1 day working at home) alongside other flexible working arrangements, these structures are not yet the mainstream. For example, some digital companies now choose the shared office as their office, which attract Generation Z's motivation to join their companies. Generation Z prefers the open working environment. It should be a consideration when more and more of Generation Z enter the job market.

Generation Z in Hong Kong is satisfied with their salary. Eighty per cent of fresh Generation Z graduates are satisfied with their first job salary, according to the 'employment status of Hong Kong's tertiary students 2018' report (JobsDB, 2019a, 2019b). In Hong Kong, fresh graduates are getting an average monthly salary of 2153.80 USD in their first jobs, which is 13% higher than the year of 2017. Over half of respondents thought it was reasonable to receive a monthly salary of 2,040 USD in their first job. Furthermore, Generation Z is concerned about the objective of companies. A survey showed that Generation Z prefers to find a company with high degree of social responsibility instead of looking for large companies (HKET, 2019). They think that it is important to contribute themselves to the society through their work. In the traditional job market, large companies with stable business are of course more popular with earners, because a good performance means that the bonus is particularly thick at the end of the year. However, Generation Z pays less attention to the company's profits than the overall market (JosDB, 2019a, 2019b). Instead, they pay more attention to whether the companies have social value and contribution. Some of Generation Z choose to work in a 'cannot be called a company' three people size studio because they feel that they can fight with their boss for better social values. This situation becomes increasingly apparent especially alongside their dissatisfaction with the government's performances.

The report also revealed that Generation Z considered 'banking and finan- cial services' as the ideal job industry and 'accounting and finance' as the ideal job category (JobsDB, 2019a, 2019b). This aligns with the strength of economic development in Hong Kong. The first choice of enterprise category is 'multina- tional companies' (35%) and the second choice is a 'government job' (19%). Nev- ertheless, only 8% of the respondents prefer to work in 'China based enterprises'. This number also reflects the political conflicts mentioned the first part of this chapter.

Besides, flexible development opportunities and novel recruitment methods can be attractive to Generation Z as well. Generation Z is always looking for learn- ing opportunities. For example, companies that change their jobs and allow them to work in different departments would be highly acceptable for Generation Z. As Generation Z is growing in the digital era, employers need to use flexible and creative recruitment methods to attract this generation. Recruiting online is a necessary action. More promotions on social platforms such as Facebook, Instagram, and LinkedIn are necessary to achieve the opportunity to reach Generation Z.

To integrate Generation Z into the team, employers must understand their motivations, strengths and weaknesses, balance the needs of each generation, encourage senior employees to impart knowledge and leadership skills to young colleagues, while young employees share new perspectives, skills, and insights. They are thereby improving the efficiency of multi-generational teams. The multi-generational workforce is the main issue happening in the workplace currently. To sum up, companies with flexible working hours, social value, and visionary, and democratic management are considered as a priority for Generation Z.

Conclusions

Generation Z in Hong Kong has a big dream, whether this is to start a business by themselves or express their attitude to political issues. Not to mention that they have to get agreement from their parents, they need to fight for themselves. Sometimes they are blamed for being too aggressive. Sometimes they are praised for being very brave; they are seeking their way. Instead of saying that 'they are too young', society should give more positive and encouraging attitudes to them.

References

admanGo. (2015). *Advertising expenditure by product category and by brand*. Retrieved from www.admanGo.com. Accessed on 28 October 2015 (by subscription)

Census and Statistics Department: The Government of the Hong Kong Special Administrative Region. (2013). Labour – Overview | Census and Statistics Department. *Census and Statistics Department*. Retrieved from https://www.censtatd.gov.hk/hkstat/sub/so200.jsp

Census and Statistics Department: The Government of the Hong Kong Special Administrative Region. (2018). *Hong Kong Monthly Digest of Statistics* (January 2016), p. 11.

Census and Statistics Department. (2018a). The Four Key Industries and Other Selected Industries – Overview | Census and Statistics Department. *Census and Statistics Department*. Retrieved from https//www.censtatd.gov.hk/hkstat/sub/so80.jsp

Census and Statistics Department. (2018b). Table 007: Labour Force and Labour Force Participation Rate – By Sex | Census and Statistics Department. *Census and Statistics Department*. Retrieved from https://www.censtatd.gov.hk/hkstat/sub/sp200.jsp?tableID=007&ID=0&productType=8

Census and Statistics Department. (2018c). Table 008: Labour Force and Labour Force Participation Rate – By Age Group | Census and Statistics Department. *Census and Statistics Department*. Retrieved from https://www.censtatd.gov.hk/hkstat/sub/sp200.jsp?tableID=008&ID=0&productType=8

Census and Statistics Department. (2019a). Press Release (2019, 19 February): Year-end population for 2018 | Census and Statistics Department. *Census and Statistics Department*. Retrieved from https://www.censtatd.gov.hk/press_release/pressRelease Detail.jsp?charsetID=1&pressRID=4419

Census and Statistics Department. (2019b). Table 002: Population by Age Group and Sex | Census and Statistics Department. *Census and Statistics Department*. Retrieved from https://www.censtatd.gov.hk/hkstat/sub/sp150.jsp?tableID=002&ID=0&productType=8

Centre for Youth Studies Hong Kong Institute of Asia-Pacific Studies, C. (2017). *Youth Political Participation and Social Media Use in Hong Kong Research Report*. Retrieved from http://youthstudies.com.cuhk.edu.hk/wp-content/uploads/2017/04/Research-Report_Youth-Political-Participation-and-Social-Media-Use-in-Hong-Kong.pdf

Chan, K. (2003). Materialism among Chinese Children in Hong Kong. *Young Consumers*, *4*(4), 47–61.

Chan, K. K. W. (2010). *Youth and consumption*. Hong Kong: City University of Hong Kong Press.

Chan, K., Leung, Y., & Luk, E. K. (2013). Impact of celebrity endorsement in advertising on brand image among Chinese adolescents. *Young Consumers*, *14*(2), 167–179.

Chan, K., & Prendergast, G. (2007). Materialism and social comparison among adolescents. *Social Behavior and Personality: An International Journal*, *35*(2), 213–228.

Chung, R., & Tai, E. (2012). *Conference on Border Crossing in Greater China: Production, Community and Identity Ethnic Identity of Hong Kong People: An Academic Question Turned Political*, 1988 (pp. 1–10).

Cindy, W. (2019). More to life than the job, say youngsters – The Standard. *The Standard*. Retrieved from http://www.thestandard.com.hk/section-news.php?id=205728

CUHK. (2015). Empowering Young Entrepreneurs Program (EYE Program) 2015 | Center for Entrepreneurship. *CUHK Business Scholl*. Retrieved from https://entrepreneurship.bschool.cuhk.edu.hk/eyeprogram

Education Centre Investor. (2014). *IEC Research: Knowledge, Attitudes and Behaviour towards Money and Debt Management*. Retrieved from https://www.ifec.org.hk/common/pdf/about_iec/IEC-research-knowledge-attitudes-and-behaviour-towards-money-management.pdf

Ejinsight. (2015). Young Hongkongers under a pile of credit card debt, says survey. *ejinsight*. Retrieved from http://www.ejinsight.com/20151014-young-hongkongers-under-a-pile-of-credit-card-debt-says-survey/

Elizabeth, C. (2017). University study find Hong Kong teenagers can be materialistic centred and distrustful. *South China Morning Post*, Hong Kong. Retrieved from https://www.scmp.com/news/hong-kong/education/article/2118174/university-study-finds-hong-kong-teenagers-can-be

G0-Globe. (2018). *Online Consumer Shopping Behavior in Hong Kong*. Retrieved from Retrieved from https://www.go-globe.hk/blog/online-consumer-hong-kong/

HKET. (2019).「廢青」「唔捱得」?Z世代打工仔更重視目標及更愛錢 – 香港經濟日報 – 中小企 – 商管策略 – D191217. *HKET*. https://sme.hket.com/article/2522038/「廢青」「唔捱得」?Z世代打工仔更重視目標及更愛錢

HKTDC Research. (2019). Economic and Trade Information on Hong Kong | HKTDC. *HKTDC Research*. Retrieved from http://hong-kong-economy-research.hktdc.com/business-news/article/Market-Environment/Economic-and-Trade-Information-on-Hong-Kong/etihk/en/1/1X000000/1X09OVUL.htm

HKU Pop. (2019a). Table – Ethnic identity – "Chinese" in broad sense. *HKU Pop Site*. Retrieved from https://www.hkupop.hku.hk/english/popexpress/ethnic/eidentity/chibroad/halfyr/datatables.html

HKU Pop. (2019b). Table – Ethnic identity – "Hongkonger" in broad sense. *HKU Pop Site*. Retrieved from https://www.hkupop.hku.hk/english/popexpress/ethnic/eidentity/hkbroad/halfyr/datatables.html

HKU POP Site. (2019a). HKU POP final farewell: Rift widens between Chinese and Hongkong identities, national pride plunges to one in four – 港大民研 HKUPOP. *HKU Pop*. Retrieved from https://www.hkupop.hku.hk/english/release/release1594.html

HKU POP Site. (2019b). Table – HKUPOP. *HKU POP*. Retrieved from https://www.hkupop.hku.hk/english/popexpress/ethnic/eidentity/halfyr/datatables.html

JobsDB. (2019a). *Over 80 % of Graduates Satisfied with their First Job as Average Monthly Salaries Rise to Almost HK $ 17K*. Hong Kong. Retrieved from https://hk.jobsdb.com/en-hk/wp-content/uploads/sites/2/static/salary-report/2019/190124_student_PR_eng.pdf.pdf?icmpid=enewsh_1202:link_art1:20190212

JosDB. (2019b). [Post-90s Pickers] Company size is not important and resists becoming "labor" of arbitrary condemnation | jobsDB Hong Kong. *JobsDB*. Retrieved from https://hk.jobsdb.com/en-hk/articles/90後揀工-公司規模不重要-抗拒淪為任意差遣的勞工/

Nielsen. (2017). Meet Today's Hong Kong Consumers. *Nielsen*. Retrieved from https://www.nielsen.com/hk/en/insights/news/2017/meet-todays-hong-kong-consumers.html

Ranstad. (2015). Only half of Hong Kong employees believe that employers can meet the needs of "Generation Z" (僅一半香港員工認為僱主能滿足「Z世代」的需求). *CTgoodjobs*. Retrieved from https//cthr.ctgoodjobsblog.hk/hr-columnist/randstadhk/2015/01/15/

Social Sciences Research Centre the university of Hong Kong. (2015). Youth in Hong Kong a statistical profile 2015: Executive summary. *The Commission on Youth*, p. 11.

Tofu gear. (2018). The digital consumer in Asia 2018. Retrieved from https://jingdaily.com/downloads/the-digital-consumer-in-asia-2018/

Yang, I. (2018). The new luxury shopper in Hong Kong. *Consumer Insights*. Retrieved from https://www.thinkwithgoogle.com/intl/en-apac/trends-and-insights/new-luxury-shopper-hong-kong/

Chapter 4

Generation Z in Japan: Raised in Anxiety

Mototaka Sakashita

Abstract

Generation Z in Japan, born between 1995 and 2010, has unique characteristics. First, they are pessimists, which is mainly because of the challenging environment in which they were raised, with long-lasting low economic
growth and multiple natural disasters. Second, they are digital natives, with a
high level of digital device literacy. Raised in a highly advanced technological
environment, they benefit in various ways by leveraging such devices. Also,
they value relationships with family and friends, forming very close intimate
relationships with their parents and broad shallow relationships with their
friends. These unique characteristics turn Generation Z into a careful spend-
er in consumption, and a stability seeker in workplaces. As consumers, they
are very knowledgeable using both online/offline information, thus, are very
selective and cautious when spending their money trying to prepare for the
possible risk in the future. As employees, they are less loyal to companies and
value their private life higher than their work life. A guideline for targeting
Generation Z in Japan is presented.

Keywords: Generation Z; Japan; consumption, work; spending; digitalisation

Introduction

Basic Information about Japan

Japan is located in East Asia, standing west of the Pacific Ocean in the Northern
Hemisphere. It is 145,936 square kilometres as of October 1, 2016 (Geospatial
Information Authority of Japan, 2016), and has 47 prefectures spreading in eight
different areas. Its capital is Tokyo, and about 10% of the population live in the
Tokyo Metropolitan Area.

The New Generation Z in Asia: Dynamics, Differences, Digitalisation
The Changing Context of Managing People, 55–70
Copyright © 2020 by Emerald Publishing Limited
All rights of reproduction in any form reserved
doi:10.1108/978-1-80043-220-820201007

Japan's population is estimated at about 126.2 million as of April 1, 2019 (Ministry of Internal Affairs and Communications [MIAC], 2019), with 61.4 million males and 64.8 million females. Japan is rapidly ageing, with the number of babies born in Japan in 2018 the lowest since records began, and its population declining rapidly (The Japan Times, December 21, 2018). The statistics say the same; out of the total population, 27.7% are people aged 65 and over; 33.5% are those aged between 40 and 64; 21.7% are those aged between 20 and 39, and 17.0% are those aged 20 and under (Statistics Bureau of Japan [SBJ], 2017).

Japan's Gross Domestic Product (GDP) is 4,873.2 billion USD, and is ranked third as of 2017 (Statista, 2019). Its main industries are automobiles, consumer electronics, computers, and other electronics (The Government of Japan, 2019). The economic growth of Japan has been sluggish since the beginning of the 1990s, and shrinkage of the working population (aged 15–64) slows it down (Ministry of Economy, Trade and Industry, 2016).

General Values and Norms

Hofstede Insights (2019) gives two interesting points about the characteristics of Japanese values and norms. First, Japan is a moderately hierarchical, less individualistic, and extremely masculine country. Since Japan values the hierarchy of society, people tend to respect the elderly or people in higher positions. Also, Japan is less individualistic, and known as a collectivistic society where people put harmony of the group over the expression of individual opinions. Finally, it is the most masculine country in the world, where people are motivated by the desire to be the best; however, this may not be the case with Generation Z in Japan, which will be explained later.

Second, both uncertainly avoidance and long-term orientation are extremely high, and indulgence level is low in Japan. This means that people tend to look for long-lasting stability in their lives, avoiding uncertainty and short-term thoughts. High uncertainly avoidance may be because Japan has been suffering from many natural disasters, thus, people like to set up rules for better predictability. Also, Japanese people tend to save money rather than spending it (Koll, 2018), which can be enhanced by their uncertainty avoidant nature. Finally, Japanese people often think indulging themselves without controlling their desire is somewhat wrong, partly because of social norms.

Preservation of Local Differences

Japan's local autonomy is secured by the Constitution of Japan, and local regions have their own local governments (MIAC, 2019). Each prefecture has multiple cities totalled at 1,719 as of 2013. Japanese language is used in all the prefectures, but each area has its own dialect.

Most of the prefectures or cities carry their own unique specialty foods or traditional crafts, and people often try to preserve them as if they were their identity. For example, each prefecture has its own famous agricultural product, such as white peaches in Okayama prefecture, strawberries in Fukuoka, mangoes in

Miyazaki, melons in Hokkaido, and so on, and local people are proud of such products. Usually people are reluctant to accept the government's policy to merge cities, because their regional culture may be diluted.

Socialisation

In Japan, social norms, family members, and schools or workplaces play a big role as a socialisation agent. First, social norms play an important role as do peers in the socialisation process in Japan. For example, Japanese people often use the term 'TPO' in many situations. TPO stands for Time, Place, and Occasion, and it means that people must behave appropriately according to each situation, so that they can maintain the harmony. Also, age-appropriateness is highly respected in fashion, so that everyone looks similar especially in ceremonies, schools or workplaces, to form a sense of harmony.

Second, family is important in the Japanese socialisation process, and often involves parental control over children (Gentina, Hogg, & Sakashita, 2017). Especially mothers play an important role in their children's (especially daughters') socialisation (Kimura & Sakashita, 2012; Sakashita & Kimura, forthcoming), given that children and parents form a highly interdependent and indulgent relationship called 'Amae' (Doi, 1962). Japanese parents usually support their children both financially and emotionally until they finish their school, and many of them keep doing so even when the children are working after graduation.

Third, schools or workplaces are also important in Japanese socialisation. Japanese people spend a lot of intimate time with their friends at schools while growing up. This interaction among friends serves as an important socialisation agent. Also, most of the schools in Japan have their own strict school rules. For example, some schools prohibit their students from dying their hair. These rules also help students' socialisation process. Likewise, some companies in Japan also have their own rules, either obvious or hidden norms. Japanese people grow up surrounded by such rules, which prescribe their socialisation.

Education

As for education in Japan, everyone is obligated to go to 6 years of elementary school and 3 years of lower secondary school, which is specified by Japanese School Education law as well as the Constitution. About 98.0% of the secondary school graduates proceed to upper secondary schools (Ministry of Education, Culture, Sports, Science and Technology [MEXT], 2019) and 57.3% of the upper secondary school graduates proceed to universities or colleges as of 2017 (MEXT, 2017). Many students are extremely stressed about severe competition with others to get into better schools, especially at universities, or sometimes even elementary school levels.

The Japanese government once tried to ease this extremely severe competition guided by cramming memorisation at schools, and it lowered the level of most textbooks so that students would have more free time to do other things. This is called 'Yutori Kyouiku (pressure-free education)', and started in 2002, which led to a big controversy (Nihon Keizai Shimbun, March 9, 2019). For example, the circle ratio was taught as '3.14' in the former education system, but it was taught as 'about 3' in Yutori Kyouiku. Some argued that the Japanese education standard would become lower because of it. Thus, the government switched back to the original education content starting from 2011; therefore, those who were born from 1987 to 2003, including Generation Z, more or less experienced this pressure-free version of education in Japan, and are called 'Yutori Sedai (pressure-free generation)'.

Basics of Generation Z in Japan: Born in a Challenging Time

Basic Information

Generation Z in Japan refers to those who were born between 1995 and 2010 in Japan. They consist of only 14.5% of the whole population, with 51.3% being male and 48.7% female (SBJ, 2017). Though small, there is heterogeneity in this group of people, thus, it might be wrong to summarise its characteristics. However, one can still conclude that they have three main characteristics (Nikkei Sangyo Shimbun, March 1, 2017).

First, members of Generation Z in Japan are 'Digital Natives' (Matsushita, 2012). The Microsoft Corporation launched Windows 95 around when they were born, and personal computers began to penetrate into ordinary homes in Japan. Surrounded by all the digital devices such as iPhones, they are more into online activities compared to the other generations. Most of the people in their twenties (born between 1988 and 1997) including Generation Z in universities possess smartphones in 2017 (94.5%), and they heavily use these personal digital devices every day for information search, e-mailing, chatting, and movie viewing (MIAC, 2017).

Second, they are 'Pessimists'. The Great Hanshin Awaji Earthquake and the subway sarin gas attack took place in 1996. When they were born, Japan was in a dark era going through a very difficult time. During their adolescent period, they experienced the Global Financial Crisis (2008) and the Great East Japan Earthquake (2011). Therefore, they tend not to believe in perfect safety in society, and often keep trying to prepare for possible disasters. The results of the survey conducted by the Japan Youth Study Group (JYSG) revealed that 72.6% of those who were born between 1992 and 1997 disagreed that 'Japan's future is bright' (Fujimura, Asano, & Habuchi, 2016).

Third, some of Generation Z belong to 'Yutori Sedai' described above. These members of Generation Z (born between 1996 and 2003) could only learn with simplified textbooks with easier learning content. Thus, they sometimes feel inferior because they did not learn as much as the other generations. Some of them often try to study hard to gain extra professional skills to cover up their insecure feelings.

Values

A nationwide inter-generational survey in 2017 conducted by Hakuhodo Inc., a leading advertising agency in Japan, found that there are two main characteristics of values that Generation Z in Japan holds. First, students of Generation Z in Japan are more diligent and serious about the future. They think study is more important than play, possibly because they like to prepare for the future, which may sometimes create stress. To avoid negativities, they often try to lower their living standard so that they can still be satisfied with their everyday lives. In fact, the results of the survey show that they think that they are 'happier' and 'more satisfied' with their lives compared to other generations, which possibly implies that they hold more humble desires.

Second, Generation Z in Japan is less materialistic compared to other generations. In Japan, most parents give allowance money to their children while in school. About 70–80% of students in elementary schools, lower middle schools, and upper middle schools received an allowance from their parents in 2015; however, members of Generation Z in Japan received less money from their parents because of the sluggish economy (Bank of Japan, 2016). Under such circumstances, coupled with their pessimistic nature, Generation Z in Japan tends to save money instead of spending it.

Media Usage

Smartphone diffusion has accelerated Internet penetration for all age groups in Japan including Generation Z, who is accessing the Internet mainly through such digital devices (Ministry of Internal Affairs and Communications [MIAC], 2017) (http://www.soumu.go.jp). What do Generation Z do online? The younger members of Generation Z tend to use video-sharing websites the most, and also often play online games (Table 1) (MIAC, 2017). However, they do not really use e-mails, homepages and blogs, or social networking services (SNS), partly because their parents prohibit them from using SNS to protect their children from interacting with unknown people. The older members of Generation Z in Japan are into video-sharing websites, free calling apps, SNS, e-mails, and online games; thus, they seem to be enjoying social interaction as well.

Now a social media service called 'LINE' has the highest penetration (around 60%) in the whole Japanese market as of 2017, followed by Facebook and Twitter (around 40%), then Instagram (around 30%) (MIAC, 2017). Members of Generation Z in Japan are also highly dependent on social networking through mobile phones and smartphones (Doi, 2014), and are heavily using LINE every day. LINE is unique in that it has many stamps (small pictures often accompanied with short messages like 'thank you' or 'hello'), so that the users can send messages without typing words. This easy-to-use characteristic of LINE seems to have captured different age groups including Generation Z in Japan.

Relationship with Parents and Friends

Members of Generation Z in Japan form unique relationships with their parents and friends. First, they have very intimate relationships with their parents, especially their mothers (Hakuhodo, 2017). Japanese mothers and their daughters in general form a close relationship, and together they engage in many activities such

Table 1. Online Activity Penetration (%)

Description	1. Age Group									
	6–12	13–19	20–29	30–39	40–49	50–59	60–69	70–79	80+	Total
E-mails	23.7	62.5	84.1	87.1	89.4	87.4	81.3	75.8	68.0	80.2
HP/Blogs	22.2	36.9	45.1	47.5	44.7	39.9	29.2	25.3	19.2	39.0
SNS	22.4	68.4	74.4	72.4	62.6	50.7	30.7	16.5	21.1	54.7
Call/Chat	24.1	72.9	77.3	71.3	59.4	51.2	34.4	19.9	14.7	55.4
Video-Sharing	74.6	75.9	69.2	67.9	55.3	45.8	24.3	13.1	10.2	53.1
Online Games	48.7	50.7	45.5	38.0	28.2	15.6	7.8	7.1	5.4	28.7
Prize Competition	2.8	11.4	22.0	25.0	28.5	25.4	15.5	10.1	11.2	20.7
Maps/Public Transportation	5.6	43.5	69.1	72.5	73.8	69.8	62.0	57.7	47.9	63.4
Weather	10.5	46.4	65.7	76.9	79.3	73.6	63.1	56.4	38.8	65.8
News	5.6	32.8	58.5	71.4	70.0	65.7	54.3	46.6	34.1	57.6
Dictionary	12.1	38.3	37.5	36.7	36.5	38.0	34.7	32.7	34.5	35.3
E-Learning	5.4	17.5	13.0	9.9	8.9	7.4	3.5	1.3	2.3	8.6
Shopping	7.4	34.5	61.7	63.7	58.3	51.4	37.5	31.4	30.5	49.1
Auction	0.4	5.3	16.1	18.6	16.8	14.6	7.4	5.5	3.3	12.7
Radio/Movie	14.5	25.1	30.1	28.2	24.7	21.9	13.5	12.6	10.6	22.6

Source: Ministry of Internal Affairs and Communication, Japan (2018).

as shopping, traveling, and even taking a bath (Gentina et al., 2018). This is typical especially for teenage daughters, but some of them continue doing so in their 20s or even beyond. This unique tendency is especially true for Generation Z in Japan; for example, they would spend most of their time in the living room with parents at home (Hakuhodo, 2017).

Second, the relationship with friends of Generation Z in Japan is diluted, selective, and homogeneous (Nagai, 2019). Looking at the JYSG comparative surveys explained above, Nagai (2019) points out that the number of friends that young people have has increased; while the average numbers of 'best friends' slightly increased from 3.8 (2002) to 4.5 (2012), that of 'acquaintances' jumped from 45.9 (2002) to 74.5 (2012). Thus, he concludes that they would prefer having wider and shallower friends. Also, some members of Generation Z in Japan seem to select friends according to different situations (Nagai, 2019). This selective nature of interpersonal relationships results not only in situation-wise homogeneity, but also diversification across different members, in terms of values, fashion, or interests.

This unique characteristic of friend relationships can never be understood without considering Generation Z's intensive use of SNS such as LINE. Especially, for the older members of Generation Z in Japan, they occasionally make friends through the Internet. One out of three in lower secondary schools is enjoying SNS in 2014, and more than 20% of them had friends whom they had met only through the Internet (Uematsu, 2016). This number is very high given that students at lower secondary schools hardly get out from their school/family/local community.

Having such relationships with friends requires Generation Z in Japan to effectively manage a wide intensive interaction with a large number of friends (Matsushita, 2012), and this may sometimes create a stressful situation for them. In Japanese society, harmony is respected, so that people are supposed to be polite to others even in a digital world. Not responding to LINE messages immediately would be impolite, thus, many of Generation Z have to constantly check their messages to reply back. Some of Generation Z are sometimes faced with too many friends and acquaintances, thus, they feel pressured, and, in some extreme cases, insecure (Doi, 2014). This would result in less friend-level competition in Generation Z, because they would rather avoid such troubles.

Members of Generation Z as Consumers in Japan: Careful Spenders

Background and Overall Characteristics

As consumers, Generation Z in Japan has three overall characteristics. First, they are humble when spending their money. Having grown up in difficult circumstances, members of Generation Z in Japan are relatively pessimistic about their future, thus, they often try to save money to prepare for possible future troubles. In fact, members of Generation Z spend a lower amount of money every year compared to other older generations (SBJ, 2014).

Second, even though they spend less, they do like shopping. The Consumer Affairs Agency (CAA, 2017) conducted a nationwide survey to compare shopping preferences among different age groups in Japan, to find that members of Generation Z have the highest shopping preference (more than 70%) compared to other older generations (around 50% or less). Though members of Generation Z in Japan do not spend much in general, they still do like shopping and selectively spend in their favourite things.

Third, members of Generation Z in Japan are efficient in spending. They are digital natives, which enables them to search the necessary information online to make a purchase decision more quickly and accurately (Hakuhodo, 2017). Male members of Generation Z in Japan spend an average time of less than 10 min on shopping per day, while older male generations spend about 15–25 min; female members of Generation Z in Japan spend less than 20 min, while older female generations spend about 25–45 min per day (CAA, 2017).

Consumption Trends

Chronologically, the overall spending of young people had decreased during 1999–2014 period (CAA, 2017), and this long-lasting decline in consumption by young people in Japan indicates that the spending of Generation Z is also very small. Generation Z in Japan is more into intangible services than tangible products. According to a nationwide survey conducted by CAA in 2016, older members of Generation Z in Japan are characterised in four ways (as seen in Table 2). First, they are very much into eating, which is the same as all the other older generations. Second, older members of Generation Z in Japan seem to be more interested in spending their money to manage their physical appearance, with high spending in fashion and hair/beauty salons, which is also found in some other younger generations. Third, unlike other generations, older members of Generation Z in Japan are spending their money on experiential services such as live sports viewing, movies, and concerts. Fourth, as previously explained, they save their money instead of spending, like other younger generations.

Values of Consumption

What do members of Generation Z in Japan value? CAA (2016) investigated what people thought was the main component of a happy life for different age groups in Japan. They found that the younger generation tends to value connections with family/friends more, compared to older age groups, as seen in Table 3. Precisely, for the older members of Generation Z in Japan (born between 1997 and 2001), the percentage of those who chose connection with family/friends as the most important component necessary for a happy life was 30.9%, while those of other generations were somewhere between 10.2% and 22.3%. Thus, older members of Generation Z in Japan are more interested in social connections, which is in line with the fact that they have a close relationship with their parents, and a broad one with a relatively large number of friends.

Table 2. Top 5 Things to Spend Money Among Different Generations.

Age	15–19	20–29	30–39	40–49	50–59	60–69	70+
Born year	1997–2001	1987–1996	1977–1986	1967–1976	1957–1966	1947–1956	–1946
Top 1	Eating (69.1%)	Eating (71.2%)	Eating (73.8%)	Eating (69.8%)	Eating (69.2%)	Eating (68.1%)	Eating (69.2%)
Top 2	Fashion (50.2%)	Fashion (52.1%)	Fashion (39.3%)	Education for children (47.7%)	Socialising (27.4%)	Medical cost (36.1%)	Medical cost (49.3%)
Top 3	Sport/Movie Concert (34.6%)	Socialising (45.2%)	Education for children (34.8%)	Housing (28.4%)	Housing (25.8%)	Travel (31.8%)	Socialising (27.8%)
Top 4	Hair/Beauty (33.9%)	Hair/Beauty (41.7%)	Housing (31.2%)	Fashion (26.5%)	Communication cost (25.4%)	Socialising (29.1%)	Hair/Beauty (27.4%)
Top 5	Saving (27.9%)	Saving (34.4%)	Saving (30.2%)	Hair/Beauty and Socialising (25.8%)	Hair/Beauty (25.0%)	Hair/Beauty (26.5%)	Travel (26.2%)

Source: Consumer Affairs Agency (2017).

Table 3.   The Most Important Thing for a Happy Life.

Age	15–19	20–24	25–29	30–39	40–49	50–59	60–69	70+
Born year	1997–2001	1993–1996	1988–1992	1977–1987	1967–1976	1957–1966	1947–1956	–1946
Money (%)	43.0	47.5	52.3	43.2	36.0	25.4	21.2	20.2
Time (%)	12.1	12.5	12.2	11.4	7.8	6.6	2.4	2.0
Connection with family/ friend (%)	30.9	17.5	14.0	22.3	20.9	19.9	15.6	10.2
Connection with local community (%)	1.2	0.0	0.0	0.0	0.0	0.2	0.2	0.2
Interaction with pets or nature (%)	1.2	1.3	1.2	0.7	0.4	0.0	0.4	0.5
Health (%)	9.7	15.0	16.9	19.2	33.4	46.0	58.3	66.9
Other (%)	0.0	1.9	0.6	0.5	0.4	0.7	0.6	0.2
None (%)	1.8	4.4	2.9	2.6	1.2	1.2	1.2	0.2

Source: Consumer Affairs Agency (2017).

Interpersonal Influence of Consumption

Typically at schools, they are deeply into LINE messaging with their friends as well as social media, which influences what and how they purchase. According to CAA (2016), the top three information sources that older members of Generation Z in Japan (born between 1997 and 2001) use when making purchase decisions were Internet websites (66.4%), family/friends (54.2%), and SNS (40.9%), while other information sources were all very low such as commercial messages on TV/Radio (27.2%), or a salesperson at a retailers (26.2%). Especially the usage of SNS is uniquely high only for Generation Z in Japan, compared to other older generations.

Members of Generation Z in Japan are very close to their parents, thus, they would also search for advice from their parents when making purchase decisions. Daughters in Japan have very close relationships with their mothers, and would go to shopping together and occasionally jointly purchase things (Gentina et al., 2018). Also, Japanese mothers often tell their daughters what kind of fashion outfits to purchase (Kimura & Sakashita, 2012; Sakashita & Kimura, forthcoming). Consumption of Generation Z in Japan is, therefore, influenced by their parents, especially the mothers.

Digitalisation in Consumption

According to the nationwide survey conducted by CAA in 2016, many members of Generation Z in Japan perceived mobile phones or smartphones as necessities: this was higher than those of other older groups. The percentage of those who used smartphones to actually purchase products/services was the highest for those in their 20s (born between 1987 and 1996) which includes the oldest members of Generation Z, with 58.9% (CAA, 2016). Though the score for younger members of Generation Z aged from 15 to 19 (born between 1997 and 2001) was relatively low (32.9%), this number is most likely to increase as they grow older.

Members of Generation Z in Japan search for more online information about the product/service and evaluations from actual users (CAA, 2016). Furthermore, such online evaluation information obtained from SNS or reviewing websites drives them to actual purchases. MIAC (2016) reports that about 90% of people in their 20s (born between 1987 and 1996) have actually bought items or services more than once because of evaluative information posted in SNS or reviewing websites. As for the influencers, they seem to be more influenced by their friends or celebrities online when making purchases (CAA, 2016).

Members of Generation Z in Japan also post messages or pictures to share their personal experiences. Both males and females in Generation Z are active SNS users, searching and sending information. CAA (2016) reported that 24.8% of males aged between 15 and 19 years old (born between 1997 and 2001) regularly share their personal experiences through SNS, which is much higher than the average (9.7%). This tendency was much stronger for females in the same age group, with 47.0% of them doing so while the average being 13.1%.

Generation Z at Work in Japan: Stability Seekers

Background and Overall Characteristics

Before Generation Z was born, Japan was enjoying high economic growth, and people's jobs were secured by lifetime employment and a steady rise in their salaries based on seniority ranking. However, these benefits could not go on after Japan entered into difficult times, and people were no longer protected. Thus, Generation Z feels insecure and often tries to prepare for the future.

Recently, Japanese companies have been facing a difficult time in hiring, because of the continuing decrease in the production age population caused by low birth rate and ageing (Cabinet Office, 2018). The situation is particularly serious in suburban areas, because of the centralisation of the population in the Tokyo Metropolitan area. Thus, the employment rate of university graduates in 2018 was the highest ever on record, with the astonishing number of 87.9% (Ministry of Health, Labour and Welfare, 2018). However, even in this optimistic situation, Generation Z is still worried about their future, having been raised in a tough time.

Work Trends

Toyokeizai Online (2019) summarises some characteristics of job hunting of older members of Generation Z in Japan (born in around 1997) in 2019. First, they prefer large companies. This is partly because big companies are relatively stable compared to other small/medium sized ones. Second, they avoid companies with business deteriorations or scandals, especially when they are widely broadcasted. Third, they tend to choose companies by industry, rather than by individual company brand names. Company brand names with a reputation used to be one of the major criteria for job hunting for university students; however, they now tend to look at the entire industry based on its image, depending on what they would like to pursue in their career.

Work Values

The Cabinet Office in Japan conducted a nationwide survey about the values of youths aged from 16 to 29 years old (born between 1988 and 2001) in 2017 (Cabinet Office, 2018). Results showed that 88.4% of students preferred full-time employment, which indicates that older members of Generation Z in Japan tend to seek stable jobs rather than temporal ones.

As for the worries that older members of Generation Z in Japan have towards working, the same survey revealed that they are most worried about their income (76.5%), followed by pension after retirement (75.4%), capability to work (73.5%), work/life blending (72.2%), and interpersonal relationships at work (71.4%). Some of Generation Z are anxious about various things at work, and the same survey revealed that they are more willing to switch between different jobs compared to other age groups. In other words, they are less loyal to the company.

Work Expectations

What does Generation Z work for? The nationwide survey by the Cabinet Office (2018) revealed that the top three things that the younger generation consider when choosing their jobs were stability (88.8%), followed by salary (88.7%), and work flexibility (88.5%). Other criteria related to job-hunting for Generation Z in Japan can be found in Table 4.

As for work–life blending, older members of Generation Z value their private lives over work. According to the same survey by the Cabinet Office, 63.7% of the younger generation (including older members of Generation Z) agreed with 'I would prioritise family and private life over work', while only 12.7% agreed with 'I would prioritise work over family and private life'. More females (69.4%) prioritise their family and private lives over work, than males (58.3%). Thus, older members of Generation Z cherish their personal lives more than their work lives.

Work Digitalisation

The hiring process in Japan is shifting towards digitalisation (Matsushita, 2012). In Japan, a typical hiring process goes through multiple steps: job seminars by companies; screening examinations; screening applications; and multiple interviews. These steps take a huge amount of time and effort, so are being replaced by more efficient digital alternative methods such as online seminars/examinations, electronic application forms, and telecommunication interviews, all of which members of Generation Z are familiar with.

Moreover, older members of Generation Z benefit from their digital information literacy in job search, by frequently checking online information and

Table 4.   (Un)important Things When Choosing a Job for a Young Generation (Born Between 1988 and 2001).

	Very important (%)	Important (%)	Unimportant (%)	Very unimportant (%)
The job is stable and I can keep working for a long time	50.0	38.8	8.3	2.9
The job pays well	46.0	42.7	8.6	2.7
The job lets me do what I want to do	42.3	46.2	8.2	3.3
The job comes with good welfare	41.1	44.1	11.1	3.7
The job gives me a lot of free time	33.9	48.3	14.3	3.5
I can commute to the workplace from home	44.3	36.0	14.6	5.2
I can use my knowledge or skills at the job	31.2	47.5	16.7	4.6
The job gives me an opportunity to improve my ability	25.0	48.2	20.6	6.2
The job benefits other people	23.7	48.1	21.4	6.9
The job allows me to take care of my kids or parents	27.4	42.7	21.1	8.8
The job is reputable in the society	16.4	40.8	33.3	9.6
I can make decisions without orders at the job	14.3	41.5	36.0	8.3
I can promote myself by the merit system at the job	14.9	36.7	36.1	12.3

Source: Cabinet Office (2018).

exchanging messages with their friends through SNS (Nikkei Sangyo Shimbun, March 1, 2017). An online service called 'Minna no Shuukatsu Nikki (Job Hunting Diary of Everybody)' offers updated information about hiring schedules, job interviews, as well as unofficial information about the working environments of current employees. Members of Generation Z in Japan also use Twitter to search for information about any particular company of their interest.

Internal and external communication at the workplace is also shifting towards digitalisation. Many younger people are using social media such as LINE or Facebook to communicate with their co-workers within their companies, as well as their customers or suppliers outside. Members of Generation Z in Japan are expected to benefit more from such digitalised communication, since they have grown up surrounded by such devices.

How to Deal with Generation Z in Japan

How to Deal with Generation Z in Japan as Consumers?

As previously explained, members of Generation Z in Japan are smart and careful consumers. First, they are very knowledgeable. They obtain the necessary information to make better purchase decisions from various online information sources such as Internet websites or social media, as well as offline information sources such as their closely related family or friends. Thus, companies are required to provide the necessary information on multiple communication media. Second, they are very careful in spending. They were raised in a difficult era when Japan was experiencing a low economic growth rate and occasional natural disasters, which made them very risk averse. Thus, they are very cautious in making purchase decisions, trying not to make mistakes. Also, they may not be really into big brand names; rather, they purely evaluate the quality of products and services. Therefore, companies should invest more in R&D so that they can provide better products and services.

Also, since members of Generation Z highly value interpersonal relationships, especially with their family and friends, companies should focus more on this aspect when targeting them. Many daughters in Generation Z go out shopping with their mothers in Japan, and companies are offering special products such as cosmetics that both of them can use, or services such as co-travel plans. Also, they value friend networks, and are more likely to be influenced by information posted by their friends. Thus, companies should offer products or services that would stimulate people's desire to post their personal experiences of the products or services. 'Insta-Bae (Looking good on Instagram)' has been a major keyword in influencer marketing in Japan, which would go down especially well with Generation Z.

Finally, digitalisation is the key when targeting Generation Z in Japan. Members of Generation Z in Japan are digital natives, using digital devices when searching and sending helpful information for better purchase experiences, or actually making purchases through smartphones. Companies are required to maximise their efforts to effectively use this technology and benefit from it, to better target Generation Z in Japan.

How to Deal with Generation Z in Japan as Employees?

Members of Generation Z in Japan are less loyal to companies, and tend to quit their companies relatively easily compared to older generations. Traditionally,

Japanese companies have been trying to educate their employees based on a long-term (even life time) employment system. These investments in employees cost a huge amount of money, however, younger generations, including Generation Z, may simply quit after receiving these benefits. Therefore, companies are required to carefully design their human development strategy.

Also, Japanese companies have been offering a yearly rise in salaries based on a seniority ranking. Older generations benefit more from such a system, leaving younger employees sometimes frustrated. Although this system is shifting to a more flexible one based on ability, some of the Japanese companies are still following the old system. However, younger employees, especially members of Generation Z, are more exposed to outside information through the Internet, such as tempting offers from other companies on websites, or unofficial internal information about the working environment of other companies through social media. Thus, companies should offer a wage system that would satisfy their needs.

Finally, members of Generation Z in Japan value their private life more than their work life. In traditional Japanese society, employees used to devote their lives to their companies, working very hard every day. However, work is just a means to live a better life with family and friends for Generation Z. Thus, companies should reduce working hours per employee, which would require efficiency improvements in the organisation. Therefore, they may want to maximise the usage of information technology so that employees can spend less time at work. Generation Z in Japan has its own uniqueness. Companies should customise their strategy to better fit them, both at markets and companies, to maximise their profitability.

Conclusions

In conclusion, members of Generation Z in Japan are digital natives with pessimistic mindsets, which makes them careful efficient spenders as consumers and risk-aversive stability seekers as workers. Raised in a challenging time, they seem to be better at dealing with the changes caused by COVID-19, with a high level of digital device literacy and a stronger psychological tolerance towards social unrest. However, Japan may economically struggle more in the after-pandemic world when they become older to play major roles in the society; they may spend less and avoid work with full devotion. Therefore, an adequate strategy is needed for Japan's brighter future.

References

Cabinet Office. (2018). Retrieved from https://www8.cao.go.jp/youth/whitepaper/h30 gaiyou/pdf/b1_00.pdf.

Consumer Affairs Agency. (2016). Retrieved from https://www.caa.go.jp/policies/policy/consumer_research/research_report/survey_001/pdf/information_isikicyousa_170726_0003.pdf.

Consumer Affairs Agency. (2017). Retrieved from https://www.caa.go.jp/policies/policy/consumer_research/white_paper/pdf/2017_whitepaper_0004.pdf.

Cabinet Office. (2018). Retrieved from https://www8.cao.go.jp.

Doi, T. (1962). Amae: A key concept for understanding Japanese personality structure. In J. Smith & R. K. Beardsley (Eds.), *Publications in anthropology* (pp. 132–139). New York, NY: Viking Fund Publications.

Doi, T. (2014). *Tsunagari wo Aorareru Kodomotachi: Netto Izon to Ijime Mondai wo Kangaeru (Children inflated towards networking: Internet addiction and bulling)*. Tokyo: Iwanami Booklet.

Fujimura, M., Asano, T., & Habuchi, I. (2016). *Gendai Wakamono no Koufuku: Fuankan Shakai wo Ikiru (Hapiness of young generation: Living in an insecure society)*. Tokyo: Kouseisha Kouseikaku.

Gentina, E., Huarng, K. H., & Sakashita, M. (2018). A social comparison theory approach to mothers' and daughters' clothing co-consumption behaviors: A cross-cultural study in France and Japan. *Journal of Business Research, 89*, 361–370.

Geospatial Information Authority of Japan. (2016). Retrieved from http://www.gsi.go.jp.

Hakuhodo, Corporate Public Relations Division. (2017). *Kodomo 20 Nen Henka: 1997, 2007, 2017 (Changes of Children in 20 years: 1997, 2007, 2017)* [Report paper]. Retrieved from https://www.hakuhodo.co.jp/uploads/2017/06/20170608_2.pdf.

Hofstede Insights. (2019). Retrieved from https://www.hofstede-insights.com.

Japan Youth Study Group (JYSG). (2012). Retrieved from http://jysg.jp/.

Kimura, J., & Sakahsita, M. (2012). Mother possessing daughter: Dual role of extended self. In A. Ruvio & R. W. Belk (Eds.), *The Routledge companion to identity and consumption* (pp. 291–301). Abingdon: Routledge.

Koll, J. (2018. September 2). Japan, savings superpower of the world. *The Japan Times Opinion*. Retrieved from https://www.japantimes.co.jp.

Matsushita, K. (2012). *Dejitaru Neitibu to Sosharu Media: Wakamono ga Umidasu Aratana Komyunike-shon (Digital native and social media: New communication from young people)*. Tokyo: Kyouikuhyouronsha.

Ministry of Economy, Trade and Industry. (2016). Retrieved from https://www.meti.go.jp.

Ministry of Education, Culture, Sports, Science and Technology [MEXT]. (2019). Retrieved from http://www.mext.go.jp.

Ministry of Health, Labour and Welfare. (2018). Retrieved from https://www.mhlw.go.jp/stf/houdou/0000184815_00003.html.

Ministry of Internal Affairs and Communications. (2017). Retrieved from https://www.soumu.go.jp/johotsusintokei/whitepaper/ja/h30/pdf/n4200000.pdf.

Ministry of Internal Affairs and Communications. (2019). Retrieved from https://www.stat.go.jp/data/jinsui/2019np/index.html.

Nikkei Sangyou Shimbun. (2017). Motto Hatarakitai (We Want to Work More). March 1, p. 1.

Nagai, J. (2019). Communication: Ongaku wo Kaishita Yuujinkankei (Communication: friendship through music. In K. Minamida, Y. Kijima, J. Nagai, & H. Ogawa (Eds.), *Ongakuka Shakai no Genzai (The latest picture of society full of music)* (pp. 89–107). Tokyo: Shinyousha.

Sakashita, M. & Kimura, J. (forthcoming). How Mother-Daughter Purchase Interaction Affects Daughter's Situational Self Construction in Japan. In J. Argo, T. M. Lowrey, & H. J. Schau (Eds.), *Advances in Consumer Research, 48*. MN: Association for Consumer Research.

The Government of Japan. (2019). Retrieved from Japan Government. (2019). Retrieved from https://www.japan.go.jp/.

Toyokeizai Online. (2019). Retrieved from https://toyokeizai.net.

Uematsu, E. (2016). Mobile media to Gakkou Kyouiku (Mobile media and school education. In H. Tomita (Ed.), *Post Mobile Shakai (Post mobile society)* (pp. 89–107). Tokyo: Sekaishisousha.

Chapter 5

Generation Z in Taiwan: Low Salaries, 'Little Happiness', and a Social-Media World in the Mix

Ryan Brading

Abstract

Diversity and uncertainty summarise Taiwan's Generation Z. Diversity because the background of fewer than 3.4 million Taiwanese, which is less than 20% of the overall population, cannot be included in a 'one-fits-all' category. As a sovereign nation, Taiwan has developed through various cultural, economic, and political stages. Democratic freedom has given the Taiwanese the right and terrain to de-Sinicise their homeland and politically construct 'Taiwanese Consciousness'. These points are essential, because this is the societal fabric given to Generation Zers. Apart from national identity, this chapter illustrates the uncertainties that Generation Zers are facing in relation to education, job opportunities, and living standards. It is suggested that conditions are easier for those that have received 'superior' education and have enjoyed family-economic support. Their consumer behaviour, Generation Z in the workplace, as well as voters are also carefully analysed in this chapter.

Keywords: Generation Z; Taiwan; consumers; family; education; work

Introduction to Taiwan

Taiwan is an island in the Western Pacific, about 100 miles away from the People's Republic of China (PRC). Taiwan's population of 23.7 million on just 36,000 km^2 makes it one of the most densely populated countries in the world. The earliest settlers came to Taiwan from the nearby islands in the South Pacific. They are known today as aboriginals. At the beginning of the seventeenth century,

The New Generation Z in Asia: Dynamics, Differences, Digitalisation
The Changing Context of Managing People, 71–85
Copyright © 2020 by Emerald Publishing Limited
doi:10.1108/978-1-80043-220-820201008

overcrowding sparked the migration of Chinese peasants to Taiwan. The majority of Chinese settlers were from Fujian province, identified by their language as Hoklo people. Nowadays, descendants of Fujianese migrants make up more than 70% of Taiwan's population. Another 15% of today's Taiwanese are Hakka people, whose ancestors also came from China (Mendel, 1970, pp. 13–14).

From 1895 until 1945, Taiwan was a Japanese colony. Even though Japanese rulers improved Taiwan's economic infrastructure and educational system, they also imposed cultural policies that denigrated Taiwan's Chinese identity and traditions. Hundreds of educated Taiwanese demanded autonomy for the island. The Taiwanese were seen as inferior people, an attitude representing both paternalism and exploitation. Japan lost Taiwan in 1945 and the Allied powers arranged for the Chinese government to accept Japan's surrender of the island, in effect handing Taiwan over to the Republic of China (ROC) (Gold, 1986, pp. 56–57).

In 1947, the Taiwanese rose up against the Chinese regime, and were violently suppressed. After the crushing of this Taiwanese uprising, this 'February 28 incident' became a taboo subject. The legacy of the initial period of KMT (*Kuomintang – Chinese Nationalist Party*) rule in Taiwan was the creation of cleavages of ethnic injustice and Taiwanese versus Chinese identity that remain significant to this day (Kerr, 1965, p. 14).

As the civil war broke out in mainland China between the ROC's ruling party KMT and the Chinese Communist Party, the defeated KMT and the surviving ROC government officials and troops took refuge in Taiwan in 1949. The ROC's priority was to rebuild its military power and recover the mainland. The KMT implemented Martial Law, which provided a legal framework for repressing dissent, censoring publications, and outlawing new political parties (Long, 1991, p. 189).

In the 1960s, the Taiwanese were permitted to elect a small number of supplementary legislators and two non-KMT candidates managed to win seats. By the late 1970s and early 1980s, the opposition Dangwai movement (which became the DPP – *Democratic Progressive Party* – in September 1986), KMT defectors and democracy activists, began to contest elections and propagated their ideals. Its main common denominator was a belief in democratisation (Tien, 1988, p. 98).

The first direct presidential election was held in 1996. However, despite President Lee Teng-hui's popularity and ability to push through political reforms, he was unable to prevent the KMT's decline. The year 2000 saw Taiwan's first election that generated change in ruling parties. Chen Shui-bian, the DPP's candidate, a humble Taiwanese to a famous dissident lawyer and trustworthy leader won the second direct presidential election.

Although democratic principles now give Taiwan's society the opportunity to politically and institutionally materialise their own sense of national identity, new external factors are adding other obstacles to this process. This identity search is even harder for Taiwan's Generation Z, because the mainland China's emerging economic and geopolitical dominance, the subtle but significant impact of globalisation, and the increasing influence of digital technology in their daily lives, add other pressures that older Taiwanese might not find as significant.

Demographics

The current dynamics of Taiwan's living population is concerning. In 2017, the crude birth rate was 8.23% compared with 7.27% for the crude death rate, compared to a birth rate of 11.65% and death rate of 5.71% in 2001 (National Statistics, 2019a). This variation in which birth rates are declining to the extent to which they are at similar levels as death rates has reached a point where by 2026, Taiwan will become a super-age society. That's because at least 20% of the population will be 65 or older. By 2065, the group of people 65 or older will take up 40% of the population (Strong, 2019).

Many Generation Zers are in their teens (ages 10–25 in 2020). During this critical teenage phase, the future prospects of each individual will be partly determined by the decisions made – such as access to education and employment opportunities available. In 2015, Taiwan's Ministry of Education announced that due to Taiwan's shrinking population – one-third of universities will be closed. By 2023, enrolment could plummet to 233,093. That is a drop of 35.84% – from 2013's 363,324 (*Focus Taiwan*, 2015). In other words, options and access to graduate and postgraduate programmes for Generation Zers will be affected.

Circumstances will be different for those that have parents who could afford overseas education. In 2018, 66,514 Taiwanese were studying abroad. The major foreign destinations are English-speaking countries (United States 21,516; Canada 5,330; Australia 18,227; New Zealand 2,070; United Kingdom 3,775). Japan was selected by 10,347 Taiwanese students (Ministry of Education, 2018). Although some of these students might not be Generation Zers, this trend of going abroad is likely to continue . For example, in 2013, 49,219 Taiwanese decided to study abroad. That's around 26% fewer students than 2018 (*Envision Recruit, 2019*). Taiwan's low birth rate is not the only reason why Taiwan's higher education system is downsizing. Many young Taiwanese have opted for 'better' alternatives abroad instead. This could be because Taiwan's higher education programmes are becoming outdated and, therefore, less attractive. By studying and living in a more developed country might also bring better career opportunities.

Those decades when Taiwan was known as one of Asia's Four Tigers has long gone. Lee Zong-rong and Lin Thing-hong state that government policies to stimulate the economy have weakened companies and led to a paradigm shift in Taiwan: from a 'miracle model' to a 'recession model'. A large part of Taiwan's economic activity occurs overseas. This arrangement offers little support to Taiwan's domestic economy. However, removing this 'life support' from the supply chain could lead to total collapse. Apparently, 'this 'artificial life support economy' has been maintained for about 15 years' (Lee & Lin, 2017, pp. 8–9).

Only a few Taiwanese businesses have actually stayed behind and really contributed to the domestic economy (Lee & Lin, 2017, p. 19). Lin's (2013, pp. 705–706) research also focusses on how the Taiwanese rank their class status. In 1995, fewer than 20% of the Taiwanese defined themselves as Working Class; by 2009, this increased to 37%. Also, in 1995, 45% of the Taiwanese defined themselves as Middle Class. This dropped to 26% in 2009. These figures provide a glimpse of Taiwan's possible social and economic downfall since the 1990s. As Runde

(2015, p. 1) notes, the success of a previously underdeveloped and resource poor island – to a regional economic powerhouse 'comes from its national commitment to investing in its people'. Although there are also other important factors, 'Taiwan has established itself as a dynamic and technology-oriented economy by improving its base of human capital'.

Still, the reduction of Taiwan's higher education system, the increased number of Taiwanese choosing to study abroad, Lee's and Lin's 'recession model' category, and a possible further decline of people's living standards – implies that circumstances mean that the government's policies in 'investing in its people' – is no longer a priority.

Basics of Generation Z in Taiwan

By the end of 2018, the population of Taiwan was 23,588,932, of which 4.24% were aged 5–9; 4.40% were aged 10–14; 5.58% were aged 15–19; and 6.58% were aged 20–24 (Ministry of Interior, 2019). These figures suggest that less than 20% of Taiwan's population can be defined as Generation Z.

Identity and Values

Democracy finally gave citizens the right to represent and vote for a pro-independence presidential candidate. During Chen's administration (2000–2008), efforts to de-Sinicise Taiwan was a pivotal part of the Taiwanisation hegemonic identity the DPP advocated. Many Taiwanese felt antagonised and previously forced to identify with the identities imposed by foreign authoritarian invaders.

Part of this emancipatory process was to rewrite the history and geography texts in the national educational curriculum. Many believed that the China-centred curriculum installed by the KMT, inculcated a foreign hegemonic identity on Taiwan's new generations. The DPP succeeded in focussing on Taiwan rather than the mainland, which was previously defined as a province of KMT's ROC. The radical reform of the curriculum for history and history-related subjects was implemented in the 2001 school year. Although Taiwan's outright independence is still taboo, the indoctrination of Chinese Consciousness in the history curriculum has shifted, and the semantics of Taiwanese Consciousness are now included in new history textbooks.

Home also has a key role in national identity. It is not possible to quantify how parental and family factors dictate the political inclinations of young Taiwanese citizens. Still, a vital element that needs to be highlighted here is the potential identity effect that foreign spouses could have upon their Taiwanese-born children. As of June 2017, 523,859 people resided in Taiwan on the basis of being local citizens' spouses. The majority were female (92.03%). About 334,583 were spouses from Mainland China (excluding those from Hong Kong and Macau). The other 173,973 were spouses from Southeast Asia (Vietnam, Indonesia, the Philippines, Thailand, Cambodia, and a few other countries). About 243,017 of these had acquired Taiwanese citizenship; 123,783 were from the PRC (National Immigration Agency, 2017; cited in Cheng, Mormesso, & Fell, 2019, p. 205).

Wang and Belanger (2008, p. 94) point out that from 2002 to 2006, 'about one in eight newborn babies has mixed parents. Grooms and in-laws expect Vietnamese female spouses in Taiwan to be wives and mothers and to do domestic work in the household'. Although there were spouses from other Southeast Asian countries, the majority are Vietnamese (Cheng et al., 2019, p. 204). Vietnamese and Chinese wives and mothers have contrasting attributes. Their ability to assimilate to this new culture, and the reception received by the main political parties have been diverse. For the DPP, Chinese immigrants acquiring ROC citizenship are 'perceived as a potential source of instability to the Taiwanese identity and to political parties' vote share' (Friedman, 2015; Cheng, 2016; cited in Cheng et al., 2019, p. 206). The mothers-in-law of Vietnamese 'were often identified as the person who expressly dictated their foreign daughters-in-law's voting decision, who were staunch DPP supporters'. The interviewed Vietnamese feel that the DPP's attempt to incorporate them 'was broadly perceived as sign of respect' (p. 209).

The KMT has been less confrontational with China and has been more accommodating in relation to immigration legislation. An interviewed Chinese spouse said: 'the majority of Mainland spouses are married to KMT members, civil servants, and elderly Mainlander veterans. These people have deep connections with the KMT' (Cheng et al., 2019, pp. 205–209). However, the KMT failed to push through crucial legislative reform before handing power to the DPP in 2016. Dissatisfied with the KMT, naturalised Chinese have founded their own political parties. Self-representation has given them the space to express their Chinese identity. Beijing has found a lot of capital from these small pro-unification political organisations. Summer camps in China for children and transnational families have been organised. A Chinese activist with a ROC citizenship said: 'there are 400,000 of us, and you should also add our family members. We are a form of power' (pp. 210–211).

Defining the identity of Taiwan's Generation Zers is a complex task. Possible changes such as political, economic, as well as family circumstances could influence the symbolic definition of Taiwanese identity, and possibly, be challenged by the gradual infiltration of Chinese nationalist sentiments from the Mainland in Taiwan's society.

Social Media

Dylan Bushell-Embling (2017) notes that by the end of 2017, Taiwan had the highest smartphone penetration in Asia Pacific. In the social media management platform *Hootsuite & We are Social,* Simon Kemp (2019) points that in January 2019, there were 28.48 million mobile subscriptions, that is, 120% of Taiwan's population. Kemp also notes that the most active social media platforms are *YouTube* (90%), *Facebook* (89%), the messenger/VOIP (Voice over Internet Protocol) platforms *Line* (84%), *Facebook Messenger* (57%), and *Instagram* (49%). It is not clear whether these percentages reflect the social media usage of Generation Zers. The results of the surveys conducted by the government-run organisation *Taiwan Network Information Center* (TWNIC) (2018, p. 44) are useful (see Table 1).

Table 1.   Usage Rate of Social Networking Brands.

(Multiple Answers) Total		Gender		Age		
N = 2044	12–65+	Male	Female	12–14	15–19	20–24
Facebook	98.5	97.8	99.2	96.1	95.4	94.7
Instagram	38.8	35.2	42.3	53.8	68.6	71.0

Table 2.   Usage Rate of Instant Messaging Brands.

(Multiple Answers) Total		Gender		Age		
N = 2455	12–65+	Male	Female	12–14	15–19	20–24
Line	99.2	99.1	99.4	96.2	97.0	100
Facebook Messenger	26.8	26.0	27.7	64.0	47.8	30.2

Although Facebook is widely used (98.5%), it appears not to be the most popular platform for Taiwan's Generation Zers. The survey also demonstrates that *Instagram* is more well-liked by young Taiwanese (particularly in the 20–24 age group), than other age groups. The *Taiwan Network Information Center* (TWNIC, 2018, p. 45) also provides valuable findings of the 'messenger/VOIP' social media platforms mentioned earlier (see Table 2).

The success of the *Line* messaging application is staggering. According to the October 2016 *Nielsen Media* survey, nearly 91% of respondents used it in the past 7 days, compared to 78% in 2014. Also, 85% of those in the 12–19 age group are regular *Line* users, as are 92% in the 20–29 age group (Zeng, 2016). Young users play a key role in this increase. The 26.8% for the total usage of *Facebook Messenger* differs from the 57% in Kemp's (2019) survey. The percentages in the above table (in the three age groups) are the highest in the TWNIC survey. Only 5.8% of those aged 65 and older use *Facebook Messenger*, compared with 98.1% using *Line*.

According to the *2018 YouTube Behaviour Survey*, *YouTube* weekly users increased from 85% in 2017 to 90% in 2018. The survey also indicates that viewing time increased from an average of 14.6 hours per week to 16.4 hours. This means, each individual spends nearly two and a half hours watching *YouTube* every day. Those in the 16–24 age group (Generation Z) are primarily behind this growing popularity (Kan, 2018).

Members of Generation Z as Consumers in Taiwan

Due to their limited income, the buying behaviour of Taiwan's Generation Zers is difficult to determine. Still, there are common traits that influence the way desires are constructed, how products and entertainment activities are designed, and what type of styles they enjoy. Hsin-I Sidney Yueh (2016, pp. 2–3) claims that Taiwan is an island of *sajiao*. *Sajiao* can be observed in daily practices, verbal/nonverbal features, rules, norms, and role expectations. *Sajiao* is an action and concept that summarises the spirit, the atmosphere, and the culture of Taiwanese society. *Sajiao* is considered as the preferred communication style for women. People believe that it helps to increase women's femininity, therefore, making them more adorable and attractive. 'Infantilising oneself as a person in need of love and attention has been portrayed to women in Taiwan as a powerful weapon' (p. 8).

Young female idols are actively marketed on television and Taiwanese entertainment websites. Images of their faces and their bodies are used for a wide range of products and services, ranging from cosmetics to video games. These idols look innocent and baby like, with big eyes, pale skin colour, and thin limbs. The media exploits Taiwan's *sajiao* culture by constructing cuteness in their marketing strategies (Hsin-I, 2016, p. 101). Taiwan's *sajiao* culture is a direct connection with Japanese popular culture. Japanese pop products like *Hello Kitty* have helped establish a big commercial empire that has motivated individuals to personify this mouthless, cute and harmless cat (pp. 104–115).

Leo Ching (2000) notes that there is a sense of identity struggle in Taiwan and historical conditions are fundamental. During Japanese rule, Japan represented the modern. Thus, Japanisation is a modernity desire. For example, the popularity of *fujoshi* in Taiwan – girls reading male homoerotic texts such as Boys' Love (BL), which originates from the fan culture of Japanese *sho ¯jo manga* (a genre of comics and animated films aimed primarily at teenage females). Chang (2017, pp. 179–180) notes that the construction and localisation of *fujoshi* culture in Taiwan is not simply the inevitable result of cultural dissemination. It has been widely recognised that Taiwan has the most noticeable 'pro-Japanese' attitude among former Japanese colonial regions in Asia.

Taiwanese *fujoshi* culture practices have constructed BL fantasies. Taiwanese mass media perceived how 'Japanophilia' was the symbolisation of an imaginary of Japan in Taiwan. Most of Chang's interviewees are Generation Z girls in their 20s. Japanese-ness plays a key role in their daily lives. They construct BL fantasies of specific members of idol groups. Some prefer to consume products such as manga, animation, music, TV dramas, or variety shows in Japanese, rather than the Mandarin translated version, 'regardless of whether they understand Japanese or not'. They fantasise of an ideal romantic partner like those observed in the BL setting (2017, pp. 180–188).

The logic of consumers is not only related to monetary purchasing. Ideals, values, personality traits and identity constructs are also fundamental components that are displayed throughout different media forms. *Sajiao* and *fujoshi* play a role in the mannerisms and behaviours of Generation Z. The notions associated with Japanese-ness have a determined input in the behaviour, consumer make-up and, therefore, the preference of Generation Z consumers. For example, 59% of skincare products are purchased from Japan. With 5,214 respondents (16 years and older), a survey conducted in July 2019 found that Korean skincare products came second with 34%. Only 20% of respondents preferred European skincare products (Statista, 2019). Although this survey is not focussing on female Generation Z; the choice of almost two-thirds of a large survey sample gives us a glimpse of the demand for Japanese beauty cultural products, thereby the significance of terms such as *Sajiao* and *fujoshi* in Taiwan's consumer culture.

Generation Z at Work in Taiwan

Until the 1980s, Taiwan enjoyed a remarkable period for growth and equality. Circumstances are now different. Based on social class, education, and ethnic backgrounds, rewarding employment and career prospects for Taiwan's Generation Z would differ. As noted earlier, Lin (2013) points out that in 2009, there was an increase of those who defined themselves as working class, and fewer believed themselves to be middle class. According to Chang (2018), inequality has become more serious after the '2008 economic depression'. The question is less about a declining middle class, but the large increase of low-income households. As the economy continues to be more influenced by a high-technology-oriented trajectory, pay differences between upper white-collar and ordinary workers will continue.

Although education in Taiwan is compulsory until the age of 18 (6–15 year-olds before 2014), those that decide to continue on further higher education – are far more likely to receive the skills the labour market requires. Even though Taiwan's population is shrinking, and by 2023, one-third of Taiwan's universities will be closed; only those students that have the economic means to invest in education overseas, or succeed in getting a place and graduating at the best universities in Taiwan – will ultimately be able to meet employers' criteria, and directly be part of Taiwan's technology-oriented economy.

Ethnic differences could also influence employment opportunities. Generation Zers with a foreign mother, that is, included in Wang and Belanger's (2008) 'one in eight new born babies with mixed parents', are likely to be brought up in a low-income household, and did not receive the same family stimulus environment to continue studying after high school. This perception also applies to other young Taiwanese whose parents are both Taiwanese born. Nonetheless, adding another level of ethnic identification and cultural coding from countries (e.g. South East Asian countries) that are economically inferior and, therefore, less developed adds another aspect for potential employers to consider.

Compared with other ages, the Generation Z unemployment rate is the highest. The overall unemployment rate of the labour force is 3.89% in Taiwan (August 2019). For those in the 15–19 age group, it is 10.51%, and 13.05% for the 20–24 age group. It drops to almost half at 6.71% for the 25–29 Millennial age group (National Statistics, 2019b). These results, in particular, for the 20–24 age group – could be because Taiwan's older Generation Zers feel that the salaries are too low, promising job opportunities are scarce, or simply, they just don't have the skills.

Pieyu Wu (2019) notes that the monthly salary of almost 50% of new recruits is less than NT\$30,000. Those that decide to work in Southeast Asia as expatriates can expect a salary that is 1.6 times higher. Based on the survey conducted by *104 Job Bank*, Taiwan's biggest online recruitment website, only 10% will receive more than NT$50,000 as a starting salary. The best jobs are for engineers. Finance- and medical-related posts are also well remunerated. In recent years, there has been a 15% increase of new graduates who are willing to go and work in Southeast Asia. However, China is still the main destination.

A growing problem in Taiwan is brain drain. In 2017, 736,000 Taiwanese were working abroad. They are mostly male. More than 70% work for Taiwanese enterprises with operations in the mainland. However, working opportunities in China are declining because mainlanders are learning the required skills (*China Times*, 2019). Unfortunately, it is not known how many Generation Zers are currently working in China.

Mr Michael Lee (2018, October 12) (Vice President – General Manager Office & Information Technology) from Advanced Semiconductor Engineering (ASE) Group stated that:

> *Many young Taiwanese have made their decision to work in China a success. However, that demand for skilled Taiwanese personnel is shrinking now. Taiwan's engineering knowledge is still more advanced than China, but Chinese training incentives are catching up with us. Working in China after graduating is not a wise decision anymore. Possibilities for career advancement are gone. With two-three years-work experience here in Taiwan after graduating – there are still career opportunities on the mainland.*

According to the www.yes123.com.tw job bank network, 90% of young Taiwanese are panicking. They are worried about economic issues and making wrong decisions. Most of them are considering going abroad: 52.2% would like to find a job in Japan, 50.3% in Southeast Asia, 43.3% in the United States, 36.6% in New Zealand, 27.9% in Hong Kong and Macau, 26.7% in China, 22.1% would like to work in Europe, 18.8% in South Korea, 17.7% in Canada, and 8.8% would consider working in India. Many believe that it might be a good idea to work and learn from Japan, and then use that knowledge to start a business back in Taiwan (CTS, 2019).

In an interview with Mr Johnny Chou (2019, September 25), 'Head of China Overseas Talent Development' at the HQ Human Resources Office of Pouchen Group (one of the world's largest footwear manufacturers in the world), Mr Chou highlights the challenges young Taiwanese are facing:

> *It is almost impossible for the young generation to buy a property with those salaries. The best salaries are for engineering graduates, those from the 'A-Class' universities: National Taiwan University, National Chiao Tsung University, National Tsing Hua University and National Cheng Kung University. Their starting basic salary is about NT$50,000. However, if they start to work for us, the starting salary is NT$35,000. World high-tech companies can pay higher*

salaries; we are a traditional manufacturing industry…Without an
'A-Class' diploma, it is very difficult for an application to pass the
shortlisting stage. We receive around 1,000 applications every year,
interview approx. 700 and 200 get job offers. Those that have diplo-
mas from top class universities, we give them 15–20% extra of the
basic monthly salary.

Basically, without the 'right' education, the chances of succeeding can be rather slim. The haves and have-nots gap is widening in Taiwan. That's why 90% are panicking because things are tough. Low salaries, pressure to study and difficulties to get on the property ladder, could make modern life depressing and difficult. Some have reacted to all these challenges by constructing their own 'Little Happiness'.

The logic of Little Happiness

'Little Happiness' is a term coined by the Japanese writer Haruki Murakami in his novel *Afternoon in the Islets of Langerhans* – first published in 1986 where he wrote: 'without this kind of small yet certain happiness, life is but a desert in drought'. Daphne Lee (2018) describes Taiwanese 'Little Happiness' as 'a steady flow of minor contentment'. According to Jingyu (2017), 'Little Happiness' is a personal lifestyle choice. Because society has become more and more unfair, 'Little Happiness' is like an ideology resisting the system. 'Little Happiness' is hoping to escape the 'Great Happiness' constructed by Western globalisation and pursue humanistic personal ideals. It has no material desire. These small businesses have an avant-garde art nature to them. Their products and services bring artistic and cultural value to Taiwan. They have retreated from unreachable expectations and the imposed competitive pressure of a consumerist-driven-modern society. Being content by simple things in life provides a sense of empowerment and temporary happiness. The idea of starting a small business and being their own boss is an exciting option. Businesses like tea houses, coffee shops, comic bookstores, craft boutique shops, private studios, and so on are the type of businesses that have popped up.

Circumstances such as there only being disheartening jobs available, depressing wages, unachievable qualifications, as well as having to compete with others who are better prepared, open the landscape for some generation Zers to accept the parameters of 'Little Happiness' to achieve some form of harmony, meaningful existence, and self-value.

How to Deal with Generation Z in Taiwan

The historical background discussed in the first section helps us to contextualise how Japanophilia and Sinicisation have influenced and, to some extent, shaped the cultural fabric of this society, as well as Taiwan's democratisation. Taiwan is a self-governed democratic state. China, however, sees Taiwan as a breakaway province. China aims to achieve peaceful unification but reserves the right to use force against 'Taiwan independence' separatists. Cross-strait economic ties are very important for both sides. However, due to the US–China Trade feud, 49.6% of Taiwanese firms in China said they intend to adjust their investment or relocate. Nearly 19% would move back to Taiwan while 22% favour Southeast Asia, mainly Vietnam as a relocation destination (Hsu, 2019). These changes could lead to more work opportunities at home as well as in Southeast Asia.

Unaffordable property prices, low salaries, and low employment opportunities for non-specialised candidates are affecting the overall development of young Taiwanese. From a marketing perspective, it is vital to differentiate Generation Z consumers, between those who are 'better-off' and those who are not. By outlining social class, education, and ethnic backgrounds, some key characteristics can be fleshed out. According to Lian Naihua (as cited in Liu, 2018), general manager of a market research consultancy, like older generations, there is no such a thing as a 'one-fits-all' category. Diversity is a dominant factor. Taiwan's Z Generation is used to wandering between the virtual and the reality world. This Market Research Consultancy conducted a survey of 1,000. About 28.2% of the respondents said that they have no ambition. They only want to have an ordinary and stable life and are more willing to spend on material things rather than investing or saving. 'Little Happiness' is commonly used. Experience and enjoyment are more important. About 16.3% of the respondents think that they are down-to-earth and believe that by being pragmatic, they could earn a living to live in a resource-poor environment. Furthermore, finding a government post or working in a state-owned company have become popular career paths to them (Liu, 2018).

Andy Huang (2014), Managing Director, *Nielsen* Taiwan, provides a still relevant Generation Z consumer analysis. 69% of the respondents 'like trendy things' and 44% are 'always the first to use a new product'. Also, 72% like to share their thoughts and feelings about what they have just bought or used. 57% identify themselves as materialistic. They are happy to spend money on leisure and entertainment rather than saving. 82% think their purchase behaviour is based on 'product feeling'. Furthermore, 77% are very responsive to advertisements. As information consumers, 68% are more likely to purchase a product simply because they like the ads. Around 67% would pay attention to what experts say, 60% listen to those around them, and 51% are influenced by celebrities. Both surveys identify that Generation Zers are consumerist driven and that enjoyment and trendiness are key attributes to them.

Politics and Generation Z

The possibilities for Generation Zers to have a major impact in the ballot box that have been rather limited. The voting age is 20. Presidential and legislative elections take place every 4 years. This means that only those that were born between 1995 and 1996 were eligible to vote in the January 2016 presidential and legislative elections. According to Tanguy Lepesant (2016), the youth voting turnout (20–29 years old) for the 2016 presidential and legislative elections was 74.5% –

compared with the 66.2% total turnout. Of these, 71% of those aged 20–23 voted for the DPP's presidential candidate Tsai Ing-wen. Some of these new Taiwanese voters were Generation Zers (born in 1995–1996).

Generation Ys' interests in politics and demonstrations against KMT rule under former president Ma Ying-yeou's (2008–2016) trade pacts with the Mainland China (the 2008 'Wild Strawberry' and 2014 'Sunflower' student-led movements) are described and analysed in another paper (Brading, 2017). At the moment of writing, Generation Yers or Zers have not challenged Tsai's administration (2016–present).

The party that has Chinese hereditary, which is the KMT, is facing a complex challenge. By remediating the imbalance in the trade flow with China, Ma hoped to bring economic stimulus. Young Taiwanese felt that Ma was instead discreetly initiating a re-unification process. Mixing economic growth and identity in Taiwan is political suicide.

Because Tsai has vaguely conceived the 'One China, with Different Interpretations' consensus, Taiwan's relations with China have been strained. Despite the pressure from China, Tsai has stood firm and strengthened her political standing – as the rightful representative of 'Taiwanese identity'.

Han Kuo-yu, latest KMT's presidential candidate and the current Mayor of Kaohsiung (Taiwan's third largest city), has shown to promote a warmer approach with Beijing. His decision to travel to Hong Kong in March 2019 – where he met with Hong Kong's Chief Executive Carrie Lam and Wang Zhimin, the director of Beijing's liaison office in Hong Kong, was a political mistake. Apart from trade agreements between both cities, it is said that this trip could have helped promote the 'one country, two systems' framework. Like Ma, Han supports the 'One China, with Different Interpretations' consensus (Cheung, 2019).

Hong Kong's political crisis, which started after Han's visit, has been seen as a reflection of what 'one country, two systems' truly entails. Indirectly, Hong Kong's student-led protests have further galvanised 'Taiwanese Consciousness' as a political symbol and made pro-China views in Taiwan's political discourse even more toxic now. The results of the Presidential Elections which were held on January 11, 2020 re-affirmed that closer ties with China undermine electoral results. Tsai secured 57.1% of the ballot. Han only achieved 38.6% of the votes.

Conclusions

Periods of colonialism, authoritarianism, economic growth, the transition towards a fully-fledged democracy, and neo-liberalism have made Taiwan a unique Asian nation. As discussed in the first section, Taiwan is an aging society. The current low birth rate level is likely to continue because the interests and opportunities for Generation Zers are different *vis-à-vis* Baby Boomers and, to some extent, Generation Xers. One-third of universities will be closed because the population is shrinking. It is stressed that the education a Generation Zer receives plays a key role in his/her future. Issues such as employment opportunities, class, ethnics, identity constructs, and aspirations like 'Little Happiness' are central subject matters in this analysis of the Generation Z in Taiwan.

Other important topics discussed are the following: their consumer behaviour (e.g. Japanophilia), the popularity of social media platforms for Generation Zers, as well as concerning issues like unemployment, low salaries, unaffordable property prices, and how the inequality gap is widening in Taiwan. This contribution to the *Generation Z in Asia* edited book concludes by warning politicians that flirting with China as a symbolic identity, as well as an influential economic force, can have profound effects on their popularity and, therefore, their success in the ballot box.

Acknowledgement

The financial support from the Ministry of Science and Technology, Taiwan (MOST 109 -2410 - H - 110 - 004 -) is acknowledged.

References

Brading, R. (2017). Taiwan's millennial generation: Interests in polity and party politics. *Journal of Current Chinese Affairs*, *46*, 131–166.

Bushell-Embling, D. (2017, December 7). Taiwan has APAC's highest smartphone penetration. *telecomasia*. Retrieved from https://www.telecomasia.net/content/taiwan-has-apacs-highest-smartphone-penetration

Chang, C.-f. (2018, December 2). Economic Inequality and Low Wages in Taiwan, *University of Nottingham – Taiwan Studies Programme*. Retrieved from https://taiwaninsight.org/2018/12/21/economic-inequality-and-low-wages-in-taiwan/

Cheng, I. (2016). Bridging across or sandwiched between? Political Re-socialisation of Chinese immigrant women in Taiwan. *Asian Ethnicity*, *17*, 414–434.

Cheng, I., Mormesso, L., & Fell, D. (2019). Asset or liability: Transnational links and political participation pf foreign born citizens in Taiwan. *International Migration*, *57*, 202–217.

Cheung, T. (2019, March 22). Beijing-friendly Taiwanese mayor Han Kuo-yu arrives in Hong for historic meeting. *South China Morning Post*. Retrieved from https://www.scmp.com/news/hong-kong/politics/article/3002782/beijing-friendly-taiwanese-mayor-arrives-hong-kong-historic

China Times. (2019, March 23). 目前約40萬台胞在陸工作 過半認為壓力大！西進競技 台灣狼煉成鋼 – At present, about 400,000 Taiwanese work in the mainland and think that the pressure is great! Xijin Athletic Taiwan wolf refining into steel. *China Times*. Retrieved from https://www.chinatimes.com/newspapers/20190323000102-260301?chdtv

Ching, L. T. S. (2000). "Give Me Japan and Nothing Else!": Postcoloniality, Identity, and the Traces of Colonialism. *The South Atlantic Quarterly*, *99*(4), 763-788.

Chou, J. (2019, September 25). Interview at *Pouchen Group HQ*, Taichung, Taiwan.

CTS. (2019, June 24). 台灣薪資太低！92.6%新鮮人想當"海漂族" – Taiwan's salary is too low! 92.6% of young people want to be "sea drifters", *CTS*. Retrieved from https://news.cts.com.tw/cts/life/201906/201906241965149.html

Envision Recruit. (2019, January 28). The number of Taiwanese students studying abroad for 2018. *Envision Recruit*. Retrieved from http://www.envisionrecruit.com/home/market-updates/in-the-news/thenumberoftaiwanesestudentsstudyingabroadfor2018

Focus Taiwan. (2015, January 15). Government to cut higher education enrolment by 35%. *Focus Taiwan.* Retrieved from http://focustaiwan.tw/news/asoc/201501150030.aspx. Accessed on January 15.

Friedman, S. (2015). *Exceptional states: Chinese immigrants and Taiwanese sovereignty.* Stanford, CA: University of California Press.

Gold, T. (1986). *State and society in the Taiwan miracle.* Armonk, NY: M.E. Sharpe.

Hsin-I Sydney, Y. (2016). *Identity politics and popular culture in Taiwan: A Sajiao generation.* Lanham, MD: Lexington Books.

Hsu, C. (2019, September 26). Yuanta-Polaris raises growth forecast. *Taipei Times.* Retrieved from http://www.taipeitimes.com/News/biz/archives/2019/09/26/2003722904

Huang, A. (2014, November 8). Getting ready for Taiwan's 'Generation Z'. *Nielsen.* Retrieved from https://www.nielsen.com/us/en/insights/article/2014/uncommon-sense-getting-ready-for-taiwans-generation-z/

Jingyu, D. (2017, October 15). 小確幸在台灣 – Little Happiness is in Taiwan. *Castnet.* https://castnet.nctu.edu.tw/castnet/article/11158?issueID=665

Kan, M. (2018, November 4). YouTube使用者持續成長 – YouTube users continue to grow. *StuffTaiwan.* Retrieved from http://www.stufftaiwan.com/2018/11/04/youtube%E4%BD%BF%E7%94%A8%E8%80%85%E6%8C%81%E7%BA%8C%E6%88%90%E9%95%B7%E3%80%80%E5%9B%9B%E6%88%90%E4%B8%AD%E9%AB%98%E9%BD%A1%E6%AF%8F%E5%A4%A9%E7%9C%8B/

Kemp, S. (2019, January 31) Digital 2019 Taiwan. *Hootsuite & We are Social.* Retrieved from https://datareportal.com/reports/digital-2019-taiwan

Kerr, G. (1965). *Formosa betrayed.* Boston, MA: Houghton Mifflin Company.

Lee D. K. (2018, November 8). Taipei, Taiwan: A Small But Certain Happiness // 小確幸. *Medium.* Retrieved from https://medium.com/@daphneklee/taipei-taiwan-a-small-but-certain-happiness-%E5%B0%8F%E7%A2%BA%E5%B9%B8-8db97a59abca

Lee, M. (2018, October 12). The Challenges of Advanced Semiconductor Engineering Group, Guest Speaker, Business Seminar Management, National Sun Yat-sen University, Kaohsiung, Taiwan.

Lee, Z.-r. & Lin, T.-h. (2017). 未竟的奇蹟：轉型中的台灣經濟與社會 / 李宗榮, 林宗弘主編 – *Unfinished miracle – Taiwan's economy and society in transition.* Taipei: Academia Sinica, Institute of Sociology.

Lepesant, T. (2016, June). Taiwan Free of China. Le Monde *Diplomatique.* Retrieved from https://mondediplo.com/2016/06/11taiwan

Lin, T.-h. (2013). The lost decade: Changing class identity and ideology in Taiwan. *Journal of Social Science and Philosophy*, 2, 695–734. Retrieved from https://www.rchss.sinica.edu.tw/app/ebook/journal/25-04-2013/4.pdf

Liu, C. (2018, August 29). Z世代大軍來了！老闆們該認識的13種面貌 – The Z-generation army is here! 13 faces that bosses should know. *Cheers.* Retrieved from https://www.cheers.com.tw/article/article.action?id=5091846

Long, S. (1991). *Taiwan: China's last frontier.* New York, NY: St. Martin's Press.

Mendel, D. (1970). *The politics of Formosan Nationalism.* Berkeley, CA: University of California Press.

Ministry of Education. (2018). The numbers of birth by nationality (by registration) – 縣市出生按身分及生母生父原屬國籍(按登記), *Department of Household Registration.* Retrieved from https://www.ris.gov.tw/app/portal/346

Ministry of Interior. (2019). Table 1. Population by Sex and 5 Year Age Group for Counties and Cities, *Department of Household Registration.* Retrieved from https://www.ris.gov.tw/app/en/3910

National Statistics. (2019a). Table 4. Number and rates of births, deaths, immigrants, marriages and divorces. *National Statistics Taiwan.* Retrieved from https://eng.stat.gov.tw/public/data/dgbas03/bs2/yearbook_eng/y004.pdf

National Statistics. (2019b). Manpower Survey Results in August 2019. *National Statistics Taiwan*. Retrieved from https://eng.stat.gov.tw/ct.asp?xItem=44670&ctNode=1830 &mp=5

Runde, D. (2015, May 26) Taiwan is a model of freedom and prosperity. *Forbes*. Retrieved from https://www.forbes.com/sites/danielrunde/2015/05/26/taiwan-development-model-freedom-prosperity/#6470a2dc670c

Tien, H.-m. (1988). *The great transition: Political and social change in The Republic of China*. Stanford, CA: Hoover Institution Press.

Statista. (2019, August). Ownership of foreign skincare products among female consumers in Taiwan as of July 2019. *Statista*. Retrieved from https://www.statista.com/statistics/1042255/taiwan-ownership-of-foreign-skincare-products-among-females/

Strong, M. (2019, February 12). Taiwan will be a super-aged society by 2016, *Taiwan News*. Retrieved from https://www.taiwannews.com.tw/en/news/3636704

Taiwan Network Information Center. (2018). Taiwan Internet Report. *Taiwan Network Information Center*. Retrieved from https://report.twnic.tw/2018/TWNIC_TaiwanInternetReport_2018_EN.pdf

Wang, H.-z., & Bélanger, D. (2008). Taiwanizing female immigrant spouses and materializing differential citizenship. *Citizenship Studies*, *12*, 91–106. Retrieved from https://doi.org/10.1080/13621020701794224

Wu, P. (2019, June 14). 社會新鮮人調查：近5成台灣月薪低於3萬，外派東南亞薪資高出1.6倍 – Social freshman survey: Nearly 50% of Taiwan's monthly salary is less than 30,000, and the expatriate Southeast Asia's salary is 1.6 times higher'. *Cheers*. Retrieved from https://www.cheers.com.tw/article/article.action?id=5094782

Zeng, W. (2016, October 20). 1700萬台灣人都在用！三張圖看LINE的使用者分析 – 17 Million Taiwanese are using it! Three graphs to see the user analysis of LINE. *Manager Today*. Retrieved from https://www.managertoday.com.tw/articles/view/53400

Part III

What the Experts Tell Us about South Asia

Chapter 6

Generation Z in India: Digital Natives and Makers of Change

Shaheema Hameed and Meera Mathur

Abstract

With a population of 472 million, Generation Z in India is the largest in the world. This chapter studies the demographic breakdown of the members of Generation Z, their political and social concerns, their career aspirations, their workplace preferences, and the changing consumer attributes. The research design for this study incorporated a qualitative approach comprising of four focus group discussions (see Appendix). Members of Generation Z in India show common behaviours and preferences with their counterparts around the world. However, members of Generation Z in India have clear opinions and ideas of how youth can contribute to a developing nation like India.

Keywords: India; Generation Z; social media; human resource; marketing; we identity

Introduction to India: the Significance of the Young Indian

India is primarily an agrarian society with 66% of the population living in villages. The urban population consists of 34% of the entire country (Ministry of Statistics and Programme Implementation, 2019). India is a diverse country in relation to geography, culture, religion, and urbanisation.

India is a democratic republic where the country is governed by people representatives chosen by the majority. As such, the diversity in relation to religion, region, culture, and language within communities lends a challenging angle to governance. The Republic of India is divided into 29 states and 7 union territories, spread over an area of 3.287 million square km (Wikipedia, 2019), each with its own cultural differences. India is also known for being the birthplace of religions such as Hinduism and Buddhism. The most followed religions of India

The New Generation Z in Asia: Dynamics, Differences, Digitalisation
The Changing Context of Managing People, 89–104
Copyright © 2020 by Emerald Publishing Limited
All rights of reproduction in any form reserved
doi:10.1108/978-1-80043-220-820201010

are Hinduism (79.8%), Islam (14.2%), Christianity (2.3%), Sikhism (1.7%), Buddhism (0.7%), Jainism (0.4%), Zoroastrianism (0.1%), and other religions (0.9%) (Shawe, 2018). Despite the diversity and magnitude, India is a country that is both collectivist and individualistic in nature (Hofstede, 2001). The collectivist aspect is reflected where Generation Z places a high value on social belongingness and family values. This is evident from the prevalent practice of joint family systems that exist within the country (Chadda, 2013). However, the predominant collectivist culture of India which stresses social linkages with an emphasis on the 'We' identity is co-existent with a focus on individualism. The individualist aspect of Indian society is seen as a result of its dominant religion/philosophy – Hinduism. Followers of Hinduism believe in a cycle of death and rebirth, with the manner of each rebirth being dependent upon how the individual lived the preceding life. People are, therefore, individually responsible for the way they lead their lives and the impact it will have upon their rebirth (Vishwananda, 2015). This explains the focus on individual concentration in an otherwise collectivist Indian society. The Generation Z in Indian society is an extension of individualistic traits.

In a country like India, where diversity is the norm, Generation Z has an advantage, be it in terms of consumerism or workplace blending. To understand this phenomenon, it is essential to understand the demographic breakdown of this generation.

Various indicators that measure the youth, such as literacy level, work status, and the age-wise population, have been disclosed by the Census of India (2011). 31% of women and 38% of men are from urban areas with 37% of women and 32% of men from the two lowest wealth quintiles (National Family Health Survey, 2009). Education is still a luxury for Indians living in rural areas though the scenario is improving with people recognising the power and impact of education. The census (conducted once every 10 years in India) reveals that 29% of women (47% of urban and 20% of rural) have over 10 years of schooling while 38% of men (49% of urban and 31% of rural) have over 10 years of schooling. Employment is highly skewed in India with 36% of women and 67% of men aged 15–24 being employed. India's workforce has fewer women than it did 6 years ago: no more than 18% in rural areas are employed, compared to 25% in 2011–2012 and 14% in urban areas from 15% in 2011–2012 (Shibu & Abraham, 2019). Despite rapid economic growth, less than a quarter (23.6%) of women aged 15 and above participated in the labour force in 2018 (compared to 78.6% of men) (Catalyst, 2019). Across all states in India, both in rural and urban areas, only 22% of the country's female population are at work, compared to men. The majority of employed women are agricultural workers; whereas there is greater diversity in male employment. Less than two-thirds of employed women (63%) earn cash for their work, compared with 88% of the country's employed men.

The report on the National Family Health Survey (2018) points out the glaring areas which need drastic measures to be taken. A sizeable proportion of the youth lacks education, even literacy. Early marriage, women burdened with childbearing and rearing, a large unmet need for family planning, poor nutritional status, and substance abuse were causes of concern. Generation Z in India is projected to contribute at least 2% annually to the Gross Domestic Product of the nation.

Economic surveys reveal that the average age of India will be a youthful 29 years in 2020. That compares to 37 years in China and the United States, 48 years in Japan, and 45 years in Western Europe. Out of the total 520 million workforce in India, over 80% (416 million) of the workforce is in the informal sector and only 100 million in the formal sector. India adds only 10 million every year to the workforce with nearly 216 million engaged in the agriculture sector, thus, becoming part of the informal economy (The Economic Times, 2018a).

The Political System in India

India is a federal republic with 29 states and six union territories. The governance is a parliamentary democracy which operates under the constitution of 1950. There is a bicameral federal parliament: the Rajya Sabha or council of states (upper house) and the Lok Sabha or house of the people (lower house). India is also the world's largest democracy. Elections to Government are held every 5 years. Paradoxically, only 6% of the leaders and ministers in the government of India are below the age of 35 (Telpande, 2018). The reluctance of youth to enter politics stems from various factors such as unpredictability in the political scenario, a fierce competition for power, and the various in-house complexities inside political parties and other agendas (Telpande, 2017).

The government of India has proactively initiated various schemes that aim at the development of the youth. The government aims to skill 400 million youth by 2020 through an unprecedented program named the 'Skill India Mission'. Various schemes like Pradhan Mantri Kaushal Vikas Yojana (PMKVY roughly translated to Prime Minister's Skill Development Plan) have been initiated to further the aim of skill development, to enable a large number of young people in the country to take up industry-relevant skills training that will help them in securing a better livelihood (Choudhary, 2018).

Entrepreneurship is a thrust area with the government encouraging young people to become job creators and not job seekers. NitiAayog, National Skill Development Centers, and the Make in India schemes have been initiated keeping this objective of entrepreneurship in focus.

Socialisation Agents: Role of Family, Peers, and Education

Family members play a major role in deciding the behaviour and the set of values that the Indian youth upholds (Sonawat, 2001). The family, in Indian society, is an institution in itself and a typical symbol of the collectivist culture of India from ancient times. The joint family system or an extended family has been an important feature of Indian culture, till a blend of urbanisation and western influence, began to affect home and hearth. This is especially true of urban areas, where nuclear families have become the order of the day (Naidu, 2018). Unlike the western countries, in India, children do not leave their homes once they turn 18; rather keeping in mind the maxim '*VasudaivaKutumbakam*' (the world is one family), it is not uncommon to see joint families still living in harmonious existence. Indian values and traditions keep the family intact.

The Indian youth has always lived in a very protective environment and this plays a major role in framing their mental makeup. Of late, the country is seeing a slow shift from a joint family setup to a more individualistic nuclear approach (Singh, 2012). Parents in India are vigilant and consistently monitor the activities and movements of their children with the purpose of guiding and protecting (Kohli & Sreedhar, 2018). The nuclear family model that predominantly exists in India nowadays results in much of the traditional role of the grandparent or aunt being taken over by strangers, whether agency-approved nannies or care takers at preschools. This interaction with 'familiar strangers' has led to a greater reliance on surveillance technology. This constant vigilance and monitoring comes in the wake of threatening exposure to dangerous games and apps on social media platforms, which takes a toll when the Generation Z is impressionable (Deepika, 2017). This might be considered authoritative and an invasion of privacy but this 'helicopter parenting'[1] slowly fades when the child transitions into adulthood. The focus of Indian parents of Generation Z is to prepare them for life and so they have higher expectations of their children (Chitnis, 2015). Generation Z in India has to face more pressure from their parents to focus on their careers, many Indian youngsters reveal that their parents put pressure on them to focus on their careers. Parents tend to encourage and push young people into conventional career options as they are unaware of new-age career options, which can create more productive lives for their children (Chakrabarty, 2019). Indian youngsters also admit that they are often asked to give suggestions on several household discussions making them active participants in decision making (Singh, 2014). Parents tend to rely on children's decisions, especially in areas of entertainment and digital purchases (Ali, Ravichandran, & Batra, 2013; Tinson & Nancarrow, 2015).

Peer dynamics are another factor contributing to the behavioural and personality development of Generation Z. The idea of loneliness makes the Indian Generation Z uneasy and anxious; they want to be surrounded by people all the time. This social anxiety could be attributed to the nuclear family setup of modern India today where the Generation Z is subject to helicopter parenting (Young, 2017).

The Education System in India

India is known for its transitional education system over the decades. The earliest form of India's education was the 'Gurukul' system where the students or disciples stayed along with the 'Guru' or teacher and learnt everything the guru taught. The Gurukul system was nature attuned and students learnt everything from languages, Holy Scriptures, Mathematics, and metaphysics (Kumar, 2011). The modern school education system was introduced in India when the nation was under the colonial rule of the British. Lord Macaulay is credited for incorporating the

---

[1]Helicopter Parenting refers to the over-controlling behaviour of parents towards their children resulting in negative repercussions on the child's ability to decide and deal with emotional issues.

modern education system in India in the 1800s. English and pure Sciences were a few of the 'modern' subjects to which the education systems were confined to.

Universal and compulsory education for all children in the age group of 6–14 years is incorporated in the constitution.[2] The medium of instruction in most primary schools is the regional language and English is introduced as the second language from grade 3 (Scholaro.com, 2018). Public examinations are conducted in two cycles (one examination after class 10, where the child is approximately 15 years old and the other after class 12, where the child would be approximately 17 years old) for the students to enter tertiary levels of education. Subjects include languages (including the regional language, English, and an elective), Mathematics, Social Sciences, Science and Technology, Art, and Physical Education. The secondary schools are affiliated with the central or the state boards who are responsible for conducting examinations every year. The Central Board of Secondary Education, New Delhi; the Indian School Certificate, New Delhi; Certificate of Vocational Education, Senior Secondary Certificate (NIOS), and Pre-University certificates are the most common boards under whose affiliation the schools belong. The tertiary education system is governed by the University Grants Commission (UGC) and is responsible for college education offering Bachelor's and Master's degrees. The UGC develops higher education on an all India level, allocates funds, and is responsible for the recognition of colleges in India. The All India Council of Technical Education (AICTE) was also established to oversee quality control of technical education. At the beginning of 2015, the Choice-Based Credit System (CBCS) was introduced by the UGC to provide for a more interdisciplinary and flexible approach to education. Generation Z in India leaves a great impact on the e-commerce industry. India's youth have started using various online learning courses to upgrade their education. They proudly display their credentials on their resumes and LinkedIn profiles. Online learning platforms like Coursera, EDX, Alison, and other platforms recognise the Indian market as a huge consumer base and design courses to the effect.

Basics of the Indian Generation Z

Social Media Life of India's Generation Z

Research by Microsoft and International Data Corporation has revealed that the giant digital transformation in India is estimated to contribute a whopping $154 billion to India's Gross Domestic Product (The Economic Times, 2018b). Technology is at the forefront in all aspects of Generation Z's lives. According to the TCS Youth Survey (2016), which traced the digital habits of teenagers in India, smartphones are the most used electronic gadget followed by laptops and personal computers. While Facebook was popular, the trend among the Indian youth today is Instagram, where self-promotion is the norm (see Appendix). Instagram users also use Facebook simultaneously (Kwarta, 2018). Privacy doesn't

---

[2]Age 4–8: primary school in classes 1–3. Age 9–15: secondary school in classes 4–10. Age 16–17: higher secondary school classes 11 and 12.

bother Generation Z much because the focus is more on self- promotion. Video calls are preferred over text messages; face-to-face interaction is more appealing to the youth.

Political Attitudes and Social Opinions

The elections in India, held every 5 years, are followed very closely by the youth of India. The Indian Generation Z is politically conscious and well aware of the fact that India needs a strong leader and politicians who are not corrupt. Optimism about the future is reflected in the satisfaction among most Indians that the country is progressing with economic gains. However, rising concerns among the Indian Generation Z about employment issues, India–Pakistan tensions, and environmental effects were reflected in the focus group discussions conducted by the researchers among the Indian Generation Z.

As many as 130 million first time voters cast their votes in the elections in May 2019. The primary concern among Indian Generation Z youth was more job creation and employment. They are willing to vote for the political party that would solve this unemployment crisis (Beniwal & Pradhan, 2018). It has often been noted that the Indian youth is a mix of conservatism and liberal attitudes. Generation Z in India is highly interested in politics (Nigam, 2013) and the Bharatiya Janata Party[3] (BJP) is the most preferred single party.

Women's equality is a rising issue among Generation Z in India. The women's movement in India has seen a rise by engaging in confronting or reforming customary practices like the *dowry system,* where the bride's family pays a hefty sum of money in cash or kind to the groom's family at the time of the wedding; *preference for sons over daughters,* which arises from a deep rooted patriarchal mindset; and the *triple talaq,* where a Muslim husband can divorce his wife instantly by uttering the word 'Talaq' thrice.

Members of Generation Z as Consumers

Consumers Changing Attitudes

The Indian Z Generation consumers are techno savvy and believe in experiencing the present with a collaborative mindset. They are conscious about their lifestyle and their social image. This is reflected in their digital connectivity and their participation in environmental safety. They believe and work towards sustainability; triggering marketers to consider their changing attributes minutely and develop products and services conforming to their expectations. The Generation Z market in India is a huge consumer base; companies need to focus on strong brand building and quality with innovation. The consumer behaviour of Generation Z can be understood using analytics and neuromarketing. This generation can be tapped

---

[3]BJP is the country's largest political party in terms of representation in the national parliament and state assemblies and is the world's largest party in terms of primary membership.

for communication and referral with the support of digital and social media marketing. Positive customer satisfaction can be expected by experiential marketing. These marketing tools will be helpful in understanding the Indian Generation Z consumers and generate returns for firms, society, and the country.

The Indian Generation Z has not seen a world without devices and uses them in all spans of life whether it be education, health, knowledge, or entertainment. In India, 71% of the members of Generation Z browse the Internet through their mobiles; 68% of them shop online for clothes, gadgets, fashion accessories, electronic items, and footwear (YouGov.com, 2019). The per capita income has risen substantially over the years giving rise to higher purchase power parity among Generation Z in India (Roy, 2018). Affordability has increased and the young generation does not need to think twice on whether they can afford products or not. The Indian Generation Z is highly aware of carbon footprints, sustainability, and environmental degradation. Generation Z in India is careful of their carbon footprints. The average young Indian leaves a per capita per capita emissions just one-quarter of the poorest 50% of those from the United States (Nason, 2019). Most companies in India make it a point to highlight their Corporate Social Responsibility initiatives to attract the Indian Generation Z consumer. Take the example of Tata, a company which is highly preferred by Generation Z in India. Tata highlights the Vasundhara (environmental) aspect of their CSR which highly motivates Generation Z to work for Tata. Many educational institutions and universities in India have student-run environmental groups that focus on plantations and sanitation (Panwar, 2018).

Generation Z at Work: Career Aspirations, Anchors, and Attitudes in India

Organisational Dynamics and Diversity

With each generation of workers entering the workforce, changes are inevitable due to the respective unique demographic characteristics of every generation. The Indian workforce has three distinct characteristics: (a) it is a young workforce; (b) the skills base of this workforce remains underdeveloped; and (c) most jobs are being created in the informal economy (Saran & Saran, 2018).

India, with its massive population of 1.33 billion (Govt. of India, Ministry of Home Affairs, 2011), as per the latest census conducted in 2011, contributes to the world economy with its youngest workforce, Generation Z, who is currently being groomed in various educational institutes across India or has just entered the workforce recently. India, in 2020, has the world's largest Generation Z cohort with 256 million of young people from this generation. It has the highest share of the youngest workforce behind the Philippines and reflects the young and growing population of Generation Z workers in India. Employees belonging to Generation Z bring a whole new perspective to the workforce as far as diversity is concerned. The Indian Generation Z believes in equality in the workplace leading to many companies incorporating inclusive programs to attract young female talent. Bringing gender parity to the workforce would increase India's GDP by 27%, as per IMF estimates. In addition, values and approaches towards environmental issues are a key area that the corporate needs to focus on as the average young Indian employee is projected to be more positive towards organisations that prioritise environmental and social issues. Employment and women's safety are the biggest concerns of young Indians (Padmanabhan, 2019). When asked to nominate the most important issue that India is facing, 18% said jobs and unemployment, 12% said economic inequality, and 9% said corruption (Economic Times, 2018).

According to a study among 500 students and 200 teachers across India in 2017 (Towbridge, 2016), 95% of the students and 91% of teachers see creativity as the driver for careers among Generation Z in India. Ninety per cent of the teachers believed that Generation Z in India would be working in careers that are currently non-existent (Bawa, 2017). The Indian Generation Z is expected to reform all the conventions and change orthodox ways of working. Young people have different expectations about their career paths and expect their employer to help them achieve them. They are interested in expanding their academic qualifications while working, having start-ups and still having enough time to pursue their passions. They have higher expectations from their employers and the organisation which they plan to serve. They are quick in making decisions and are hyperactive in nature. They prefer straight forward conversations and an open work environment. There's no stigma associated with failure and the Z Generation Indian is practical but risk-averse (Meghani, 2018). Despite the fact that globally, young Indian workers of Generation Z are projected to bring about a marked change in organisations, the scenario requires further scrutiny in India. This is because the 'skills gap' between academia and corporate is a very real hurdle that needs to be crossed. According to a study by the Varkey Foundation on Generation Z across the world in 2017, only 10% of the Indian Generation Z was interested in pay compared to 37% of the respondents of the study, who wanted to develop their skills.

The Start-up Culture

Young Generation Z Indians would prefer their own start-ups and ventures rather than being bound to a job that imposes strict working hours (Patel, 2017). This could be due to the fact that the urban youth in India remains pessimistic about job prospects, with 65% of Generation Z stating that it is extremely difficult to land a job (LiveMint, 2018b). They picture a venture where they are not bound down by authoritative norms and are masters of their domain. This reiterates the aversion of the Indian Generation Z to being led by others. This presents a challenge to companies who will have to train and develop strategies to attract and retain this particular set of employees. Despite the technology overload in the hands of the youngsters, this generation more than any other will suffer from the growing gap between the highly skilled and the unskilled. The technical skill gap is huge, but the non-technical skill gap is even more pervasive.

Managing the Indian Generation Z requires a huge remedial effort on broad transferable skills such as work habits, interpersonal communication, and critical thinking and a huge investment in remedial technical training. A research study at Harvard states that 60% of Indian Generation Z students in top colleges between the age group of 18 and 21 stated that they don't feel ready for a job (Raina, 2016).

Attracting Generation Z: Suggestions and Strategies

Approaches in Marketing

Attracting Indian Generation Z to buy a product requires more strategic thinking and a plan of action rather than mere advertising. With the massive Z Generation population of India, marketers have a never before opportunity of tapping into the demographic. Generation Z in India is a socially conscious generation. Meaningful advertisements that bring out social issues such as Surf Excel detergent (promoting religious harmony), All-out (#standbytoughmoms), Myntra Fashion (Bold is Beautiful), and Vogue India (Boys don't cry) are examples of products that have captured the market due to advertising with social messages in them (Sharma, 2016). The Indian Generation Z needs to feel that they are creating a social impact when they purchase products (King, 2018). The Indian brand FabIndia, which sells handmade products, furniture, essential oils, and craft items, are an example to this. Rural artisans in India stand to gain with the expansion and growth plan of FabIndia. Each customer feels that he/she is making a difference in the lives of the rural worker. Since this is an important factor for a Generation Z consumer, companies are likely to capture a higher market share if their consumers feel that they are making a social impact.

The environmental concern among Generation Z in India has led to a rise in Collaborative consumption that was non-existent before. The 'sharing economy', which may be due to a collectivist culture in India, is a huge market for collaborative consumption. Companies such as OLX[4] (used goods buy and sell platforms), ZoomCar[5] and UBER[6] (Car rentals), AirBnB[7] (home stays), and the Lending-Club[8] (where people borrow money from each other instead of banks) are examples of the rise of collaborative consumption in India. (Zain, 2016).

The Indian Generation Z looks for novelty in any product they consume, be it food (novel toppings at Pizza Hut), holidays (women only tours, adventure tourism), or the shows they watch, marketers would likely garner bigger shares of the Generation Z market if they innovate their products constantly. Take for example, in the 2016 Olympics, when badminton shuttler P. V. Sindhu of India and wrestler Sakshi Malik of India won medals, Pizza Hut advertised by giving free pizzas to girls whose names were 'Sindhu' or 'Sakshi' (Challapalli, 2018).

---

[4] www.olx.in
[5] www.zoomcar.com
[6] www.uber.com
[7] www.airbnb.co.in
[8] www.lendingclub.com

The FMCG marketers in India are appealing to the Indian Generation Z's pride in their heritage and tradition (Chauhan, 2018). Companies like Hamdard,[9] whose trademark product is RoohAfza[10] (a summer drink made with traditional ingredients), are now seeking to revamp this traditional brand to the Generation Z by appealing to the youngsters with its history. So is the case with AMUL[11] (India's largest milk co-operative) whose advertising campaign shows their range of products catering to the Generation Z and making them aware through various media about the positive social impact they are making. The Indian members of Generation Z love their lineage and heritage and companies are designing marketing strategies revolving around this.

Approaches in Human Resource Management

The process of recruitment and selection itself has undergone changes since the Indian Generation Z uses diverse methods of job hunting. Traditional public sector companies in the Automobile and Information Technology sectors such as Tata Steel and Mahindra and Mahindra are changing their image in a bid to attract Generation Z. Attracting and retaining workers from Generation Z is a daunting task; nevertheless, certain strategies could be the key to hold on to them and reap organisational benefits.

The Indian Generation Z is one that is used to the 'instant' culture, where information and opinion are instantly and openly expressed. In an organisational setting that places emphasis on mentoring, managers giving feedback and looking out for the Z Generation are more likely to retain them for much longer (Singh, 2017).

The Indian Generation Z wants a workplace that is 'fun' to work in. There is an overall environment of optimism and growth despite concerns of employment. The social and environmental agenda of organisations will come to the forefront and hyper-specialisation and need for autonomy will make portfolio careers more a norm than an aberration (Alaganandan, 2019).

Conclusions

Generation Z in India is on the cusp of bringing change to the world economy with their very presence. The start-up culture, strong opinions, and actions on current events and environmental concerns are common key points in the Indian Generation Z. The outlook of Generation Z in India is optimistic, positive, techno-savvy, and adaptable. Drawing from a rich culture and history, the Generation Z of India has the power and ability to bring positive additions to the world economy.

---

[9]www.hamdard.in
[10]http://www.hamdard.in/product/roohafza
[11]www.amul.com

References

Alaganandan, P. (2019). *Indian workplace of 2022: Are organizations ready for the future?* New Delhi: PricewaterhouseCoopers India.

Ali, A., Ravichandran, N., & Batra, D. (2013). Children's choice of influence strategies in family purchase decisions and the impact of demographics. *Vision: The Journal of Business Perspective*, *60*, 27–40.

Bawa, K. (2017, December). *90% of teachers feel their Gen Z students will have careers that do not exist today: Survey*. Retrieved from www.hindustantimes.com: https://m-hindustantimes-com.cdn.amproject.org

Beniwal, V., & Pradhan, B. (2018). *India's Z Gen voters have a simple message for politicians*. Retrieved from https://m-ecomonictimes-com.cdn.amproect.org

Catalyst. (2019). *Women in the workforce – India: Quick Take*. India: Catalyst.

Chadda, R. K. (2013). Indian family systems, collectivistic society and psychotherapy. *Indian Journal of Psychiatry*, *55*, 299–309.

Chakrabarty, R. (2019, February). *93% Indian students aware of just seven career options: What are parents doing wrong?* Retrieved from https://www.indiatoday.in/education-today/news/story/93-indian-students-aware-of-just-seven-career-options-what-are-parents-doing-wrong-1446205-2019-02-04

Challapalli, S. (2018, February). *The Hunt for Cool*. Retrieved from www-thehindu businessline-com.cdn.amproject.org

Chauhan, G. (2018, June). *Target: Millennials*. Retrieved from https://www-fortuneindia-com.cdn.amproject.org

Chitnis, S. (2015). *Why Indian parents should learn to let go*. Bangalore: Outlook.

Choudhary, A. (2018). *Skill India: 70% of Indian youth don't even know about government's skill development programmes*. New Delhi: The Financial Express.

Deepika, K. (2017). *Children on Social Media-a predicament for parents and schools*. Bengaluru: The Hindu.

Economic Times, India. (2018). *94% of engineering graduates are not fit for hiring, says this IT stalwart*. Retrieved from https://economictimes.indiatimes.com/jobs/only-6-of-those-passing-out-of-indias-engineering-colleges-are-fit-for-a-job/articleshow/64446292.cms?from=md

Hameed, S., & Mathur, M. (2019). The disruption of the Z Gen *Employee: Change strategies for a smoother workforce induction. *International Journal of Innovative Technology and Exploring Engineering*, *8*(6C), 69–74.

Hofstede, G. (2001). *Culture's consequences: Comparing values, behaviors, institutions, and organizations across nations*. Thousand Oaks, CA: Sage.

King, M. (2018, July). www.forbes.com. Retrieved J from Three things you need to know about marketing to Gen Z: https://www-forbes-com.cdn.amproject.org

Kohli, D., & Sreedhar, N. (2018). *Honey, I'm watching the kids*. Retrieved from https://www.livemint.com.

Kumar, A. (2018, October 9). *Women in Workforce: What it would take to achieve gender parity in India*. Retrieved 2020, from www.yourstory.com: https://yourstory.com/journal/women-in-workforce-what-it-would-take-to-achieve-g-pare59syolk

Kumar, A. (2018). Women in workforce: What it would take to achieve gender parity in India. *YS Journal*.

Kumar, D. V. (2011, December). *The education system in India*. Retrieved from www.gnu.com: https://www.gnu.org

Kwarta, N. (2018, August). *Why Instagram has become the next Facebook*. Retrieved from https://www-livemint-com.cdn.amproject.org

LiveMint. (2018b). *Young India not so hopeful about job prospects*. New Delhi: YouGov-Mint.

Meghani, V. (2018). *The zing thing: Gen Z redefining work and workplaces*. India: Forbes India.

Ministry of Statistics and Programme Implementation. (2019). *Population of India*. United Nations (World's population Prospects).

Naidu, V. (2018). *Why the Indian family is a great institution*. New Delhi: The Economic Times.

Nason, V. (2019). *Gen Z's smaller carbon footprint still may not be enough*. Retrieved from https://www.salon.com/

National Family Health Survey. (2009). *Analysis of NFHS3 Data*. New Delhi.

Nigam, A. (2013). *More youth showing interest in politics, says CSDS survey*. New Delhi: The Business Line.

Padmanabhan, V. (2019). *A new generation takes charge of our destiny*. New Delhi: LiveMint.

Panwar, R. (2018, July). *Making students environment-conscious*. Retrieved from: https://www.thehindubusinessline-com.cdn.amproect.org

Patel, D. (2017, April). *How Gen Z will shape the future of business*. Retrieved from www.forbes.com/sites/deeppatel/2017/how-gen-z-will-shape-the-future-of-business/ampshape-the-future-of-business/amp

Raina, S. (2016, November). *How Talerang is preparing our country's youth to be work ready*. Retrieved from https://sheroes.com/articles/shveta-raina-shares-how-talerang-is-preparing-our-country-s-youth-to-be-work-ready/MjUyMA==

Roy, S. (2018, March). *The Indian Consumer Market and its changing dynamics*. Retrieved from https://qrius-com.cdn.amproject.org

Saran, S., & Saran, V. (2018). *The future of the Indian workforce: A new approach for the new economy*. New Delhi: Observer Research Foundation.

Scholaro.com. (2018). *Education system in India*. Retrieved from www.scholaro.com: https://www.scholaro.com

Sharma, D. (2016). *Top 10 Best Indian Advertisements on Social Media*. Retrieved from https://listsurge-com.cdn.amproject.org

Shawe, B. E. (2018, July). www.worldatlas.com/articles/society. Retrieved from https://www.worldatlas.com/articles/major-religions-in-modern-india.html

Shibu, J., & Abraham, R. (2019, July). *Share Of Regular Salaried Work Rises, But Women More Likely To Be Self-Employed*. Retrieved from https://www.indiaspend.com/more-women-are-self-employed-in-india-fewer-hold-salaried-jobs/

Singh, A. (2014). Challenges and issues of Generation Z. *IOSR Journal of Business and Management (IOSR-JBM)*, *16*(7), 59–63.

Singh, P. (2017). *Make way for Generation Z*. New Delhi: LiveMint.

Sonawat, R. (2001). Understanding families in India: A reflection of societal changes. *Psicologia: Teoria e Pesquisa*, *17*(2), 177–186.

Telpande, J. U. (2017). *Why-is-Indian-youth-not-entering-politics*. Retrieved from www.youthkiawaaz.com: https://www.youthkiawaaz.com/2018/05/why-is-indian-youth-not-entering-politics/. Accessed on August 2019.

Telpande, J. U. (2018, June). *Why The Indian Youth Is Not Entering Politics*. Retrieved from www.youthkiawaaz.com: https://www.youthkiawaaz.com/2018/05/why-is-indian-youth-not-entering-politics/. Accessed on May 2019.

The Economic Times. (2018a). *Demographic dividend will drive India's future growth*. New Delhi: THG Publishing Pvt Ltd.

The Economic Times. (2018b). *Evolving technologies: India's big leap into the digital world*. Mumbai: Bennett Coleman & Co. Ltd.

Tinson, J., & Nancarrow, C. (2015). The influence of children on purchases: The development of measures for gender role orientation and sopping savvy. *International Journal of Market Research*, *47*(1), 5–27.

Towbridge, T. (2016, June). *Gen Z in the Classroom: Creating the Future.* Retrieved from www.theblog.adobe.com: https://theblog.adobe.com/gen-z-in-the-classroom-creating-the-future/. Accessed on August 2019.

Vishwananda, S. (2015, April). *How does Hinduism encourage Individualism?* Retrieved from https://hinduism.stackexchange.com: https://hinduism.stackexchange.com/questions/6965/how-does-hinduism-encourages-individualism/6971#6971. Accessed on August 2019.

Wikipedia. (2019, April). *en.wikipedia.org/wiki/Geography_of_India.* Retrieved from www.wikipedia.org: https://en.wikipedia.org/wiki/Geography_of_India. Accessed on May 2019.

YouGov.com. (2019, February). The age of digital natives: An understanding of the Indian Millennial, Mumbai.

Young, J. L. (2017). *The Effects of 'Helicopter Parenting'.* Retrieved from https://www.psychologytoday.com/us/blog/when-you-adult-child-breaks-your-heart/201701/the-effects-helicopter-parenting.

Zain, A. (2016, February). *The rise of the sharing economy and why it will work in India.* Retrieved from https://yourstorycom.cdn.amproject.org

Appendix A: Focus Group Discussion

Research Method	Qualitative	
Research Objective	1. Assess the behavioral competencies of Generation Z	
	2. What makes the Indian Generation Z different from their counterparts?	
Universe of the study	Generation Z; MBA/PGDM graduates born in or after 1995	
Period of study conducted	July 2019-December 2019	
Composition of the focus group	4 groups of 5 Members each (Members assigned numbers to maintain confidentiality)	
Gender composition in each group	Male	12
	Female	8
Religious composition of the subjects	Hindu	16
	Muslim	3
	Christian/Other	1
Educational Qualification	High School	0
	Graduate	13
	Post Graduate	7
Family Structure	Joint	2
	Nuclear	18

Appendix B: Selected Analysis Used for the Study

Topic	Quotes
SOCIAL MEDIA USAGE	*"I love sharing my pictures and Insta provides me the best platform to do that. I share my sketches and creative work on Insta and I have a lot of followers. This encourages me to work on developing my skills better. I cannot imagine a life without their mobile phones. From shopping to studies, from food to communication; it is technology that keeps us on the right track"*
	Akansha Yadav; M2 Group 3
	"I was a hardcore Facebook user but I find the double taps on Insta much more fun. Also WhatsApp, Snapchat and Facetime are the best means to socialize."
	Nisha Raghav; M1 Group 1
BIGGEST CONCERNS OF LIVING IN INDIA TODAY	*"Employment is our biggest worry in today's times. We receive education but are unsure how applicable it will be in the real world."*
	Devrat Choudhary, 22, M3 Group 4
	"I feel that environmental concerns are paramount. We feel responsible for doing our bit to preserve the environment…even if it means planting one tree"
	Twinkle Jain, 21, M4 Group 2
	"Definitely Women's safety is a concern in India. The laws should be made stricter with criminals"
	Drishti Singh, 18, M1 Group 3
STRONGEST COMPETENCIES IN TERMS OF BEHAVIOR	*"I feel an advantage in today's times. No doubt it's the technology. This gives me the ability to multi-task across devices"*
	Aditi Agarwal, 20, M4 Group 4

Topic	Quotes
WORKPLACE PREFERENCES AND ATTITUDES	*"I am eager to work…I'm looking forward to it; I'd like to work for a company that gives me the freedom to learn and grow…Corporate settings such as Google seems attractive to me. I like the open workspaces and fun atmosphere it has…"* Celestee Singh, 18, M4 Group 4
WHERE DO YOU SEE YOURSELF 5 YEARS FROM NOW?	*"I want to be my own boss after sometime… maybe develop something that's profitable and sustainable, my own company, for starters"* Mayank Jain, 22, M3 Group 2

Chapter 7

Generation Z in Pakistan: Individualistic and Collectivist in Orientation

Ahmad Jamal

Abstract

An estimated 52% of Pakistan's population is under the age of 25, and like their counterparts elsewhere around the globe, Generation Z in Pakistan was born into a world overrun with technology, Internet, and social media. This generation of consumers possess information processing ability that is much faster than any other generation. Generation Z consumers in Pakistan are active users of social media platforms connecting with local and international users, brands and exchanging information, photos, videos, ideas, and opinions with people inside and outside Pakistan. To develop insights into the consumption patterns, preferences, attitudes, and preferences of this segment of consumers, this chapter provides an overview of cultural and social values underpinning consumption choices and social media preferences. The chapter identifies and discusses the dynamic nature of Generation Z in Pakistan by identifying some of its defining features: the generation consists of confident, able, and multilingual consumers who are largely collectivists in orientation but shows strong individualistic tendencies. Such consumers have a global outlook and actively seek engagement with brands via digital platforms and influencer marketers expecting authenticity, respect, and equality. The chapter discusses work-related implications such as the need for providing transformational leadership and training programs to harness the intellectual skills of Generation Z in Pakistan. The chapter concludes by identifying and discussing issues relevant to handling Generation consumers in Pakistan including effective marketing strategies.

Keywords: Generation Z; Pakistan; digitalisation; consumption; marketing; leadership

The New Generation Z in Asia: Dynamics, Differences, Digitalisation
The Changing Context of Managing People, 105–117
Copyright © 2020 by Emerald Publishing Limited
All rights of reproduction in any form reserved
doi:10.1108/978-1-80043-220-820201011

Introduction to Pakistan

Pakistan's population was 207 million in 2017 (Pakistan Bureau of Statistics, 2017) making it the fifth most populous country in the world. According to the Human Development Report (2019) published by the United Nations Development Program, Pakistan's Human Development Index value (which is a measure of its long-term progress in three basic dimensions of human development: a long and healthy life, access to knowledge, and a decent standard of living) increased from 0.404 to 0.560, an increase of 38.6% between 1990 and 2018, whereas its Gross National Income (GNI) per capita increased by about 62.4% during the same period.

Most Pakistanis are young as 51.7% of Pakistan's population are aged under 25 (Index Mundi, 2019). Pakistan is experiencing a decline in its mortality and fertility rates, which means that there are huge opportunities for Pakistan to benefit from a demographic dividend, enhance education and health provision, and expand the capacity of the labour market to absorb young labour productively (Jehan & Khan 2020). Pakistani young adults are concerned with completing their education, securing a job, having a secure future in financial and material terms, and are keen to emigrate and/or study aboard (Khan, 2018).

Pakistan has witnessed dramatic social and cultural changes which have ushered in a new era of urbanisation leading to the creation of megacities such as Karachi and Lahore. An estimated 36% of Pakistan's population are city dwellers in comparison to 25% in Afghanistan, 34% in India, and 75% in Iran (World Bank Data, 2020). People in Pakistan are now enjoying much better life expectancy (around 68 years as per Index Mundi, 2019) than ever before due to improved medical facilities and better educated health professionals being available in the country.

Pakistan's economy largely relies on agriculture (notably cotton), manufacturing, and foreign remittances. Since the late 1980s, the country has favoured policies that encouraged private enterprise, privatisation of state-owned banks, and manufacturing enterprises. Pakistan became an independent country in 1947 and, since then, its gross domestic product (GDP) averaged 4.92% from 1952 until 2018 (Trading Economics, 2020). A large proportion of urban Pakistan are English speaking, and, since 2018, the country has been making steady progress in relation to improving the country's business environment, increasing tourism, reducing its dependence on foreign loans, and widening the country's base. To boost economic development, Pakistan and China are implementing the China–Pakistan Economic Corridor (CPEC) with $60 billion in investments targeted towards energy and other infrastructure projects. According to Moody's Analytics (2019), Pakistan believes that CPEC investments will enable growth rates of over 6% of GDP by laying the groundwork for increased exports.

While Pakistan's cultural heritage dates back thousands of years to the period of the Indus civilisation, people in Pakistan take great pride when identifying with the Islamic culture. People in Pakistan value and admire modesty in dress and often have conservative expectations when it comes to interactions between men and women. Increasingly, women are working outside the home and traditional gender roles are changing with men, especially from the urban middle-income group, becoming more relaxed about role of women in and outside the home. Pakistani women now appear prominently in traditional and new media and many of the distinguished scholars, politicians, doctors, journalists, teachers, and even entrepreneurs are women.

People in Pakistan, like Muslims elsewhere (e.g. Jamal, Yaccob, Bartikowski, & Slater, 2019), are inspired and motivated by Islamic beliefs, values, and altruistic attitudes, which means that they show a real concern for others irrespective of their religious, cultural, or ethnic backgrounds. People in Pakistan are well known for expressing sympathy and empathy towards the poor, elderly, and needy individuals. Philanthropy is an integral part of Islam and Pakistan is one of the most charitable nations in the world. Amjad and Ali (2018) report that Pakistan contributes more than 1% of its GDP to charity. This compares very well with much wealthier countries like the United Kingdom (1.3% of GDP) and Canada (1.2% of GDP). On an average, people in Pakistan give an estimated Rs. 240 billion (more than $2 billion) per year to charitable causes (Amjad & Ali, 2018). This culture of generosity is underpinned by the Islamic emphasis on charitable giving such as *Sadaqa* (donations seeking blessings and forgiveness from God) and *Zakah* (giving a set proportion of one's wealth to charity).

People in Pakistan love listening to religious (*hamd* and *naat*), traditional (*qawwali, ghazals,* etc.), Indian, and Western popular music. Pakistan is home to multiple cultural and ethnic groups with each ethnic group valuing and cherishing their own modern and ancient cultural traditions including music but also language, dress styles, and literature. People's preferences for music, thus, reflect this cultural diversity with each ethnic music following its own form and poetic style. Music in Pakistan includes diverse elements from different parts of South Asia, South East Asia, Central Asia, Persian, Turkish, Arabic, and modern-day Western popular music (Siddiqui & Sibghatullah, 2014). Pakistanis' love for music comes to life during wedding ceremonies which can last from 3 to 6 days and have a lot of music and dance. People in Pakistan also play and appreciate many sports (e.g. hockey, squash, badminton), especially cricket as the country has raised one of the world's best cricket teams (Gulwani, 2019).

Pakistan is a federal parliamentary democratic republic and since becoming an independent country in 1947, there have been 13 elections in Pakistan (Shah & Sareen, 2018). Nationally, Pakistanis vote to elect a bicameral legislature known as the Parliament of Pakistan which consists of a lower house called the National Assembly and an upper house called the Senate. People of Pakistan also vote to choose members of provincial assemblies and local governments. Generation Z Pakistanis, depending on their age, may have strong memories of the twelfth general elections (held in May 2013), whereby a relatively new political party led by the cricket legend Imran Khan managed entry to the Pakistan Parliament with 32 members (Evolve Magazine, 2013). His party also managed to form a government in one of the local provinces called Kyber Puktoon Kawah (KPK). Imran Khan led the Pakistani cricket team to a World Cup victory against England in 1990 and constructed a state-of-the art cancer research hospital in Lahore. He subsequently became the Prime Minister of Pakistan after the 13th general election held in July 2018.

Basics of Generation Z in Pakistan

Like their counterparts in other regions of the globe, Generation Z in Pakistan (especially those who were born in urban areas) lives in a world of continuous updates involving social media and Internet use. As per Siddiqi (2018), Generation Z enjoys an information processing ability that is much faster than any other generation. Compared to Millennials, Generation Z Pakistanis have higher expectations and were born into a world overrun with technology, Internet, and social media use, hence, the significant popularity of Apps like Facebook, Instagram, and Tik Tok among Pakistani youth.

Thirty-seven million people in Pakistan use social media (Ali, 2020) and online communication channels (e.g. Facebook) and multimedia platforms (e.g. YouTube, Instagram) allow Pakistani Z to connect with local and international users and exchange information, photos, videos, ideas, and opinions. Such an engagement with social media sites satisfies Pakistani Generation Z's need for socialisation and building social capital both at local and global levels.

Generation Z Pakistanis are born into a society that remains strongly patriarchal, with many people living with extended families, often in the same house or compound. Generation Z Pakistanis are likely to see their father as the main controlling figure at home (in financial terms) and hold mothers with very high esteem. This is because they are guided by Islamic teachings which instruct Muslims to be very kind, obedient, and gentle to both parents especially mothers.

Although Generation Z Pakistanis were brought up in a largely collectivist society (e.g. Triandis & Gelfand, 1989), they nonetheless greatly value individuality and are less likely to be as tribal and as susceptible to interpersonal norms and group thinking as previous generations (Zaidi, 2018). Generation Z in Pakistan seeks uniqueness in key domains of life such as family, work, and entertainment. They do not like to be told things by their parents or elders and are often honest and outspoken in expressing their needs (Siddiqi, 2018). According to Zaidi (2018), Generation Z in Pakistan is more likely to have working mothers, more likely to have been raised by a single parent, and more likely to have had parents who met each other independently of their families than any other Pakistani generation before them.

While considering the individualistic characteristics of Generation Z in Pakistan, it is also important to bear in mind that parental styles can still shape Generation Z's development outcomes such as their engagement with wider society and marketplace activities in Pakistan. A parental style is defined as 'a constellation of attitudes toward the child that are communicated to the child and create an emotional climate in which the parental behaviours are expressed' (Darling & Steinberg, 1993, p. 493). A study conducted by Fatima, Dawood, and Munir (2020) investigated adolescents' perceptions of parenting styles, moral identity and prosocial behaviours in Lahore, Pakistan taking a sample of 236 adolescents (aged 12–18). The study found that, unlike a permissive parental style, an authoritative parental style of both the mother and the father is positively associated with moral identity and prosocial behaviours. Findings point to the paradoxical nature of Generation Z in Pakistan. Unlike their counterparts in the Western world, Generation Z Pakistanis are expected to focus not only on self-reliance, independence, and hedonism but also on deference to authority and preservation of harmony in the context of hierarchical relations such as those involving parents (Shavitt, Lalwani, Zhang, & Torelli, 2006). Accordingly, they are expected to value individualism but also familism revealing some degree of normative feelings of allegiance, dedication, and reciprocity to parents.

While individualistic and family oriented, Generation Z Pakistanis are also likely to be influenced much more by friends and celebrities than their preceding generations. About 15–20 million Generation Z Pakistanis are regularly online on platforms such as Facebook, Instagram, and Twitter (Bradri.com, 2018) and, in Pakistan, the idea of social media influencers is gaining significant momentum with a number of influencers enjoying a massive fanbase on multiple media platforms (Bradri.com, 2019). As per media reports (Bradri.com, 2019), the many influencer marketers includes Ali Gul Pir (became famous through a viral post involving a song titled 'wadeiray ka beta'), Taimoor Salahuddin (celebrity vlogger known as Mooroo), Faiza Saleem (known for her hilarious videos often on Facebook), Junaid Akram (famous for his hilarious commentary on the current affairs of the country or global pop culture), Hira and Hemayal (renowned for fashion and lifestyle blogging), Irfan Junejo (known for his vlogging skills), and Humna Raza (a famous blogger on Instagram).

However, engagement with social media and new technology also creates negative consequences such as depression, anxiety, and stress for Generation Z in Pakistan (The Express Tribune, 2019). Extreme use of social media and the Internet is making members of Pakistani Generation Z susceptible to isolation as they limit themselves to their own private space/rooms and neglect opportunities to interact with close family members.

More broadly, Generation Z in Pakistan is being shaped by country's political and economic instability, global terrorism, the aftermath of September 11, wars in Afghanistan, Iraq, and Syria and highly volatile relations with neighbouring countries like India (e.g. Kashmir conflict). Accordingly, Pakistani Generation Z is born into the notion of conflict and instability, has lived through conflict, and is equipped to process, manage, and survive conflict (Zaidi, 2018).

The charismatic persona of Pakistani Prime Minister, Imran Khan, relies on an overwhelming support from Pakistani youth, including Generation Z, who feels strongly disconnected with major political parties associating them often with corruption and have a very strong desire for change (Nabi, 2011) creating a new or Naya Pakistan free of corruption. As argued by Mehboob (2018), Pakistani youth (including Generation Z) are interested in political candidates that are better educated, have competence, integrity, and a clean reputation. They are also most worried about the quality of education they receive, low levels of unemployment, and a lack of sport/leisure facilities in the country. They also feel that they are not being heard by major political parties and, hence, want to bring a change to the existing system. They aspire to have greater accountability and enhanced transparency (Aziz & Chughtai, 2018).

Like youth elsewhere, young people in Pakistan have been less enthusiastic about electoral activity in the past, but since 2013, Pakistani youth have been fiercely involved in political participation (Aziz & Chughtai, 2018) as evidenced by the list voters published by the Election Commission of Pakistan (ECP) prior to the 2018 general election. There were almost 29 million (or over 27% of the total votes) registered voters aged 26–35 and about 17.5 million (17% of the total) voters of the 18–25 age group making youth (aged 18–35) a formidable 44% of the total voters in Pakistan (Mehboob, 2018).

Accordingly, major political parties have been publicising youth centric manifestos promising self-employment schemes for youths, provision of low interest loans, increased access to community banks, creation of jobs, and enterprise via skill development and vocational training programs (Khan, 2018). In 2020, the Pakistani government led by the Prime Minister Imran Khan launched a National Youth Development Programme (called Kamyab Jawan) in association with the United Nations Development Programme. The programme includes a range of schemes such as youth entrepreneurship, skills for all, start-up Pakistan, the green youth movement, and a national internship.

Members of Generation Z as Consumers in Pakistan

Like their counterparts elsewhere (IBM, 2017), Generation Z in Pakistan prefers to use mobile phones rather than computers when accessing Internet and expect faster downloading speeds, easy to use apps, and websites. Online shopping is gaining momentum in Pakistan with sales driven mostly by Generation Z who tends to buy items such as accessories for mobiles, laptops and similar gadgets, clothes, and gift items (Khan, Ilyas, & Rehman, 2016; Nazir, Tayyab, Sajid, Rashid, & Javed, 2012). Generation Z tends to buy online (Siddiqui, 2018).

According to Shahzad (2018), Generation Z in Pakistan is interested in engaging with brands that they see as authentic and showing sincerity towards them. They are also quality conscious consumers seeking greater value from their shopping experiences. Accordingly, and to build strong relationships with Generation Z in Pakistan, brands need to show transparency and demonstrate authenticity. Generation Z also very much likes to receive advertisements and promotional offers in their social media feeds for products and services based on their shopping interests.

Pakistani Generation Z is global in its outlook and global consumer culture has become an inescapable aspect of their day-to-day life (Cleveland & Laroche, 2007). The retail landscape in Pakistan is experiencing a transformation from traditional to modern retail formats and a range of modern outlets such as Lucky One in Karachi and Packages Mall and Emporium Mall in Lahore showcase international brands. Pakistan's retail market is estimated at $152 billion as per Planet Retail, an international retail forecasting firm and modern local supermarket chains (e.g. Imtiaz Super Market and Chase Up in Karachi) compete against their international counterparts such as Hyperstar (a local version of French Carrefour) and Metro Cash and Carry, a German retail and wholesale giant (Zahid, 2017).

The interaction and engagement of Pakistani Generation Z with global and foreign mass media and social media platforms exposes it to a repertoire of ideologies, messages, and brands that subtly disseminate foreign (largely Western) cultural ideals and customs. This generation is also likely to have cosmopolitan traits (Thompson & Tambyah, 1999) because of its willingness to engage with different people and cultures with the confidence and ability to do so. This openness and desire to emulate foreign cultures makes it possible for Pakistani Generation Z consumers to draw from a variety of ideas, lifestyles, and products triggering self-identification not only with their own culture but also with the global consumer culture (Cleveland & Laroche, 2007). Accordingly, Pakistani Generation Z is most likely to be comfortable with multiple identities than any generation preceding it (Zaidi, 2018).

Most members of Pakistani Generation Z are multi-lingual as they can speak not only Urdu (Pakistan national language) but also English and at least one local language such as Punjabi, Pushto, Sindhi, or Balochi. Scholarly work states that 'an individual's choice of language signals a specific social identity and/or belonging to a particular community' (Luna & Peracchio, 2005, p. 760) and, hence, Pakistani Generation Z's preference for English suggests a desire to emulate Western cultural values and traditions. The degree to which Pakistani Generation Z perceives Pakistani and Western cultures as either compatible or clashing can be described as a bicultural identity integration mechanism and this has important implications when it comes to targeting this generation.

The interaction and engagement of Pakistani Generation Z consumers with social media and the Internet can also be explained via the phenomenon of acculturation which refers to learning of new a culture (Jamal, Peñaloza, & Laroche, 2015). Acculturation 'refers to the process in which individuals learn and adopt the norms and values of a culture different than the one in which they grew up' (Cleveland & Laroche, 2007, p. 250). Generation Z is fully immersed into this process of culture change. Social interactions involving international travel, social/digital media engagement, contacts with people around the globe, exposure to marketing activities of global brands in Pakistan, and an openness and desire to emulate global consumer culture facilitate this process of learning among Generation Z in Pakistan.

Acculturation to global consumer culture by Generation Z consumers in Pakistan (Cleveland & Laroche, 2007) is triggering changes in food and media consumption patterns, dress choices, language, and friendship preferences. This explains the tremendous popularity of international cuisine (e.g. Chinese, Lebanese, Turkish, Middle Eastern, etc.), fast food restaurants (Burger King, Pizza Hut, McDonalds, etc.), and coffee shops (e.g. Gloria Jean's Coffees, New York Coffee) among Generation Z Pakistanis specially in the key urban areas of Pakistan, such as Lahore, Islamabad, and Karachi.

To fully understand the dynamics of Generation Z consumer behaviour in Pakistan, one needs to understand their susceptibility to interpersonal influences both from a theoretical perspective (e.g. Bearden & Etzel, 1982; Park & Lessig, 1977) and also from a practical perspective. For example, when Generation Z Pakistanis are faced with uncertainty and need to seek information, they are likely to be influenced by influencers such as others on the social media. Informational influence (e.g. Bearden & Etzel, 1982; Park & Lessig, 1977) is based on the desire to make informed decisions and Generation Z Pakistanis are very likely to keep up with how social media spreads information around so that they are quite informed and educated about how the world is. As Generation Z Pakistanis frequently share product-related reviews and experiences with others via social media platforms, they serve the informational needs of their own Generation Z members. Generation Z in Pakistan is also acting as an 'information provider' for own family members. For example, it is very common for Generation Z Pakistanis to educate and inform elder members of their own family (e.g. educating mum or dad about how to use Internet or mobile applications). Furthermore, Generation Z consumers in Pakistan are socially conscious consumers as they wish to contribute to their communities and protect the environment (Jamil, 2020). They are very likely to be influenced by corporate social responsibility programs that aim to reduce poverty, enhance employment opportunities for the youth, and create gender balance at work.

Generation Z at Work in Pakistan

According to the Pakistan National Human Development Report (2017) published by United Nations Development Program (UNDP), Pakistan has been witnessing the most rapid demographic transition in its history resulting in a youth bulge which means that young adults are entering the labour market at an unprecedented rate. Such a transition, according to the same report, represents a golden opportunity for Pakistan.

A report by Lenovo Pakistan (2017) provides a number of interesting insights into the workplace implications given that Generation Z is seen as digital native, tech-savvy, and immersed in the Internet from birth. First, employers should make sure that Generation Z Pakistanis (specially born and raised in urban areas) have access to up to date workplace technology, provide employees with autonomy, and acknowledge their expertise.

Second, companies may find it difficult to recruit Generation Z Pakistanis given that the generation is expected to be looking for careers that have a positive and real-world impact. Accordingly, companies need to develop and sustain an organisational culture that is supportive to Generation Z in fulfilling their ambitions to innovate, develop their entrepreneurial spirit, and pursue purpose-driven work. A strong training programme is also expected to harness the intellectual skills of Generation Z Pakistanis.

For example, Shafi, Lei, Song, and Islam (2020) investigated the effects of transformational leadership on employee creativity within the IT industry of Pakistan using a sample of 164 employee–supervisor dyads, which also included Generation Z Pakistanis (13% of employees and 21% supervisors were aged between 20 and 24). Citing previous literature, the study conceptualised transformational leadership as the one that motivates employees, through a number of mechanisms such as role modelling, inspirational motivation, intellectual stimulation and listening to and solving employee problems, to work devotedly to achieve organisational objectives. These authors found that transformational leadership dimensions such as inspirational motivation, idealised influence, and intellectual stimulation had a positive and significant effect on employee creativity.

Accordingly, employees in Pakistan, including those belonging to Generation Z, depend on transformational leaders to motivate them for creative performance. It is, therefore, important for managers to adopt transformational leadership style at workplace as it seems to be quite compatible with the psychological needs of Generation Z employees in Pakistan who may be seeking to perform innovatively to enhance their productivity.

Third, companies need to be imaginative and transparent in their efforts to engage with new recruits from Generation Z in Pakistan as this Generation is expected to favour a diverse and an outward-looking workplace. Generation Z Pakistanis are expected to able to juggle careers, fight for flexible working hours and flatter management structures, and argue for equal pay for equal work (Fakhr, 2019). There is abundance of talent in Pakistan especially among the youth and Generation Z has lot to learn from young Pakistani entrepreneurs that have already gained international acclaim in recent years.

However, Cho and Majoka (2020) report that a high percentage of Generation Z in Pakistan (aged 15–24) are not in education, employment, or training and, therefore, highlight the need to create more jobs to induce potential workers who are currently out of the labour force to engage in it. Authors recommend a number of measures to address this issue including strengthening training and entrepreneurship youth initiatives, providing job search assistance (e.g. job fairs), providing opportunities to build workplace skills and experience (e.g. on-the-job training and internships/apprenticeships), and enhancing the focus on soft skills (e.g. effective communication and creative thinking, etc.). In response, the current Pakistani government has recently launched a programme to develop human capital through the Prime Minister's Youth Program aimed largely at Generation Z in Pakistan.

How to Deal with Generation Z in Pakistan

Jamil (2020) outlines four essential strategies for marketing to Generation Z in Pakistan. The first strategy is about focussing on innovation on digital channels which includes having a robust social media presence on platforms such as Facebook, Twitter, Instagram, and Snapchat. She also argues for considering the fact that Generation Z in Pakistan uses social media for different purposes and, hence, marketers need to avoid placing the same content on all social media platforms. In support of the first strategy, she cites the examples of famous brands in Pakistan such as Ufone which has a very clear strategy of placing different contents on different platforms (e.g. Facebook for building a community of customers and engaging with them via crafted content, Instagram for addressing consumer queries, Twitter for posting well-shot images, and YouTube for uploading video ads and bundles).

A second strategy is to focus on using influencers instead of celebrities as Generation Z in Pakistan turns to digital media for product reviews and endorsements from common people with whom they can relate instead of celebrities who are out of their reach. In support of this strategy, Jamil (2020) cites the example of a fashion retail store called So Kamal. The retailer is owned by Kamal Limited, which is one of the oldest and foremost textile manufacturing houses of Pakistan.

The store has branches in main cities of Pakistan: Lahore, Karachi, Islamabad, Faisalabad, and Multan. The retail brand actively engages with influencers and student ambassadors for their marketing campaigns especially on Instagram.

A third strategy is to connect with Generation Z in Pakistan using authentic corporate social responsibility programs as Generation Z tends to include socially conscious consumers who care a lot about their communities and environmental issues. This is in line with Porter and Kramber (2007) who suggest that a growing number of firms are leveraging their unique capabilities and value chain activities to encourage the adoption of desirable behaviours such as a healthy lifestyle and sustainable consumption practices. In Pakistan, a telecommunication company called Telenor Pakistan, a wholly owned subsidiary of Telenor Group, has successfully used #TweetAMeal for their Share Your Meal campaign through which consumers were asked to tweet pictures of the meals they had in the holy month of Ramazan. The income generated based on the number of tweets was then used to distribute food supplies among hunger struck families in Thar, Pakistan.

A fourth strategy is to incorporate user input (e.g. trending hashtags, picture contests, testimonials, etc.) from Generation Z in marketing campaigns. The strategy allows Generation Z to feel connected with the brand. For example, Coca Cola is famous among Generation Z for using hashtag campaigns such as #Shareacoke along with personalised Coca-Cola bottles, to encourage the sharing and gifting of Coca-Cola bottles. This can be supplemented by partnering with talented members of Generation Z in Pakistan and showcasing their achievements in a variety of life domains such as art, drama, music, and sports. Companies like Procter and Gamble, Unilever, Nestle, Pepsi Cola, Coca Cola, Reckitt Benkister, and Telecom companies dominate the advertising landscape in Pakistan but are shifting their expenditure towards digital media at a fast pace given that more and more consumers, specially Generation Z, spend more time on digital media, particularly on mobiles, compared to TVs (Narula, 2017).

However, marketers face a number of challenges in their efforts to target Generation Z consumers in Pakistan. One challenge in appealing to Generation Z consumers in Pakistan is that members of the Generation Z may be at different stages of learning and engaging with multinational brands with varying levels of receptiveness to marketing efforts in targeting them through TV and digital media platforms. For example, brands like McDonalds, Pizza Hut, and Nike are highly symbolic of the United States and Western cultural traditions. Generation Z consumers can differ in the extent to which they perceive their Pakistani identity as compatible and integrated or oppositional and difficult to integrate with foreign culture and its ideologies (Haritatos & Benet-Martínez, 2002).

A further challenge is to stay relevant with Generation Z consumers in Pakistan who are quite savvy and discriminating when it comes to buying local versus international brands. For example, Zahid (2017) reports Pakistani brands such as 14th Street Pizza finding great success among Generation Z consumers against their global counterparts (e.g. Pizza Hut) by adopting aggressive marketing tactics involving digital media and offering at-par product and service quality.

Another challenge is the lack of reliable and quality consumer research data making it difficult for marketers to make informed strategic choices. Global brands may, therefore, benefit by working closely with local marketing communications agencies as there is always a need for developing marketing campaigns quickly and work with country-specific digital platforms to target Generation Z consumers in Pakistan.

Conclusions

Generation Z represents the future of Pakistan as the generation has significant capabilities and comprises the major portion of the demography in Pakistan. While many Generation Z consumers in Pakistan seek uniqueness in key domains of life such as family, work, and entertainment valuing self-reliance, independence, and hedonism, there are strong indications that Generation Z wants to preserve social harmony and parental values. Generation Z consumers in Pakistan are strong advocates of transparency, authenticity, and brand engagement through active participation via digital platforms such as Facebook. However, there is a lack of empirical research investigating digital and brand engagement, shopping habits, and buying patterns within Generation Z in Pakistan. Moreover, and beyond media reports, there is also little empirical research focussing on their entrepreneurial expectations, work–life blending issues, behaviours, employee, and managerial approaches within organisational context. The chapter, therefore, concludes with an urgent call for empirical research investigating Generation Z in Pakistan providing insights into their general consumer behaviour, digital and brand engagement behaviours and tendencies, influencer marketing orientations, and work-related attitudes and entrepreneurial orientations.

References

Amjad, S. M., & Ali, M. (2018). Philanthropy in Pakistan: Why civil society organizations get bypassed in favour of donations to individuals. *Stanford Social Innovation Review*. Retrieved from https://ssir.org/articles/entry/philanthropy_in_pakistan. Accessed on March 19.

Ali, S. A. (2020). The effects of social media and youth in Pakistan. *Daily Blochistan Express*, February 26. Retrieved from https//www.bexpress.com.pk/2019/12/the-effects-of-social-media-and-youth-in-pakistan/

Aziz, S., & Chughtai, A. (2018). How do young Pakistanis plan to vote in the general election? *Aljazeera Feature Report on Pakistan Elections*. Retrieved from https://www.aljazeera.com/indepth/features/young-pakistanis-plan-vote-general-election-180719220256511.html

Bearden, W. O., & Etzel, M. J. (1982). Reference group influence on product and brand purchase decisions. *Journal of Consumer Research*, 9(2), 183–194.

Bradri.com. (2018). How to sell to Pakistani millennials with influencer marketing. Retrieved from https://bradri.com/blog/how-to-sell-to-pakistani-millennials-with-influencer-marketing/. Accessed on August 8.

Bradri.com. (2019). Pakistani influencers who are making the most out of influencer marketing. Retrieved from https://bradri.com/blog/pakistani-influencers-who-are-making-the-most-of-influencer-marketing/. Accessed on April 11.

Cho, Y., & Majoka, Z. (2020). Pakistan jobs diagnostic: Promoting access to quality jobs for all. Retrieved from http://documents.worldbank.org/curated/en/848471581443849598/Pakistan-Jobs-Diagnostic-Promoting-Access-to-Quality-Jobs-for-All

Cleveland, M., & Laroche, M. (2007). Acculturaton to the global consumer culture: Scale development and research paradigm. *Journal of Business Research, 60*(3), 249–259.

Darling, N., & Steinberg, L. (1993). Parenting style as context: An integrative model. *Psychological Bulletin, 113*(3), 487–496.

Evolve Magazine. (2013). General elections in Pakistan: A brief history. Retrieved from http://www.evolvemagazine.com.pk/general-elections-in-pakistan-a-brief-history/

Fakhr, A. (2019). The ABC of Gen Z. The News on Sunday, Special Report. Retrieved from https://www.thenews.com.pk/tns/detail/568090-abc-gen-z. Accessed on July 7.

Fatima, S., Dawood, S., & Munir, M. (2020). Parenting styles, moral identity and prosocial behaviors in adolescents. *Current Psychology*. Published online 22 January. Retrieved from https://doi.org/10.1007/s12144-020-00609-3

Gulwani, N. (2019). 13 Things you should know about Pakistani culture. Retrieved from https://theculturetrip.com/asia/pakistan/articles/13-things-you-should-know-about-pakistani-culture/

Haritatos, J., & Benet- Martínez, V. (2002). Bicultural identities: The interface of cultural, personality, and socio-cognitive processes. *Journal of Research in Personality, 36*(6), 598–606.

Human Development Report. (2019). Inequalities in human development in the 21st Century. Retrieved from http://hdr.undp.org/en/countries/profiles/PAK

Index Mundi. (2019). Pakistan demographics profile. Retrieved from https://www.index-mundi.com/pakistan/demographics_profile.html

Jamal, A., Peñaloza, L., & Laroche, M. (2015). Introduction to ethnic marketing. In A. Jamal, L. Peñaloza, & M. Laroche (Eds.), *The Routledge companion to ethnic marketing* (pp. 1–12). London: Routledge.

Jamal, A., Yaccob, A., Bartikowski, B., & Slater S. (2019). Motivations to donate: Exploring the role of religiousness in charitable donations. *Journal of Business Research, 103*, 319–327.

Jamil, A. (2020). Generation Z: The first generation of true digital natives. Retrieved from https://pas.org.pk/generation-z-the-first-generation-of-true-digital-natives/. Accessed on January 8.

Jehan, Z., & Khan, F. A. (2020). Demographic changes and economic growth in Pakistan: Role of capital stock. *Pakistan Development Review, 59*(1), 1–24.

Khan, S. (2018). Pakistan's youth: An untapped resource by Pakistan's political parties. Retrieved from https://www.cato.org/blog/pakistans-youth-untapped-resource-pakistans-political-parties. Accessed on July 24.

Khan, A. A., Ilyas, M., & Rehman, C. A. (2016). Generation 'Z' is coming, are you ready? A wakeup call for HR strategists in Pakistan. *Review of Public Administration and Management, 5*(10), 171–182.

Lenovo Pakistan. (2020). How generation Z will impact the workplace. Retrieved from https://www.lenovo.com/pk/en/solutions/smb/how-generation-z-will-impact-workplace

Luna, D., & Peracchio, L. A. (2015). Advertising to bilingual consumers: The impact of code-switching on persuasion. *Journal of Consumer Research, 31*(4), 760–765.

Mehboob, A. (2018). A large youth vote bank in Pakistan: What it means for political parties? Retrieved from https://pildat.org/blog/a-large-youth-vote-bank-in-pakistan-what-it-means-for-political-parties

Nabi. Z. (2011). Connecting the Youth: Young Pakistanis flock to Imran Khan. *News Line Magazine*, November. Retrieved from https://newslinemagazine.com/magazine/connecting-the-youth-young-pakistanis-flock-to-imran-khan/

Moody's Analytics. (2019). Economic Indicators. Retrieved from https://www.economy.com/pakistan/indicators#ECONOMY

Nazir, S., Tayyab, A., Sajid, A., Rashid, H. U., & Javed, I. (2012). How online shopping is affecting consumers buying behavior in Pakistan. *International Journal of Computer Science Issues, 9*(3), 486–495.

Narula, T. T. (2017). The world of advertising – An overview. *Pakistan Today*, May 28. Retrieved from https//www.pakistantoday.com.pk/2017/05/28/the-world-of-advertising-an-overview/

Park, C. W., & Lessig, V. P. (1977). Students and housewives: Differences in susceptibility* to reference group influence. *Journal of Consumer Research, 4*(2), 102–110.

Pakistan National Human Development Report. (2017). Unleashing the potential of a young Pakistan. Retrieved from http://hdr.undp.org/en/content/national-human-development-report-2017-pakistan

Pakistan Bureau of Statistics. (2017). Population Census, 2017. Retrieved from http://www.pbs.gov.pk/content/population-census

Porter, M. E, & Kramer, M. R. (2007). Strategy and Society: The Link Between Competitive Advantage and Corporate Social Responsibility. *Harvard Business Review, 84*(12), 78–92.

Shah, K. M., & Sareen, S. (2018). *Pakistan general elections 2018: Analysis of results and implications.* Special Report no. 78. Observer Research Foundation, December. Retrieved from https://www.orfonline.org/research/pakistan-general-elections-2018-analysis-of-results-and-implications-46324/

Shahzad, S. K. (2018). What does 'Generation Z' expect from brands? *Daily Times*, August 2. Retrieved from https://dailytimes.com.pk/277008/what-does-generation-z-expects-from-brands/

Shafi, M., Lei, Z. Z., Song, X., & Sarker, M. N. I. (2020). The effects of transformational leadership on employee creativity: Moderating role of intrinsic motivation. *Asia Pacific Management Review*. https://doi.org/10.1016/j.apmrv.2019.12.002

Shavitt, S., Lalwani, A. K., Zhang, J., & Torelli, C. J. (2006). The horizontal/vertical distinction in cross-cultural consumer research. *Journal of Counselling Psychology, 16*(4), 325–356.

Siddiqi, K. (2018). Behold generation Z. *The Express Tribune*, March 5. Retrieved from https://tribune.com.pk/story/1651342/6-behold-generation-z/

Siddiqui, K., & Sibghatullah, A. (2014). Perceptions towards music preferences in Pakistan, *European Journal of Business and Management, 6*(14), 203–208.

Thompson, C. J., & Tambyah S. K. (1999). Trying to be cosmopolitan. *Journal of Consumer Research, 26*(3), 214–241.

Trading Economics. (2020). Pakistan GDP growth rate. Retrieved from https://tradingeconomics.com/pakistan/gdp-growth

Triandis, H. C., & Gelfand, M. J. (1998). Converging measurement of horizontal and vertical individualism and collectivism. *Journal of Personality and Social Psychology, 74*(1), 118–128.

World Bank Data. (2018). Urban population (% of total population). Retrieved from https://data.worldbank.org/indicator/SP.URB.TOTL.IN.ZS

Zahid, W. (2017). Pakistani brands who found success against their global competitors. *The Express Tribune*, June 16. Retrieved from https://tribune.com.pk/story/1426359/pakistani-brands-found-success-global-competitors/

Zaidi, M. (2018). Pakistan's awesome generation Z. *The News*, March 6. Retrieved from https://www.thenews.com.pk/print/288811-pakistan-s-awesome-generation-z

Part IV

What the Experts Tell Us about Southeast Asia

Chapter 8

Generation Z in Indonesia: The Self-Driven Digital

Zahrotur Rusyda Hinduan, Adilla Anggraeni and Muhamad Irfan Agia

Abstract

Despite several similarities, Generation Z in Indonesia has specific character-istics that might differentiate them from their colleagues from other countries. Socio-cultural factors such as national values shape their behaviours in many aspects of their life. Specific significant life events in Indonesia such as inhu-manity among minorities and damaging natural disasters are also believed to contribute to the development of the specific characteristics of Generation Z in this country. The aim of this chapter is to describe these characteristics as well as the behaviours of Generation Z in personal and professional contexts, including their consumer behaviours. Based on literature and publications re-lated to the topic, it can be seen that people from this generation are realistic but confident with their abilities, especially in using technologies. However, there is a need for social interaction, especially with experts such as their su-perordinates particularly during difficult times. These characteristics will lead to specific behaviours from Generation Z in Indonesia.

Keywords: Generation Z; Indonesia; work; consumers; technologies; social interaction

Introduction: Indonesia at a Glance

Socio-Cultural Aspects of Indonesia

Indonesia is located in South East Asia, between the Indian and Pacific oceans. This country is the world's largest island country that is very rich with natural resources, such as oil and gas, tin, copper, and gold. Agriculture is mainly rice, palm oil, coffee, tea, cacao, and spices. Indonesian spices have been well known

The New Generation Z in Asia: Dynamics, Differences, Digitalisation
The Changing Context of Managing People, 121–134
Copyright © 2020 by Emerald Publishing Limited
All rights of reproduction in any form reserved
doi:10.1108/978-1-80043-220-820201012

among Asian and European countries for a long time. Many foreign countries, such as Portugal, the Netherlands, the United Kingdom, and Japan came to Indonesia and several of them took its natural resources. As a result, since at least the seventh century, Indonesia has been one of the important regions in Asia for trade.

After almost 350 years of colonialism by several European countries (Portugal, the Netherlands, and the United Kingdom) and Japan, Indonesia declared its independence in 1945. In general, there are several characteristics of Indonesia. (1) There are many linguistic groups, but it has a national language, called 'Bahasa Indonesia' that unites all people who live in this archipelago. (2) The national motto is 'Bhinneka Tunggal Ika' that means unity in diversity. The motto was inspired by a fourteenth century poet sage of Majapahit, a Hindu empire in South East Asia, based on the island of Java. This spirit of religious tolerance of Hinduism and Buddhism that was essential for the empire. Today, the motto means we are of many kinds, but we are one. It is a doctrine that shows the essential unity of its members despite ethnic, social, regional, and religious differences. There are hundreds of distinct native ethnic groups in Indonesia, with the largest group being the Javanese. This group was originally from Central Java, East Java, and Jogjakarta. Today, the Javanese people are concentrated on the island of Java and spread across various part of Indonesia. (3) Indonesia is a Muslim-majority country. This country recognises six official religions: Islam, Catholicism, Protestantism, Hinduism, Buddhism, and Confucianism.

Although Indonesian Muslims claim themselves as Moderate Muslims, in recent years, they have embraced more overt signs of religiosity and shifted towards Arab style in fashions, names, and terminologies. Although Islamic principles are one of the factors that influence political decision making in Indonesia, the current government has banned a puritan Islam that calls for Islamic law to replace a unifying ideology of this country called Pancasila. Pancasila means five principles: Belief in one God, Humanism, Indonesian Nationalism, Democracy, and Social Prosperity. Both cultural values and religions influence many aspects of life of people in this country (Mangundjaya, 2013).

Socio-Demographic Aspects of Indonesia

Right now, Indonesia is the fourth most populous country in the world. The population is over 261 million and about 57% people of Indonesia live on Java Island. Based on the population census data in 2018, 67.6% of the Indonesian population is of productive age (15–64 years old). The pyramid structure of the population in Indonesia is bulging in the middle. It is predicted that in 2020–2030, Indonesia is having a demographic bonus or the condition in which the population that is of productive age outnumbers the non-productive population. This might lead to an increase of economic productivity (Suharyadi, Purwanto, & Faturohman, 2012). This condition means that the country has an expanding youth population, known as Generation Z. The demographic bonus can be a bonus if the Indonesian Government can provide good education, facilities, and policies for this generation.

National Culture

According to Hofstede (2011, p. 3), culture is 'the collective program of the mind that distinguishes the member of one group or categories of people from others'. This term is most commonly applied to nations. In a study conducted in the early 2000s regarding work values, Indonesia was high on (1) power distance (78) (*leaders play important roles in decision-making*) but low on (2) individualism (14) (*goals of a group are more important than individual goals*), (3) uncertainty avoidance (48) (*feeling comfortable in unstructured situations*), and (4) masculinity (46) (*gender roles are overlapping*) (Hofstede, 2001). However, a recent study among 2,025 employees in an Indonesian's state-own company indicates that there is a shift in values among Indonesian employees from collectivists to individualists and from feminine to masculine (Mangundjaya, 2013).

It is argued that these shifts might due to a more complex situation in the country that demands tight competition. Undeniably, Indonesia has faced several unfortunate situations during the past several years. (1) The Asian financial crises in 1997 and 2008. The immediate effects of the crisis were accelerating inflation, food prices had risen by 30%, job losses, unemployment, and underemployments among workers, especially in urban areas and poverty (Sherlock, 2008). (2) Indonesia is located in 'the ring of fire'. It means that there are many active volcanoes in this country. Numerous natural disasters have happened in this country, such as floods, earthquakes including tsunamis, and volcanic eruptions. (3) The increase in the number of ethnic-, religious-, and gender-based violence in the country (Varshney, Panggabean, & Tadjoeddin, 2004).

Power distance in Indonesia has always been high (78) since the early days of the country. There were unequal rights between power holders and non-power holders during the 350 years of colonialism. This condition can also be dated back to the very strong gap between government and military to its citizens several decades ago. These unequal rights were extremely normal between older generations and were considered as normal, especially during the pre-reformation era in 1998 (the fall of the second president of Indonesia's regime). Between students, this translated to seniority that could become extreme.

After the reform era, people in Indonesia including the younger generation experienced freedom of speech, opinion, and information as well as more balance between power holders and non-power holders. Perceived power distance to government officials has reduced significantly compared to the previous generation. There is a balance between the executive and legislative branches of government. The military forces (army and police) have lost their authoritarian power and improved their professional standards. Civilians can also control their power. Thus, in the current generation, power distance based on age might remain but has been lessened significantly. The issue of bullying in school has slowly become less acceptable.

The level of individualism among Indonesians is low (14). This means that Indonesia is a collectivist society. The loyalty to their in-groups is high and persons in this country identify themselves as 'we'. However, the practices of collectivism in Indonesia, especially in urban areas, have decreased significantly.

Communal work is rarely to be seen among young people in big cities. Moreover, an empirical study among 1,455 workers in four big cities revealed that there are several new values among respondents. One of them is individualism (Sihombing, 2013). It is argued that globalisation affects value changes by spreading western culture, such as individualism. Another study about the intergenerational transmission of values across three generations in Germany and Indonesia has also showed that the Indonesian sample is less individualist than the German sample, but the transmission of individualistic values was higher in the Indonesian sample (Albert, Trommsdorff, & Wisnubrata, 2009). It was argued that the change of values might be transmitted since the next generation might face a different situation and the old values might not be suitable for this.

Indonesia has a balanced masculinity spectrum with a slight inclination to more feminine values in the past (Hofstede, 2001). It is important for Indonesians to have status (a position that a person holds) and outward appearance. Material gain was not a main force in the past. However, there is a slight shift in Indonesia to be more masculine in relation to achieving material success. For example, a study among Chinese Indonesians yields the results that they tend to be masculine. They are goal oriented and independent (Suharnomo, 2017). Chinese Indonesian is a minority group in this country but contributes significantly to the economic development in Indonesia. A majority of firms in the country are owned by 15 Chinese Indonesian families and they control more than 60% of the shared trading in Indonesia (Lawrence, 2013).

In this chapter, we would like to describe the characteristics of Generation Z in Indonesia, especially those who live on the Java Island.

Basic Information of Generation Z in Indonesia

Shared Significant Life Events

As mentioned above, there are three major shared significant life events for Generation Z in Indonesia. The first is the monetary crisis. The monetary crises that happened around 1997 and again in 2008 were caused by the structural financial crisis across the Asian countries. Each crisis affected Indonesia through bad debt of private companies that were measured in the US Dollar while their source of income was in the Indonesia Rupiah. The Indonesian currency weakened significantly against the US Dollar at that time. The unemployment rate increased, meaning that many families struggled in raising a child. Generation Z experienced controlled spending in relation to many items in life, things that are usually seen as ordinary became luxurious. Therefore, almost half of Generation Z in Indonesia see money as one of the top factors that cause them anxiety in life (Varkey Foundation, 2017).

The second is the Internet dot-com boom. The Internet boom in Indonesia lagged behind the dot-com boom in the US market. The wide spread of Internet usage was started by the popularity of Internet cafes that in Indonesia are commonly called '*warung internet* or *warnet*'. At that time, the price of Internet through subscription was too expensive for the general population and a computer was also a luxury for most families. Moreover, because of the small number of business participants in this dot-com boom, the economy was not significantly affected.

The third set of events would be the many natural disasters that have happened in Indonesia in 2000s, starting from tsunami in Aceh, earthquakes that have shattered Lombok and Sulawesi, as well as volcanic eruptions and constant floods in the capital city of Indonesia. These natural disasters may have provided Generation Z with a sense of togetherness, as in general, crowdfunding and donations have been highly encouraged during the difficult times.

Generation Z, Internet, Social Media, and Technology

According to the Nielsen Consumer & Media View (CMV) report from the second quarter of 2016, the main sources of information for Generation Z in Indonesia are television, Internet, and radio. This survey of Nielsen included 17,000 respondents aged 10–19 and was conducted from 2010 to 2016 in 11 cities in Indonesia, including Jakarta, Bandung, Yogyakarta, Semarang, Surakarta, Surabaya, Denpasar, Medan, Palembang, Makassar, and Banjarmasin. Among other sources, TV is the most popular media for Generation Z in Indonesia during the pre-teen life. However, the Internet plays a more and more important role during teen life. Only 9% of this group read printed media, with newspapers as the most popular media followed by magazines and tabloids.

While most Indonesian consumers are predominantly on Facebook, Generation Z's social media channel preferences are more diverse, with an almost equal proportion accessing Facebook, YouTube, and Instagram daily (Kantar Research, 2017). Based on AdReaction Kantar Research in 2017, as mentioned previously, TV is also an important medium to reach them, as they watch TV for about 1.8 hours daily. But mobile is where they spend most of their screen time. On an average, Generation Z spends 3.5 hours accessing the Internet on their mobile daily – about 13% longer than the average Millennial. Based on Tirto ID Research, 90% of Generation Z in Indonesia uses a smartphone daily and 35.2% uses social media for Information Access. Instagram & Line are social media platforms that are used the most for this purpose (Tirto Media Research, 2017a, 2017b).

As previously mentioned, AdReaction's (2017) research suggests that Indonesia's social media users do not really interact with the rest of the world and often create their own community. Unlike China, the reason is not because of governments' imposed Internet constraints. Low English literacy contributes in creating a significant language barrier for such a strong and intense interaction. However, along with better education, English literacy is improving although at a slow pace.

Indonesia is one of the largest mobile markets in Asia and is characterised as a highly dynamic market (Statista Research Department, 2019). By 2022, the number of smartphone users is expected to increase by two-thirds compared to 2013 to around 90 million. Almost all socio-economic groups in Indonesia have mobile phones. The widespread access of smart phones allows the pervasive access of the Internet. This also creates the huge potential and influence of Indonesia's social media industry. In the real world, the dynamic social power amongst Generation Z is enough to periodically create multiple new terms and new words. Often there exist more formal appropriate words already that convey the same expression.

Generation Z and Current Trends

A UNICEF report from February 2014 claimed that 30 million Indonesian young people are now online, mostly on social media. Hence, there has been a socio-cultural transformation, with particular influence from the West, Japan, and Korea. Handajani (2005, 2010) claimed that the Indonesian teen print media tends to take on western representations of how models look and dress (e.g. revealing dress), but the content still portrays a sweet girl image. Earlier, Japanese culture became popular in Indonesia via animated films, pop music, and food (Setiowati, 2013). More recently, Korean popular culture has been more influential (Jung, 2011). In fact, in 2010, Indonesian young people caused a spike in Twitter trending topics for the K-pop boyband, Super Junior. Some also observed that there is a hybridisation of Islamic and popular cultures in Indonesia, for example, the concept of trendy hijabers (hijab-wearers/muslim-clothes-wearers). These trendy hijabers wear clothing that is recommended by Islamic teaching, albeit with some modifications to make it more fashionable.

Generation Z and Well-Being

Primasari and Yuniarti (2012) reported that family is the main source of happiness for Indonesian young people. Relations with others include relationships and bonding with families, friends, and events related to love and being loved, while self-fulfilment consists of events related to achievements, use of leisure time (hobbies), and money. Achievement of the younger generation is not only aimed at personal happiness but also dedication to other people, their parents, for example. Money and leisure time are also not only there to fulfil personal desire and needs but also to nurture friendships (e.g. go shopping together, play sports together), indicating that self-fulfilment in this context is not entirely for oneself, but also for social relationships.

Interestingly, spirituality (relation with God) is also an important source of happiness for young people in Indonesia. They believe that there is a reciprocal relationship between individuals and God (Gao, 2018). They feel the existence of positive emotions when they relate to God, in the form of a sense of security, composure, comfort, feelings of fortune, and even as a form of coping against pressure. It is important to note that the Indonesian education curriculum strongly facilitates students to have a relationship with God. Religion subjects (Islam, Christianity, Hinduism, and Buddhism) are delivered in the school curriculum starting from kindergarten, primary, secondary, high school, and the first year of university.

On the other hand, even though youngsters in Indonesia still have religious values, materialism has started to become a part of the youth sub-culture of Indonesia. This includes the increased need to follow trends (dressing, hanging out at 'cool' places, carrying the right bag, knowing the most updated information, etc.), which is very deeply ingrained among the Indonesian youths (BVABDRC.com, 2019). The existence of more options for technological devices have increased this materialism tendency, possibly distracting their devotion to practice religion which some feel portrays a 'less modern image' (BVABDRC.com, 2019).

Generation Z and Life Priorities

Generation Z in Indonesia is generally more optimistic about the future as they have a practical mindset that sets their course of actions compared to the Millennials (Jakartapost.com, 2019). This is caused by them growing up in a recovering economy in their recent years. However, the economic crisis in their childhood created price sensitivity across most socio-economic segments. Generation Z rarely takes time to arrive at a purchase decision. However, there are some factors that guide the decision behaviour of Generation Z. Product popularity is often used as a benchmark of product quality. Recommendations from friends and acquaintances easily substitute any quality assurance.

Consumer Behaviours

Generation Z in Indonesia as Consumers: the Self-Driven Digital Natives

Consumer behaviour is heavily influenced by fast-growing digital technology and connectivity. A report by Euromonitor International in 2017 also highlights that social media play an important role in how consumers make decisions throughout the year, as digital natives and the most connected consumers compared to other generations. Before they want to buy something as a consumer, 63% of them seek information and other perspectives from the Internet. They use social media to gather information, comparing things, and following people or brands that inspire them. This social media trend takes them to a new level of experience in finding and using information that they will use to make decisions. The majority of Generation Z in Indonesia use on an average three social media channels: most of them use Facebook (82%), Twitter (42%), and YouTube (27%) (Universum, 2017). There are three relevant trends that shaped Indonesian consumers' behaviour today and will define consumer behaviour in the future – the connected consumer, premiumisation, and experience (Euromonitor International, 2018). These trends are growing with the help of rapid Internet usage by Generation Z.

Generation Z also drives the purchase decisions for vacations and electronic goods in the majority of households in Indonesia. A report from Nielsen Consumer and Media View in 2016 that focussed on Generation Z stated that 47% of children (10–14 years old) have an influence on the buying decision for vacations and 33% have an influence on the buying decision for electronic goods. Teenagers (15–19 years old), on the other hand, have a stronger influence with 67% having an influence on buying decisions for vacations and 62% influencing the buying decision for electronic goods.

Based on the data above, we can see that most of Generation Z in Indonesia decide what brand or products they want to buy or use by themselves: they are self-driven as a consumer. More than 70% of Generation Z in Indonesia decide on the brands and models of fashion products (clothes, shoes, and bags) that they want to buy (Tirto Media Research, 2017a, 2017b).

Not only they are self-driven in their decision making as a consumer, but they also put in extra effort to buy the product they want by saving their money given to them by their parents or even side income (Tirto Media Research, 2017a, 2017b). The other interesting finding from the Tirto research is that almost all of the respondents in the study (90% of young people) said they preferred to buy fashion products in stores or malls or markets. It indicates that they really want to know exactly what kind of products they will buy or use by seeing and feeling it first. Offline shopping enables them to try the product first before deciding to buy.

Payment Preferences: Cashless

Cashless payments are one of the important developments that help people to spend. Digital payments are expected to grow as the number of people owning smartphones is on the rise. Data from Statista in September 2019 stated that the number of e-wallet users is expected to amount to 75.9 million in 2023. It indicates that the trend of going cashless globally is increasing.

In Indonesia, cashless payments are becoming more and more popular since the government started the cashless society campaign in 2016. Until November 2019, there were 40 institutions registered as E-Money providers in Bank Indonesia and 504,386 e-money machine readers across Indonesia (Ipsos, 2020). Cashless payments do not directly encourage people to spend more, but can actually create a seamless and unique experience. Cashless payments also increase convenience and influence consumers to purchase more things in the long run.

A report from Alvara Research Center called 'Indonesia Gen Z and Millennial Report 2020: The Battle of Our Generation' found that 20.6% of Generation Z in Indonesia use e-wallet for digital payment. Based on the study, 78.2% of Indonesian Generation Z's digital payment is for online transportation. They are increasingly mobile and prefer to use and book online transportation, since it shortens the duration time of waiting and searching for this. They prefer the cashless method for the payment since the method is already integrated within the online transportation App. A recent study by asset management firm Piper Jaffray (2018) also suggested that Indonesian members of Generation Z are budget-conscious consumers. They are more likely than the older consumers to use payment technology that allows them to share or split purchases with friends.

A study from Microsoft (2019) (Understanding Consumer Trust in Digital Services in Asia Pacific) indicates that Indonesian consumers feel that IT companies need to build consumer trust. This study also shows how these consumers believe that the government plays a role in building consumer trust (30%). Government in Indonesia has a huge role in pushing the industry to become cashless with the national policy of National Payment Gateway.

Moreover, this study shows that for Asia Pacific consumers, only Generation Z believes that IT companies should be the pioneers in building customer trends. In Indonesia, there are some IT and digital start-ups which have become the main option for Generation Z's digital payments: OVO, Gopay, Dana, and LinkAja. Ease (convenience), perception of lower prices, varieties of products, and time efficiency are the most common reasons for Generation Z in Indonesia to use digital payment and online shopping (Simangunsong, 2018). Fashion has become the most purchased item category in e-Commerce by 80.2% of Generation Z in Indonesia (Alvara Strategic Report, 2020).

Generation Z in Indonesia will push further the traditional banks and payment players to innovate and think beyond the functional aspects of mobile payment apps to create an engaging customer experience. Moreover, findings from the IPSOS report 'Indonesia The Next Cashless Society' found that Generation Z in Indonesia is not likely affected by promotional offers. Generation Z in Indonesia will still use Digital payment despite of lack of promotional offers, because they already perceive that digital payment eases their pain of transaction (Ipsos, 2020).

Generation Z at Work

As mentioned in the first part of this chapter, Indonesia is one of the countries in the world that will employ Generation Z on a large scale due to the demographic bonus (Business Digest, 2016). In this section, the characteristics of this generation in Indonesia in the workplace will be discussed in more detail.

Work Values: Realistic Generation

A work value is 'the goal of what individuals pursue in their work and is a direct influence on individual's choice and abilities' (Ye, 2015). These values might differ from time to time, from one group to another, and from one generation to another. This means that the end states that Generation Z in Indonesia wants to achieve in the workplace will be different from (1) other generations and (2) their colleagues from outside Indonesia. These differences might relate to the differences in shared significant life events. As mentioned earlier, Generation Z in Indonesia has faced some hard situations during their earlier life, such as economic recession, damaging natural disasters, and inhumanity. This condition might contribute to the development of realism among this generation in Indonesia. They, therefore, want to achieve realistic goals in the work setting. A study that was conducted among university students from this generation on important work goals shows that this generation is willing to work harder and to be relocated to another cities or countries for (1) higher pay, (2) job security, and (3) better work opportunities (Dwidienawati & Gandasari, 2018).

Another study among high-school students from this generation in Indonesia suggests that the aspiration of this generation to work in a multinational company is a realistic one. According to the study, the most important aspect for them is stability at work or ability to maintain a job for a certain amount of time (Business Digest, 2016). Moreover, the study also suggests that there is an increasing interest in work–life balance. Information from western countries about this concept might influence this generation in this country.

Dream Jobs of Generation Z in Indonesia: Working with Technology and Entrepreneurship

One of the characteristics of Generation Z globally, including Indonesia, is being technology savvy. This characteristic might influence how they want to work with technology. Dell Technologies Research (2017) 'The Gen Z Effect' conducted in Indonesia showed that 94% of Generation Z in Indonesia wants to work in a company that uses the most advanced technology. Ninety-nine per cent of them mention that technology literacy is important and 76% of them are willing to share their knowledge and become a technology mentor for their co-workers. Generation Z in Indonesia needs a work culture which allows them to explore and enhance their knowledge in the technology field. Sixty per cent want jobs that allow them to be involved in technology development and 41% believe their job must be able to give them new skills and experience in the workplace. This survey was also conducted globally. Compared to their colleagues in South East Asia, this generation in Indonesia shows more self-efficacy in using technology.

Moreover, entrepreneurship is also one of dream jobs among this generation. Almost 90% of respondents want to start their own companies. Compared to the other 46 countries (on an average 55%), the Indonesian Generation Z is the most entrepreneurial. Moreover, a study that aimed to compare entrepreneurial intention among this generation and previous generations (Generation X and Y) shows that Generation Z has higher self-efficacy and perceived instrument readiness. They think that they have enough social networks, information, and access to capital to start their own business and they are optimist that they can make it (Setiobudi & Herdinata, 2018).

Communication at Work: The Importance of Face-to-Face Communication

The Dell Technologies Research (2019) also revealed that Generation Z in Indonesia still respect the human element and need human interaction in the workplace. Almost 80% of them hope that they can learn about their work from colleagues directly, not by online learning. More than half of the respondents stated that face-to-face communication is the method of communication they want to have with work colleagues. This result is supported by other research conducted by Dwidienawati and Gandasari (2018). According to this study, face-to-face communication such as feedback sessions or opinion sharing among supervisors and colleagues is very important. Guidance from superiors is important for them, especially when they face difficulties at work.

Generation Z in Indonesia: How to Deal with Them

Shopping

Generally speaking, Indonesians are loyal to brands and indicate a strong preference for local brands (McKinsey, 2014). Generation Z as teenagers have needs in the range of technology, entertainment, food, and beverages and fashion. With the rising trend of mobile connectivity, Generation Z in Indonesia is also look-ing for a variety of experiences as their expectations are also rising. Brands must offer different shopping experiences and services to their consumers. For example, brands can use live streaming experiences to showcase the products with some people reviewing them.

Workforce Challenges

Generation Z in Indonesia is ready to be a part of digital transformation. This will be a challenge for companies because they have to invent strategies with the right offer to attract potential employees. With Generation Z being the newest member of the workforce, companies will be filled with multi-generation employees and, therefore, need to understand how to treat them based on their characteristics.

The first challenge for companies is fulfilling Generation Z's desire to contrib-ute to the greater good. In a Universum study in 2017, 88% of Generation Z in Indonesia say they would like to start their own company to change the world for the better, to be their own boss, and to have the flexibility in their work life to spend more time with their family and doing the things they like. Companies, therefore, need to clearly display the right values, culture, and opportunity for work–life balance to motivate Generation Z in doing their best work in the com-pany. Generation Z in Indonesia will no longer choose a company based on the industry or corporate brand but based on its culture, its environment, and its purpose.

Generation Z also wants to work with the latest technology in their environ-ment. In addition, they also are willing to share their knowledge about this. Even when they have high digital maturity, they prefer to communicate in a more direct and conventional way.

Education

Parents are still the most significant decision makers and influencers for Genera-tion Z in Indonesia when it comes to choosing education and careers (74%) based on the Universum study in 2017. Educational Institutions need to make sure that they offer a safe feeling to parents while promoting their programmes and high-lighting how their children will excel and grow.

Generation Z is also determined to become a global citizen of the world by planning to study abroad. Research from AFS, Mapping Generation Z in 2016, reveals Generation Z in Indonesia's continued enthusiasm for studying abroad and intercultural learning. Forty-four per cent of Generation Z as a student expressed that their motivation to study abroad is for cultural exploration. Gen-eration Z in Indonesia shows a safety concern in relation to studying abroad at the rate of 47%, which points to an increased awareness of the global security situation.

In relation to barriers, affordability remains a significant challenge for Gen-eration Z in Indonesia (AFS Global Research, 2016). Forty-five per cent of all respondents from Indonesia indicate that they would not be able to afford an exchange abroad without receiving a full scholarship. In terms of destinations for study abroad, 86% Generation Z in Indonesia prefer English-speaking countries including the United States, United Kingdom, and Australia. Generation Z in Indonesia decides to go studying abroad by themselves (94%).

Conclusions

Generation Z in Indonesia is evidently unique and possesses different characteristics that their predecessors (Generations X and Y) may not have. As evident in this paper, Generation Z views themselves as connected and knowledgeable consumers, even more so than previous generations due to their status as digital natives.

References

AdReaction. (2017). Engaging gen X, Y, and Z. Retrieved from https://www.millwardbrowndigital.com/resources/adreaction-engaging-gen-xy-and-z/. Accessed on August 8, 2019.

AFS Global Research. (2017). Mapping generation z in Indonesia: Attitudes toward international education program. Retrieved from https://afs.org/research/. Accessed on July 31, 2019.

Albert, I., Trommsdorff, G., & Wisnubrata, L. (2009). Intergenerational transmission of values in different cultural contexts: A study in Germany and Indonesia. In *Proceedings from the 18th international congress of the international association for cross-cultural psychology*, Grand Valley State University, Michigan.

Alvara Strategic Report. (2020). Indonesia Gen Z and Milennial Report 2020. Retrieved from https://alvara-strategic.com/indonesia-gen-z-and-millenial-report-2020/. Accessed on January, 2020.

Business Digest. (2016). Nestlé Indonesia gets ready for the gen z wave. Retrieved from https://business-digest.eu/en/2016/03/01/nestle-indonesia-gets-ready-for-the-gen-z-wave-interview/. Accessed on July 24, 2019.

BVABDRC.com. (2019). Yang muda yang bergerak: The evolving youth of Indonesia. Retrieved from https://www.bva-bdrc.com/projects/yang-muda-yang-bergerak-evolving-youth-indonesia/. Accessed on October 19, 2019.

Dell Technologies. (2017). The gen Z effect. Retrieved from https://www.delltechnologies.com/en-us/perspectives/gen-z.htm. Accessed on July 31, 2019.

Dwidienawati, D., & Gandasari, D. (2018). Understanding Indonesia's generation Z. *International Journal of Engineering & Technology*, 7(3), 245–252.

Euromonitor International. (2018). *Generation Z: The Next Wave of Consumers*. Retrieved from https://www.euromonitor.com/generation-z-the-next-wave-of-consumers/report

Gao, R. (2018). We Asked Gen Z About Their Spending Habits: "It's Always Comes Back to Food". Retrieved from https://www.vice.com/en_us/article/d3kd7q/we-asked-gen-z-about-their-spending-habits. Accessed on July, 2019.

Handajani, S. (2005). *Globalizing local girls: The representation of adolescents in Indonesian female teen magazines* (Unpublished doctoral dissertation). Perth: University of Western Australia.

Handajani, S. (2010). *Selling alternative masculinities: Representations of masculinities in Indonesian men's lifestyle magazines* (Unpublished doctoral dissertation). Perth: University of Western Australia.

Hofstede, G. (2001). *Culture's consequences: Comparing values, behaviors, institutions and organizations across nations* (2nd ed.). Thousand Oaks, CA: SAGE Publications.

Hofstede, G. (2011). Dimensionalizing cultures: The Hofstede model in context. *Online Readings in Psychology and Culture*, *2*(1), 3.

Ipsos. (2020). Indonesia The next cashless society. Retrieved from https://www.ipsos.com/sites/default/files/ct/news/documents/2020-01/ims-2020-summary-v1.pdf. Accessed on January 15, 2020.

Jakartapost.com. (2019). Millennials and gen z are increasingly pessimistic about their lives, survey finds. Retrieved from https://www.thejakartapost.com/youth/2019/05/21/millennials-and-gen-z-are-increasingly-pessimistic-about-their-lives-survey-finds.html. Accessed on October 19, 2019.

Jung, S. (2011). K-pop, Indonesian fandom, and social media. In R. A. Reid & S. Gatson (Eds.), *Race and ethnicity in fandom*, Special issue *Transformative works and cultures*. Melbourne: Victoria University.

Kantar Sea Insights. (2017). 8 Ways to engage gen Z consumers. Retrieved from https://sea.kantar.com/business/brands/2017/8-ways-to-engage-gen-z-consumers/. Accessed on July 24, 2019.

Lawrence, P. (2013). Does Asia have capitalism right? Retrieved from https://theconversation.com/does-asia-have-capitalism-right-10917. Accessed on August 17, 2019.

Mangundjaya, W. (2013). *Is there cultural change in the national cultures of Indonesia?* Australia: Congress of the International Association for Cross Cultural Psychology, University of Melbourne.

McKinsey Report. (2014). The evolving Indonesian consumer. Retrieved from https://www.mckinsey.com/business-functions/marketing-and-sales/our-insights/the-evolving-indonesian-consumer. Accessed on August 11, 2019.

Microsoft. (2019). Understanding consumer trust in digital services in Asia Pacific. Retrieved from https://news.microsoft.com/apac/2019/04/16/microsoft-idc-study-only-31-of-consumers-in-asia-pacific-trust-organizations-offering-digital-services-to-protect-their-personal-data/. Accessed on July 31, 2019.

Nielsen Consumer & Media View. (2016). Gen Z: Kosumen potensial masa depan. Retrieved from https://www.nielsen.com/id/en/press-releases/2016/GEN-Z-KONSUMEN-POTENSIAl-MASA-DEPAN/. Accessed on July 23, 2019.

Piper Jaffray. (2018). Piper Jaffray 37th semi-annual generation Z survey. Retrieved from https://www.businesswire.com/news/home/20190408005596/en/Piper-Jaffray-Completes-Semi-Annual-Generation-Survey-8000. Accessed on July, 2019.

Primasari, A., & Yuniarti, K. W. (2012). What make teenagers happy? An exploratory study using indigenous psychology approach. *International Journal of Research*, *1*(2), 53–61.

Setiobudi, A., & Herdinata, C. (2018). Difference in entrepreneurial intention on generation X, Y, and Z. *International Journal of Academic Research in Business and Social Sciences*, *8*(7), 49–58.

Setiowati, D. (2013). *Perkembangan film animasi cheburashka di Jepang: Sebuah kajian tentang dampak perubahan ideologi dan globalisasi di era federasi Rusia*. (Unpublished doctoral dissertation). Depok: University of Indonesia.

Sherlock, P. L. (2008). Doing a bit more for the poor? Social assistance in Latin America. *Journal of Social Policy*, *37*(4), 621–639.

Sihombing, S. O. (2013). Identifying changing in Indonesian values and its impacts to Indonesian consumer behavior. *The Internet Journal of Language, Culture, and Society*, *36*(2), 101–109.

Simangunsong, E. (2018). Generation-z buying behaviour in Indonesia: Opportunities for retail businesses. *MIX: Jurnal Ilmiah Manajemen*, *8*, 243.

Statista Research Department. (2019). Smartphone market in Indonesia – Statistics and facts. Retrieved from https://www.statista.com/topics/5020/smartphones-in-indonesia/. Accessed on July, 2019.

Suharnomo, S. (2017). Understanding business behavior of the Chinese Indonesian: A study using Hofstedes cultural framework. *Jurnal Dinamika Manajemen, 8*(1), 11–19.

Suharyadi, A. N., Purwanto, S. K., & Faturohman, M. (2012). *Kewirausahaan: Membangun usaha sukses sejak usia muda.* Jakarta: Salemba Empat.

Tirto Media Research. (2017a). Kelahiran generasi Z, Kematian media cetak. Retrieved from https://tirto.id/kelahiran-generasi-z-kematian-media-cetak-ctLa. Accessed on July 10, 2019.

Tirto Media Research. (2017b). Mengikuti keseharian generasi Z golongan pertama. Retrieved from https://tirto.id/mengikuti-keseharian-generasi-z-golongan-pertama-ctLk. Accessed on July 11, 2019.

UNICEF. (2014). *Indonesia annual report.* UNICEF Annual Report, 28.

Universum. (2017). *Generation Z grows up.* Stockholm: Swedish Press.

Varkey Foundation. (2017). *What the world's young people think and feel.* London: Varkey Foundation.

Varshney, A., Panggabean, R., & Tadjoeddin, M. Z. (2004). *Patterns of collective violence in Indonesia (1990–2003).* Jakarta: USFIR.

Ye, L. (2015). Work values and career adaptability of Chinese University students. *Social Behaviour & Personality: An International Journal, 43*(3), 411–422.

Chapter 9

Generation Z in Vietnam: The Quest for Authenticity

Linh Hoang Nguyen and Hoa Phuong Nguyen

Abstract

Vietnam is an emerging economy in the South East Asia region. Its Generation Z is gradually taking the lead in the country. But rather than breaking away from the previous generations, this generation also shows a strong preference towards local values and solid commitment to social issues. Thus, traditional culture elements are increasingly integrated in every aspect of Generation Z's life, such as advertising and fashion. Instead of hanging out at coffee places, they go for bubble tea. They still appreciate the traditional values but integrate them within a modern context. Brands chase after these young people by adapting their values into their products and services. In the work place, the Vietnamese Generation Z is less confident. They are partially lost in career development with poor career counselling in the education system. They desire new experience and new learning opportunities. Generation Z, who were born beginning in 1995, emerges in Vietnam as a fresh and promising force.

Keywords: Generation Z; Vietnam; values; career; education

Introduction: A Young Generation in a Moving Economy

Vietnam is an emerging economy in South East Asia. After the Vietnam War, the country was one of the poorest in the world. Post-war per-capita Gross Domestic Product (GDP) was under $100 (World Bank, 2020). The country was also embargoed by the United States and in tension with its neighbour countries, especially China. The post-war internal policies and international political situation

The New Generation Z in Asia: Dynamics, Differences, Digitalisation
The Changing Context of Managing People, 135–148
Copyright © 2020 by Emerald Publishing Limited
All rights of reproduction in any form reserved
doi:10.1108/978-1-80043-220-820201014

drove the country into an economic crisis, with inflation reaching up to 700% in the 1980s. By 1986, the government introduced an economic and political reform called 'Doi Moi' aimed at transforming the war-torn country into a socialist-oriented market economy. This bold move set forth decades of economic growth, putting Vietnam into the spot light as a promising emerging market. Vietnam achieved on an average 7% of growth rate and had a robust manufacturing industry and modern infrastructure. As a result, its placement in Global Competitiveness rose to the 67th in 2019 (Schwab, 2019). The economic outlook of Vietnam remains to be positive at 5.4% until 2030 (Economist Intelligence Unit, 2019). The Vietnamese benefited greatly from this change. In terms of GPD per capita, Vietnam has strived to achieve US $2,566 in 2018, a dramatic jump from just US $94 in 1989 (Wordbank, 2020). Statistics showed that poverty not only dropped to 9.8% in 2016, the poor often escaped from it (World Bank, 2018). This healthy growth is attributed greatly to increasing domestic demands, strong export activities, and continuous economic reforms. AT Kearney's (2019) Development Index put Vietnam's retail market among the top in its development index thanks to its low saturation level and the highest GDP growth in the South East Asia region (Vietnamnet, 2018). The arrival of international retailers, such as Aeon[1] and Lotte,[2] both of which are present in Vietnam, will surely drive the country's economy ahead.

Along with the rapid change in economy, Vietnam's demography and society is also experiencing significant transformation. By 2020, there were 96,990,666 people in total (danso.org, 2020). The country enjoys a young and educated workforce, with 45% being under 30 years old (PwC, 2017). Notably, 33% of the population lives in urban areas as of 2016 and, by 2035, this figure will increase to 50% of the total population, or nearly 54 million people (World Bank, 2016). With this trend, the country can be said to have a sustainable source of workers, especially when Vietnam is poised to be the next Asian manufacturing centre thanks to its lower wages and proximity to China (PwC, 2017).

According to Nielsen (2018a), the local consumers' confidence continues to remain at a very high level over the years. This growth is attributed to the optimism about personal finances and a strong willingness to spend. However, the Vietnamese consumers' concerns are still very traditional, namely job stability and health (Nielsen, 2018a). As the Vietnamese become more urbanised, the local middle class is also on the rise. World Bank (2018) reports that 13% of Vietnam's population earn enough to belong in the global middle class, and this figure is moving up with 1.5 million more each year. A typical middle-class Vietnamese is projected to earn around US $15,000 per year in 2035 and up to US $30,000 by 2050 (PwC, 2017). This group will be the main driver for more sophisticated services and higher quality consumer goods.

---

[1] Aeon is the largerst shopping mall developer and operator in Asia, based in Japan.
[2] Lotte Corporation is a South Korean multinational conglomerate, with a very strong retail division.

Table 1.   Reasons Why Generation Z Like New Food.

Famous Brand	Unique Packaging	High Price	New Flavour	Good Taste	Imported Goods	Other
9.68%	9.97%	12.01%	26.22%	21.38%	13.04%	7.7%

Source: Younet Media (Brandsvietnam, 2018).

Basics of Generation Z in Vietnam: it's all About Digital

A Digital Community

A study from Nielsen (2018b) on 370 respondents, of which 160 are Millennials and 210 are Generation Z, found that the Vietnamese members of Generation Z spend a large portion of their time on social media. They engage and express themselves online. Thus, this will have a huge impact on their consuming behaviours. These young people are reported to be much more influential to their family purchase decision. For example, more than half of the questioned Generation Z in Decision Lab (2015)'s survey (n=710) indicated that they are the main decision makers in various domains, such as entertainment, out-of-home dining, and technology-related purchases. Nguyen (2019) notes that the brands of the technology products are entirely decided by these young consumers, with nearly half of the respondents admitting having the last say in these matters. Consequently, Vietnamese brands are increasingly trying to connect with members of Generation Z by associating themselves with this generation's values. Notable examples include Momo (the number one e-wallet app in Vietnam)'s activities to increase users' traffic by introducing interactive games in multiple events, or OPPO (a leading smartphone brand in Vietnam)'s communication strategy to reach the young consumers with their mix of traditional family values and a modern, always connected life-style.

In the next few years, the Vietnamese Generation Z will be the causes of great changes in social and consumption patterns. With 13,000 billion VND (Viet Nam Dong – the local currency) or roughly US $600,000,000 in out-of-home dinning spending, they will be the golden consumers in the near future, when these young people begin to enter the workforce. Internet was introduced in the country in 1997, Facebook was launched in 2004, and YouTube was online in 2005, being born from 1995 onward, they grew up with these technologies already mature. Thus, these people are dubbed 'digital natives'. They are the new kind of consumers: every aspect of their life has been digitalised to a certain extent.

Many Real Differences

Generation Z is making their first steps into the world. A study on Vietnamese young consumers by Decision Labs in 2015 found that these young people have an average income of US $100 per month, despite having no official salary. Vision Critical (2018) predicts that members of Generation Z are the future of the global economy. Their number is equivalent to that of the Millennials. In 2018, they will consume US $200 billion globally, and indirectly influence another US $600 billion in their family's purchase. Generation Z, according to some experts (Brandvietnam, 2018), is trendsetters in various fields, from entertainment, fashion to consumer goods.

Results from Social Listening and Data Analytics from Younet Media (Nhip Cau Dau Tu, 2018) suggest that online activities such as social networks, movies, music, and instant messaging are favourites of Generation Z. According to Mr Trieu, Director of Younet Media, members of Generation Z in Vietnam are rebellious and like to challenge the status-quo. They are willing to spend and have their own style in cuisine and fashion. They have a preference for global and international trends, taking them from social networks and the Internet. However, they show a clear interest towards traditional values. Consequently, brands have tried to capture this generation by introducing product lines incorporated with Vietnamese patterns.

Nhip Cau Dau Tu (2018), a Vietnamese investment magazine, interviewed industry experts and revealed many interesting insights. Mr Nguyen Thanh Tong, founder of Idea Guru, an advertising consulting agency, suggests that Generation Z was born in the economic reform period called 'Doi Moi', in which the country opened up to the outside world, imported international technology, and was exposed to global values. As a result, these young people are naturally more globalised than the previous generations. The influx of new thinking will inevitably clash with the old traditions. In other words, the Vietnamese Generation Z is swimming in the soup of conflict, between the new and the old, the nationalist and the globalist, the conservatism and the evolutionism. Notably, Generation Z speaks foreign languages and has a wide range of knowledge (Anphabe. com, 2018). The exposure to global values has overthrown the traditional balance between professional work and personal life. Vietnamese young people place higher priority on their own freedom and aim for financial achievements. This poses serious challenges to employers in Vietnam because this is completely unlike employees from previous generations.

Generation Z as Consumers in Vietnam: Desire for Local Values and a Higher Purpose

Unfollow the Older Generations

In a country where GDP per capita reaches roughly US $2,400 (World Bank, 2019), Generation Z's average monthly spending of 2,400,000 VND or equivalent of US $100 (Decision Lab, 2015) is surprisingly high. Young people in Vietnam are dining out more often and at different places than their predecessors (Decision Lab, 2016). Generation Z in Vietnam prefers to frequent canteen and fast service restaurants and goes less to street food stalls and fast casual places. Bubble tea also topples coffee and alcoholic drinks as the favourite beverage (Nielsen, 2018b). Decision Lab (2016) surveyed 19,089 consumers and found that visits to bubble tea increased 117% in 2016, while coffee shops (the popular beverage for older generations) saw a 6% drop. This difference in spending leads to some level of ideological conflicts between generations.

The philosophy of Confucius lays the foundation to the structures of the Vietnamese and Chinese society (Williams, 1992). It emphasises harmony with others, especially with family members. The social hierarchy is of the utmost importance because to improve one's self, he/she must respect and learn from the elders' wisdom. Thus, values such as humility, lack of competitiveness, and thriftiness are highly appreciated (Yeung, 2008). These were tough times economically and belt-tightening was part of life, even a worthy 'trait'. But that is no longer the case.

'What we see here is an interesting generational gap, but not the gap between parents / grandparents and their children', Phan Tuong Yen, a psychology lecturer at Hoa Sen University in Saigon, told VnExpress International in October, 2017. 'It's much closer than that and it's clearly a conflict of personal values'. It's those born from the mid-1990s onward who have welcomed a strong cultural wave that carried the concepts of freedom, individuality and right to indulge along with an economic boom. This generation 'feels they are part of this booming wealth, more so than in the earlier days of austerity', said Yen. 'Therefore, the notion of freedom between these two generations somewhat differs, and so does the concept of cautious spending'.

Seeking Authenticity

Similar to the Generation X consumers, Generation Z consumers in Vietnam are fully immersed into the virtual world. Nielsen's study in 2018 (Hanoitimes.vn) on 210 Generation Z consumers found that 99% of them have a Facebook account, 77% are on Zalo (a local social network app equivalent to Facebook), and 90% still watch television every day. And they do buy online. The Internet is likely their first touch point for a product and most still shop at established and reputed e-commerce sites, but many are turning towards social media or chat apps as an alternative. Moreover, Generation Z's Vietnam is an e-sport giant. Their teams are more performative and have been dominating the regional leagues. The developer of League of Legends, a popular e-sport game, reserves an entire competitive region for Vietnam (Bishop, 2018). This is a big privilege since it guarantees the Vietnamese a slot in major international competitions such as the Mid-Season Invitational or Worlds, to which other countries have to fight for.

Although being online is an essential part of their life, they do not trust the information on the Internet as much as their parents or grandparents. They have a high level of scepticism over online sources, especially online reviews (Forbes, 2018). This is really surprising because just a few years ago, online reviews were still regarded as one of the most effective advertising tools. KPMG (2017)'s survey on Vietnamese online shoppers of older generations found that that consumers generally trust online information and online reviews. About 9.9% of the Vietnamese respondents relied on online reviews to make their purchase decisions. Furthermore, another 8% would pick them as a reliable information source, after only friends and relatives (11.5%), social media (8.3%), and online shop

(8.2%). Instead, they overwhelmingly rely on their parents for accurate information (Nielsen, 2018a). This scepticism is accompanied by a fickle loyalty towards brands (Nielsen, 2018a).

Furthermore, the young Vietnamese desire Vietnamese values and cultures embedded in their products and service (Nielsen, 2018a, 2018b). Knowing this, marketers have been aiming to incorporate traditional values into their products and marketing campaigns. Notable examples are Style Z, who put Hang Trong Pictures patterns into their ready-to-wears, or even The Pizza Company, which blends masterfully traditional Vietnam culture into its Italian cuisine. Since 2014, OPPO, one of the local top smartphone brands, has been pursuing an emotional approach in their marketing strategies to target Generation Z. In their TVCs such as 'Giu Tet tryen thong, song Tet hien dai' (2016), family connection, a long standing and traditional value of Vietnamese people, is celebrated.

Generation Z in Vietnam also has a strong desire to engage with social issues. Nielsen's study in 2018 pointed out that animal protection, gender equality, and environment are among the top five on their list. It should be noted that these young people buy environmentally friendly products because they see themselves as such (Nguyen, Lobo, & Nguyen, 2017). Huge social movements in Vietnam in the recent years include #savesondoong and #truongsahoangsalacuavietnam. The former is a campaign against the construction of cable car system inside the world biggest cave (Son Doong) while the latter are the protests against Chinese aggression in South China Sea. All those movements are largely dissipated in the population via social networks and with the significant contribution of young activists and people. This eagerness to act is very likely to make them rally behind a brand that shows great purpose. Since 2014, OPPO, one of the local top smartphone brands, has been pursuing an emotional approach in their marketing strategies. Their latest campaigns targeted specifically Generation Z. The overarching theme is the real family relationship advocating a real-life connection with others. In their TVCs 'Lam cha can ca doi tay' (2014), 'Trong the gioi bi mat cua me' (2015), or 'Giu Tet tryen thong, song Tet hien dai' (2016), family connection, a long standing and traditional value of Vietnamese people, is highlighted. Other brands have begun to follow suit. Tiger, a beer company, launched an annual campaign called 'Buc Tuong Tiger' (translation: Tiger Wall) promoting moderate drinking behaviours among the youth. As Generation Z grows in size and purchasing power, we will hopefully see many positive influences on society.

Generation Z at Work in Vietnam: Investing for Long-term Benefits

An Irrelevant Degree

TopCV (2018) in Vietnam looked at their database of 30,000 companies, 1.6 millions of over 18-year-old applicants, and conducted more than 2,000 interviews. They found that sales is the number one job that young people apply to. 31% of all applications are in sales positions. Human Resources, Marketing, and Customer Services follow the lead. The traditional high-earning professions, such as real-estate and insurance, are quite unattractive, with under 2% of applications.

TopCV assumes that the lack of recruiting channels is the culprit of this situation. 'VietnamWorks', the number one job site in the country, suggests in their 2018's Digital Recruiting Handbook that social media is now one of their most effective platforms. They stress that using social networks is not only about attracting talent but also engaging with potential applicants. With Generation Z's deep immersion into the digital world, long-standing companies in the real-estate and insurance business may fail to catch up with younger applicants.

This may sound strange to foreigners not familiar with the recruiting scene in Vietnam but working in a profession other than your training is very popular in Vietnam. It is estimated that 60% of these applicants work in fields other than their formal degree (Dinh & Nguyen, 2018). Career orientation in the Vietnamese education system has been always criticised as inefficient. This activity is often misunderstood at the high-school level as an introduction to the universities' programmes, rather than as guidance based on students' talents and backgrounds (Le, 2018). The curriculum, thus, lacks orientation and focusses entirely on test-taking (Dinh & Nguyen, 2018). Consequently, only 50% of university graduates manage to find a job matching their degree (Tran, 2019). Furthermore, in a study of young employees aged under 25 conducted in Ho Chi Minh city by Bamboo in 2017 (Brandvietnam, 2017), 65% of respondents indicated that they have no clear direction in the future. It is interesting to note that only 25% of the respondents admit that their career choice is based on analysis of market trend. In this way, TopCV (2018)'s results make sense. Jobs that are deemed practical such as Sales, Shop Keeping, or Human Resources require little specialised knowledge and, thus, attract a large pool of applicants. However, relevant diplomas or working experiences are usually the criteria for traditionally high-earning positions, such as real-estate or auditors. Young applicants with no determined career path naturally turn away from these jobs.

There is an old saying 'Sĩ Nông Công Thương' (Intellectuals, Farmers, Technicians, and Business in hierarchical order) which shows a long-standing social and economic prestigious impressions of these jobs. Even though the development of the economy has somewhat reversed the traditional order into a modern version 'Nhất Y Nhì Dược tạm được Bách Khoa' (Medicine is the best, Pharmacy is second, and Technology is acceptable), the pressure from parents for their children to pursue 'higher class' jobs prevails. There is also a dissent of society towards 'lower-class' trades such as technicians or welders. In a country where 75% of high-school students take the national university entrance exam, there will not be enough places for college-level jobs (Nhandan.com.vn, 2013). With the alternative of being unemployed, having any kind of job suddenly appears much more attractive.

Unfortunately, applying to a position without the relevant training is not always easy. According to TopCV (2018), business-related jobs are the ones with the most personnel having no suitable degrees, with banking and press leading the figures. Technology-oriented jobs, such as IT or engineering, are naturally harder to access without suitable training. Sadly, Uber and Grab drivers are emerging as a popular employment for degree holders (Tuoitrenews.vn, 2018).

Beyond Formal Education

The answer for this problem lies in the country's inefficiency in integrating the needs of corporations with the education authorities. The education system is blamed for its surreal curricula, which are built upon what the schools have, not on what society demands (Vnexpress.net, 2019). The high unemployment rate among university graduates suggests a large gap between their actual skills and what the companies demand (Demombynes & Testaverde, 2018). Lucky individuals, who are able to pursue their dream career, must survive on a salary that gives them little room to breathe. For example, a newly recruited law officer in Quang Ngai Province reportedly earns 2.5 million VND (US $110)/month full-time, which translates to an annual income of US $1,320, only slightly more than half of Vietnam's 2016 GDP per capita of US $2,185.69, as reported by the World Bank (Tuoitrenews.vn, 2018). This pushes many skilled young workers, university educated, to labour intensive positions. To bring that number into focus, the same law officer could earn a maximum monthly wage more than six times higher if he or she was to join Uber. It makes sense to see young Vietnamese turn to Uber in droves to seek easy money. A college student working part-time as an Uber driver can earn as much as four million VND (US $175)/month, which is significantly more than working part-time as a private tutor, waiter, or teaching assistant. For those prepared to go full-time, they can earn up to four times as much, with some drivers regularly pocketing monthly salaries of around 20 million VND (US $700). The extreme mobility in the Vietnamese job market seems to affect those who are in stable positions. TopCV (2018) found that 95% young applicants are constantly looking for new opportunities, no matter what their current condition is.

The number one concern for their first jobs is not financial rewards for Vietnamese young people. Over 50% of TopCV (2018) respondents were willing to stay with the companies that offer a positive environment for learning and promotion. Failing to adhere to this demand means that the companies will lose many young workers sooner or later. Among the reasons why they gave up their job, the first was the lack of promotion opportunities, low salary, and bad bosses. Thirty-nine per cent of respondents would even accept a 10% lower income if the new employers offered a better environment and better chance to improve (TopCV, 2018). This poses a challenge, and, at the same time, an opportunity for companies to adapt themselves to the new wave of Vietnamese employees from Generation Z.

How to Deal with Generation Z in Vietnam

In the Marketplace: Go Digital, Go Mobile.

As 'mobile generation', Generation Z will open an era in which all transactions with all kinds of goods will be completed wirelessly. Using mobile phones is not just a habit, it's a way of life. The banking industry is among the first to realise the importance of smartphones in capturing the younger consumer. Technologically speaking, the Chinese have already implemented mobile payment on a mass scale. Payment apps such as Alipay or WeChat Pay dominate the Vietnamese market and almost eradicate cash in everyday purchases. From paying home applicants to buying snacks, all they need to do is to scan the recipient's QR code using their smartphone. At the 2017 Retail Banking Forum held in Hanoi, Mr Tran Nhat Minh, Deputy General Director of VIB Bank, affirmed that future payment services will be led by the Z generation (Vietnamnet, 2017). Mobile phones will be substituted for bank branches to eliminate the need for queues, counters, and physical stores. Most banks in Vietnam now offer their clients Internet and mobile banking services. Balance checking and money transferring via mobile are now the norm. Some banks, such as Techcombank and VIB, go even further by allowing money remittance via Facebook and ATM access without physical cards.

However, payment is no longer the exclusive domain of banks. The development of MoMo e-wallet in Vietnam is an example. As an all-in-one solution, its users can not only pay utilities bills and services but also make peer-to-peer payment by topping up their MoMo accounts. Furthermore, with integration to bank accounts and credit/cards, MoMo has the potential to replace cash as the dominant payment method in the market. Its strong growth is credited to the banks' inability to provide convenience experience to its customers (Theasianbanker.com, 2018). To make a transaction, MoMo users need to make two steps, a massive improvement when compared to the eight steps of other apps. With eight million current users, along with the growing Z Generation, MoMo aims to increase the number of its users to 50 million by 2020. Banks and payment services are just one of many changes for the market to adapt to Generation Z.

To date, only a small number of Vietnamese brands are interested and have successfully implemented digital and mobile channels. Because Generation Z consumers spend a significant amount of their time on social media, brands have to follow. An advertising campaign by the Vietnamese shoe maker, Biti's for its Hunter product line is one notable example. By cooperating with Son Tung MTP, a famous local singer, in his new video clip uploaded on YouTube, Biti's has managed to revitalise its entire existence. The music video, named 'Lac Troi', features the singer dancing and singing in the new Hunter shoes in front of Vietnamese mountainous scenery in a fantasy setting. It hit seven million views after its first 48 hours and helped Biti's to sell out in only 7 days (Vnexpress.net, 2017). The success of Son Tung MTP's case makes other brands change their perspectives. In the following years, other brands spend heavily on music videos featuring their products or services. For example, Tiki, the Vietnamese equivalent of Amazon, announced 'Accompanying the Vietnamese stars' to produce exclusive contents for popular social networks (Advertisingvietnam.com, 2019).

Nhip Cau Dau Tu (2018) features an interview with Cao Thi Ngoc Dung, Chairman of PNJ's Board of Directors. She remarks brands need tactics to help connect with Generation Z on the phone, re-thinking about physical and wealth locations, and provide a good experience from the beginning to the end of the customer's journey. Embracing the new trend towards Generation Z consumers, PNJ has also spent much effort. The company invested more than US $8 million in deploying an omni-channel system in recent years. Instead of relying solely on demographic indicators such as gender, income, and age, PNJ go deeper into analysing buyers' behaviour to offer products that are separate services for each person. Its online revenue is expected to increase five times in 2018, from 30 billion in 2017 and reach at least 1,000 billion in 2021. In the end, it is important to note that even though social media is essential to Generation Z consumers, it is not their everything. Traditional mediums such as Television can still be as effective as Facebook content (Nielsen, 2018a, 2018b). To successfully capture Generation Z consumers in Vietnam, brands need to get the right message at the right time on the right platform.

In the Workplace: Find the Right Z

These young people benefit from a low employment rate of 2.17% (General Statistic Office, 2019) and a bright economic outlook (PwC, 2017). With a higher education level and economic standing than their predecessors, thanks to the economic reforms 'Doi Moi', Generation Z is better equipped to face the new challenges of a fast-emerging economy. As in the year 2019, many Vietnamese Generation Z of different educational backgrounds have begun to join the professional world. Eventually, these young employees will hold many important positions, so it is essential that companies understand how to recruit and nurture the right persons the right way.

When it comes to search for a job, social networks are also a major source for information (Adecco, 2019). Therefore, they are the first place to hunt for potential candidates. According to VietnamWorks (2018), Facebook is the most effective platform for recruitment in Vietnam, especially for well-known brands. They found that fan pages of those companies generate more interactions and attract a higher number of members. Recruitment activities of big corporations like Coca-Cola or Unilever are gradually digitalised. And to compete for better candidates, they also get more creative. Notable examples in Vietnam are Next Generation Leader and Coke Spark from Coca-Cola. These two programmes attract the local Generation Z population by distributing creative and playful messages on social networks, such as 'Crush on Coca-Cola' contents or the cartoonish polar bear recruiting message (Coca-Cola, 2019).

To the social engaging Generation Z in Vietnam, social responsibility is another factor that companies have to consider. Generation Z is especially vocal on social issues, proven via various campaigns such as #SaveSonDoong or the annual VietPride parade (an LGBT supporting manifestation). The activities surrounding SonDoong Caves cable car campaign or the South China Sea disputes show the significance of having their voice recognised for Generation Z. Companies need to integrate their operation with activities contributing to society, such as environment protection. Vingroup, the local giant agglomerate, has multiple established funds, such as the Kind Heart Foundation, to undertake missions meant for local's communities' well-being and development. But these works have to be read by the right people. As VietnamWorks (2018) has suggested, popular social networks such as Facebook and Zalo generate more engagement and reach more Vietnamese people than traditional channels.

When it comes to accommodating Generation Z in Vietnam, it is important to note that degrees do not tell much about the applicants' potential. Since most of them are likely to work in a different field than their respective training (Brand-vietnam, 2017), they would be more committed to earn experience. Therefore, companies need to create an environment where Generation Z employees in Vietnam can have opportunities to learn new things. Many companies, both local and international, have applied these principles and achieved great results. Vinamilk, awarded 'Vietnam Best Place to Work 2018', retains its young employees by proposing flexible work hours, learning opportunities and constant challenges at work. They follow pre-established career paths and are provided necessary training and education to move forward in a fair and encouraging environment (Anphabe, 2018).

However, Vietnam is a country where hierarchical authority is valued in organisational culture (Truong, Hallinger, & Sanga, 2018). There is concern whether the rebellious Generation Z can thrive in the professional world. Since working in a different educational field is common in Vietnam, Generation Z is assumed to lack the necessary skills and knowledge to thrive in their positions. Thus, they need to be guided and trained on the job. The hierarchical culture of Vietnam may pose great challenges in establishing an open environment, where Vietnamese young people can discuss and express themselves freely. They may not raise their ideas, but to submit to their supervisors'. This prevents the companies from reaping the benefits of introducing a fresh flow of perspectives in their teams. Members of Generation Z in Vietnam can be creative and innovative but they need a certain degree of encouragement. It is the job of the top management to introduce the necessary push to move things forward.

Conclusions

The opportunities that the Vietnamese Generation Z have are unprecedented. On the one hand, the young Generation Z embraces modern technology to express themselves and to lead the country's development in their own way. On the other hand, we can see a strong sentiment towards the traditional values. Unlike the assumption that Generation Z will be truly global, these young Vietnamese aspire to build their identity as a blend of both global and local values. For both marketers and employers, to communicate with this generation using their language would be the decisive element for their success.

References

Adecco. (2019). *The result of career choices & the motivation survey 2019 is out now.* Retrieved from https//adecco.com.vn/vn/knowledge-center/detail/wm-2019-results

Advertisingvietnam.com. (2019). *Chien Luoc Cua Tiki La Gi Qua Du An Tiki Di Cung Sao Viet*. Retrieved from https//advertisingvietnam.com/2019/05/chien-luoc-cua-tiki-la-gi-qua-du-an-tiki-di-cung-sao-viet/

Anphabe. (2018). *Bao cao khao sat: noi lam viec tot nhat viet nam 2018*. Retrieved from https://www.anphabe.com/survey-report/

AT Kearney. (2019). *The 2019 Global Retail Development Index*. Retrieved from https://www.kearney.com/global-retail-development-index/2019.

Bishop, S. (2018). Vietnam is now its own competitive region in Leagues of Legends. Retrieved from https://www.gamereactor.fr/vietnam-is-now-its-own-competitive-region-in-league-of-legends/.

Brandvietnam. (2017). *Insight cua gioi tre trong viec dinh huong nghe nghiep*. Retrieved from https://www.brandsvietnam.com/congdong/topic/6376-Insight-cua-gioi-tre-trong-viec-dinh-huong-nghe-nghiep

Brandvietnam. (2018). *Oppo goc nhin gen Z*. Retrieved from https://www.brandsvietnam.com/campaign/231-Oppo-Goc-nhin-Gen-Z

Coca-Cola. (2019). *Talent Programs Page*. Retrieved from https://en.cocacolavietnam.com/careers/talent-programs

Danso.org. (2018). *Daily Statistics, Vietnam section*. Retrieved from https://danso.org/viet-nam/

Decision Lab. (2015). *Genzilla's report*. Retrieved from https://www.decisionlab.co/download-material-genzilla-vietnam

Decision Lab. (2016). *Out of home dining trend*. Retrieved from http://www.decisionlab.co/hubfs/Download_materials/Decision%20Lab_OOH%20trends_Mailer-official.compressed-updated-prices.pdf

Demombynes, G., & Testaverde, M. (2018). *Employment structure and returns to skill in Vietnam: estimates using the labor force survey*. Policy Research Working Paper. Retrieved from http://documents.worldbank.org/curated/en/965641520866682470/Employment-structure-and-returns-to-skill-in-Vietnam-estimates-using-the-labor-force-survey

Dinh C. K., & Nguyen V. D. (2018). Vai trò của chính quyền thành phố trong việc hỗ trợ kết nối doanh nghiệp và các cơ sở đào tạo. Conference Proceeding: "Liên kết giữa nhà trường và doanh nghiệp trong việc giải quyết việc làm cho sinh viên sau khi tốt nghiệp" (pp. 29–36). Ho Chi Minh: UEH Publishing House.

Economist Intelligence Unit. (2019). *Country report: Long term outlook*. Retrieved from https://country.eiu.com/article.aspx?articleid=127183396&Country=Vietnam&topic=Economy&subtopic=Long-term+outlook&subsubtopic=Summary

Forbes. (2018). *Understanding Vietnam's Generation Z*. Retrieved from https://www.forbes.com/sites/davisbrett/2018/02/03/understanding-vietnams-generation-z/#53c719687529

General Statistic Office. (2019). *General Statistic Office Homepage*. Retrieved from https://www.gso.gov.vn/default.aspx?tabid=382&idmid=2&ItemID=19136

Hanoitimes.vn. (2018). *Generation Z Leave Marked Impact on Vietnam's Consumer Landscape*. http://www.hanoitimes.vn/economy/2018/10/81e0cdda/generation-z-leave-marked-impact-on-vietnam-s-consumer-landscape-nielsen/

KPMG. (2017). *KPMG International Survey: What really matters to online shoppers?* Retrieved from https://home.kpmg/vn/en/home/insights/2017/02/kpmg-international-survey-details-what-really-matters-to-online-shoppers.html

Le, D. H. (2018). Thực Trạng Nhu Cầu Về Các Hình Thức Tư Vấn Hướng Nghiệp Của Học Sinh Một Số Trường Trung Học Phổ Thông Tại Thành Phố Hồ Chí Minh. *Tap chi giao duc, 427*, 15–18.

Nguyen, H. Q. (2019). Gen Z next in line. *Vneconomic Times*. Retrieved from http://www.vneconomictimes.com/article/business/gen-z-next-in-line

Nguyen, T. N., Lobo, A., & Nguyen, B. K. (2017). Young consumers' green purchase behaviour in an emerging market. *Journal of Strategic Marketing, 26*, 583–600.

Nhandan.com.vn. (2013). Nearly one million Vietnamese highschool students begin crucial exam. *Nhan Dan*. Retrieved from http://en.nhandan.com.vn/society/education/item/6313002-nearly-one-million-vietnamese-high-school-students-begin-crucial-exam.html

Nhip Cau Dau Tu. (2018). The He Z: Tuong Lai Cua Kinh Te Toan Cau. *Nhip Cau Dau Tu*. Retrieved from https://nhipcaudautu.vn/chuyen-de/the-he-z-tuong-lai-cua-kinh-te-toan-cau-3324816/

Nielsen. (2018a). *How to engage with Generation Z in Vietnam*. Retrieved from https://www.nielsen.com/apac/en/insights/news/2018/how-to-engage-with-generation-z-in-vietnam.html

Nielsen. (2018b). *Vietnam Consumer Confidence Index Q3 2018*. Retrieved from https://www.nielsen.com/apac/en/insights/article/2018/vietnam-consumer-confidence-index-q3-2018

PwC. (2017). *Spotlight on Vietnam*. Retrieved from https://www.pwc.com/vn/en/publications/2017/spotlight-on-vietnam.pdf

Schwab, K. (2019). *The Global Competitiveness Report 2019*. Retrieved from http://www3.weforum.org/docs/WEF_TheGlobalCompetitivenessReport2019.pdf.

Theasianbanker.com. (2018). How Fintech outgrew banks in the mobile wallet market in Vietnam. *The Asian Banker*. Retrieved from http://www.theasianbanker.com/updates-and-articles/how-fintech-outgrew-banks-in-the-mobile-wallet-market-in-vietnam

TopCV. (2018). *Bao Cao tuyen dung nhan su 2018*. Retrieved from https://blog.topcv.vn/tham-khao-bao-cao-tuyen-dung-nhan-su-2018-cua-topcv-de-biet-minh-biet-ta-tram-tran-tram-thang/

Tran A. T. (2019). Dự Báo Nhu Cầu Thị Trường Lao Động Qua Đào Tạo Việc Làm Sinh Viên Sau Khi Tốt Nghiệp – Liên Kết Giữa Nhà Trường Và Doanh Nghiệp Tại Tp. Hồ Chí Minh. *Liên kết giữa nhà trường và doanh nghiệp trong việc giải quyết việc làm cho sinh viên sau khi tốt nghiệp* (pp. 9–28). Ho Chi Minh: UEH Publishing House.

Truong, T. D., Hallinger, P., & Sanga, K. (2016). Confucian values and school leadership in Vietnam. *Educational Management Administration & Leadership*, *45*, 77–100.

Tuoitrenews.vn. (2018). Nation doomed as skilled young Vietnameses turn to uber and grab in droves. Retrieved from https://tuoitrenews.vn/news/city-diary/20180122/nation-doomed-as-skilled-young-vietnamese-turn-to-uber-grab-in-droves/43722.html

Vietnamnet. (2017). Digital banking grows to support new customers. *Vietnamnet.vn*. Retrieved from https://english.vietnamnet.vn/fms/business/192192/digital-banking-grows-to-support-new-customers.html

Vietnamnet. (2018). Retailers Flock to Vietnam as Consumer Spending Soars. *Vietnamnet.vn*. Retrieved from https://english.vietnamnet.vn/fms/business/198382/retailers-flock-to-vietnam-as-consumer-spending-soars.html

VietnamWorks. (2018). *VietnamWorks publishes Vietnam digital recruiting handbook – Guideline for hiring in digital age*. Retrieved from https://www.navigosgroup.com/vietnamworks-publishes-vietnam-digital-recruiting-handbook-guideline-hiring-digital-age/

Vnexpress.net. (2017). *Housing crisis brews in vietnam as low income homebuyers are forgotten*. Retrieved from https://e.vnexpress.net/news/business/housing-crisis-brews-in-vietnam-as-low-income-homebuyers-forgotten-3525825.html

Vnexpress.net. (2019). *Chu Tich Tp HCM: 60% Sinh Vien Lam Viec Trai Nganh, Gay Lang Phi Lon*. Retrieved from https://vnexpress.net/giao-duc/chu-tich-tp-hcm-60-sinh-vien-lam-viec-trai-nganh-lang-phi-lon-3866656.html

Williams, M. C. (1992). *Vietnam at the crossroads*. New York, NY: Council on Foreign Relations Press.

World Bank. (2016). *Vietnam 2035 : Toward Prosperity, Creativity, Equity, and Democracy*. Retrieved from https://openknowledge.worldbank.org/handle/10986/23724.

World Bank. (2018). *Climbing the ladder: Poverty reduction and shared prosperity in Vietnam*. Retrieved from http://documents.worldbank.org/curated/en/206981522843253122/pdf/124916-WP-PULIC-P161323-VietnamPovertyUpdateReportENG.pdf

World Bank. (2020). *Vietnam's Data*. Retrieved from https://data.worldbank.org/indicator/NY.GDP.PCAP.CD?locations=VN

Yeung, J. C. K. (2008). Role of traditional values on coping with stress among manufacturing workers in China: An empirical study. *International Journal of Management, 25*(2), 224–236.

Chapter 10

Generation Z in Malaysia: The Four 'E' Generation

Fandy Tjiptono, Ghazala Khan, Ewe Soo Yeong and Vimala Kunchamboo

Abstract

Generation Z in Malaysia is currently the largest age group representing 29% of the overall population, with a monthly disposable income of US$327 million. The Malaysian Generation Z is an electronically engaged generation and is heavily dependent on their smartphones and social media, spending an average of 8 hours a day on the Internet. They are also well educated, empowered, and entrepreneurial. As consumers, Malaysian Generation Z is influential and independent in their decision-making process. At the workplace, members of Generation Z in Malaysia are curious, caring, competent, and confident. These unique characteristics and behaviours provide specific challenges to deal with them as consumers, workers, and entrepreneurs.

Keywords: Generation Z; Malaysia; digitalisation; education; work; consumers

Introduction to Malaysia: Truly Asia

With its multi-ethnic and multi-cultural background, Malaysia has a strong image as 'Truly Asia' (Tourism Malaysia, 2019). Malaysian ethnic groups consist of Malay (69%), Chinese (23%), Indians (7%), and other ethnic minorities (1%) (Department of Statistics, 2019). As with other developing nations in Asia,

The New Generation Z in Asia: Dynamics, Differences, Digitalisation
The Changing Context of Managing People, 149–163
Copyright © 2020 by Emerald Publishing Limited
All rights of reproduction in any form reserved
doi:10.1108/978-1-80043-220-820201015

Malaysia registers a high proportion of youths among its 32.6 million people (Department of Statistics Malaysia, 2019), with a median age of about 28 years old (Santander, 2019). In comparison to the Baby Boomers (13%) and Generation X (18%), Generation Y (26%) and Generation Z (25%) represent the largest generational cohorts in Malaysia (Worldometers, 2020). The majority of Generation Z is composed of Malay ethnicity, followed by Chinese and Indian. The male population of Generation Z stands at 52% and the female 49% (Worldometers, 2020). Over the years, a decline in birth rate has resulted in smaller family size with an average household size of four people (Hirschman, 2019). Consequently, members of Generation Z live in smaller households with the fewest siblings in Malaysian history. Most of them (78%) live in urban areas (Worldometers, 2020). The statistics indicate a high literacy rate of 97% for both males and females among Generation Z in Malaysia (UNESCO, 2016).

Over the last few decades, the country has experienced economic boom and rapid development. Between 2000 and 2018, Malaysia recorded a Gross Domestic Product (GDP) annual growth rate of 4.80% which resulted in a lower poverty rate, good access to education, and improved living conditions and health (Department of Statistics Malaysia, 2019). Malaysia succeeded in drastically reducing the poverty rate from 49.3% in 1970 to 0.6% in 2018 (Department of Statistic Malaysia, 2019) through various initiatives, including The New Economic Policy and National Development Policy developed to address ethnic economic disparities and other measures, such as tax reduction strategies and financial aids (Prime Minister's Office of Malaysia, 2019). The Gini Coefficient ratio (ratio of 0 refers to equal distribution of wealth) for Malaysia shows a significant drop from 0.51 in 1970 to 0.428 in 2018 (Knoema, 2020), indicating a reduction in income inequality. However, a stable growth of GDP may not necessarily indicate a better standard of living. Beginning in the mid-2015s as a result of political instability and misconduct, the country is experiencing economic slowdown and widening economic growth disparities, impacting standard of living (Rao, 2019). The gap among the rich, middle class, and the poor is prevalent, where Malaysia is more unequal than most of its neighbouring countries in the Southeast Asian region (Ng & Tan, 2018). A sizable 40% of the 7.5 million households are classified as relatively poor (The Star, 2018a, 2018b). In addition, income disparities among the major ethnic groups have widened. Median monthly income disparities between the Malay and Chinese ethnic groups, and between the Chinese and Indian ethnic groups have increased fourfold between 1989 and 2016 (Ministry of Economic Affairs, 2019).

Although the Malaysian unemployment rate has remained stable over the last decade, youth unemployment indicates a gradual increase. In 2019, the youth unemployment rate at 10.9% represents 60% of the currently unemployed population (Malay Mail, 2019). A main criticism is of the expansion of private and public universities locally, resulting in mass production of graduates. Nearly all participants in a study commissioned by Dell Technologies on Generation Z in Malaysia indicated concerns about their lack of soft skills and job experience sought by future employers (Focus Malaysia, 2019). Although Generation Z is equipped with knowledge, there seems to be much criticism from existing employers that there is a lack of practical and problem-solving skills among this generation. Despite the government's efforts to address these issues through the Malaysian Education Blueprint 2015–2025 (Ministry of Education Malaysia, 2015), the effectiveness of the initiatives and their outcomes rely heavily on the implementation of the plan and labour market situations.

Since 1997, there has been a boom in the Malaysian telecommunication industry. Currently, the majority of households have Internet connections and own mobile phones. By 2016, 92% of the population had 3G data coverage and 64% had 4G data coverage (Lau, 2018). Generation Z is the first generation in Malaysia to be exposed to digital technologies since their earliest youth, and found to be tech-savvy and adaptive to rapid technological advancement. Parented by Generation X, who are highly educated compared to Baby Boomers, members of Generation Z are introduced to technology by their parents at a very young age. This group with 98% of Internet and 99% smartphone penetration (The Star, 2019a) are early adopters of the fast-changing technology and their lives are strongly tied to social media, with a high usage of Instagram, Snapchat, Twitter, Reddit, and related products and services.

In the political field, Malaysia experienced a historic change when the ruling party of over six decades was ousted by the opposition coalition in the 2018 general election. As they experience a transformational political era, Generation Z in Malaysia shows an increased awareness and interest in political issues. The change in the ruling party brought along several critical challenges to the government to rebuild the nation. A particular focus is to employ the youth segment, specifically Generation Z due to their size and social impact to reform the economic, political, and social situation. In 2019, the Youth Societies and Youth Development Act was passed to establish a new definition of youth by lowering the youth age range from 15 to 40 years to 15 to 30 years (The Star, 2019b). In the same year, the voting age was lowered to 18 from 21. News tabloids identify this new generation as game changers with the power to create political kingmakers as approximately 1.5 million voters from this generation were added to the voting list (The Star, 2019a). The newly elected government has since initiated various economic policies and interventions including The Shared Prosperity Vision 2030, a short-term plan to restructure a failing economy and to address widening disparities among income groups and ethnicities. The framework defines strategic initiatives and outlines policy measures for economic transformation by focussing on fostering innovation, creativity, digitalisation, and knowledge building. The success of this model demands a highly skilled knowledge-based workforce. Generation Z has begun to join the workforce. Hence, the Malaysian government initiatives focus on skill development and entrepreneurship targeting this new generation. The entrance of this cohort to the workforce is expected to intensify competition in the job market. Generation Z is driven by global aspirations with a completely different outlook than previous generations. As one of the largest segments of its population, Malaysia is largely dependent on them in building the nation.

Basics of Generation Z in Malaysia: The 4E

Malaysian Generation Z tends to be family oriented and, in general, enjoys spending time with family. The majority of them were either raised by live-in maids or grandparents (Paul, 2019), which may influence the close relationships they enjoy with their families. The family closeness and pampered living may also be explained by their unwillingness or awkwardness to interact with the outside world. Generation Z likes sheltered lives at home (Tieu, 2015) and is helped by digital connectivity. Optimum Media Direction (OMD) Malaysia named this phenomenon 'perpetual child syndrome'. In layman's term, a perpetual child can be defined as a person who is forever young. This, in turn, may make it difficult for Malaysian Generation Z to deal with stress and life pressures (The Star, 2015).

Based on an in-depth literature review, the main characteristics of Malaysian Generation Z can be summarised into 4E: Electronically engaged, Educated, Entrepreneurial, and Empowered.

Electronically Engaged

Like their global counterparts, Malaysian Generation Z is a digital native generation. With 99% smartphone ownership, they have not known life without the Internet and digital technologies (The Star, 2019c). They prefer to express their feelings via stickers or emojis, and use social media frequently (Manimaharan, 2019). The top five social media platforms among Malaysian youths are Facebook, Twitter, Pinterest, Instagram, and YouTube (Statcounter, 2020).

Malaysian young people are frequent seekers of online knowledge. Approximately 71% of Malaysian Generation Z get their news from social media, and 43% from instant messaging. Surprisingly, 44% still get their news from television (Nielsen, 2019). This digital savviness may be used to influence older family members in many ways, including doing online transactions (such as paying bills and booking an airline ticket or taxi online), connecting to others using social media (e.g. Facebook), and checking directions using Google Maps. For them, there is no difference between the digital world and the real world (Ong, 2015). They live a very digitally focussed social life and 80% of them look at one to three screens daily (Emran & Rahim, 2016) and spend an average of 8 hours a day on the Internet (Dhesi, 2018). Staying connected is important for these young people, as Generation Z has a fear of missing out (Ong, 2015).

Educated

Malaysian Generation Z places great emphasis on education and believes that it is essential for a successful life (Focus Malaysia, 2019). They have global awareness, value knowledge, and aspire to achieve higher education qualification compared to their parents. Interestingly, a study undertaken by Dimensional Research involving 724 Malaysian Generation Z found that 98% of them have used technology as part of their formal education and about 64% rated their education as excellent or good in preparing them for their future careers (The Sun Daily, 2019). Malaysian young people are characterised as active learners and are motivated to gain specific skills in specialised disciplines (The Star, 2018a). They indicate a preference for skill development via interactive and practical learning and are less inclined to traditional classroom-based approaches. They are motivated to learn outside school, aided by digital tools such as online forums and Skype.

The Malaysian Generation Z is financially literate, places a high importance on financial stability, and has learned to manage their finances (Emran & Rahim, 2016). Financial literacy comprises of knowledge and understanding of financial concepts and risks, and the necessary skills, motivation, and confidence to apply the acquired knowledge to make sound and effective decisions across a range of financial contexts (Lusardi, 2015). Financial literacy helps to improve the financial well-being of individuals and society and enables participation in economic life (Lusardi, 2015).

As consumers, financial literacy of Generation Z is likely to influence their savviness. According to Hoyt (2019), financial savviness is an important component of financial literacy, whereby young people learn to manage money and are in control of their finances. This financial savviness of Generation Z may in turn influence their consumption choices, information search and possibly modes of payment. Financial savviness is reflected in their shopping behaviour, whereby heavy emphasis is placed on value for money. For instance, a recent study, conducted by Nielsen (2019) on Malaysian Generation Z, reported that before making a purchase online, 85% of online shoppers would compare prices at physical stores and that approximately 82% would take the shipping rates into consideration before making a purchase decision.

Entrepreneurial

A study on more than 500 Malaysian Generation Z respondents showed that a significant number among them (about 31%) were interested in becoming entrepreneurs (Mariappan, 2015). Another study by the Asian Institute of Finance (The Star, 2018a, 2018b) reports an even higher proportion of Malaysian Generation Z who want to start their own business (about two-thirds of 978 respondents). This job-creator mindset (instead of job-hunter perspective) is mostly driven by monetary reasons (The Star, 2018a, 2018b). Malaysian Generation Z perceives that earning potential is much higher as an entrepreneur than working for someone else.

Empowered

In relations to the political field, Malaysian Generation Z is exposed to political instability and has been a voice to bring about the recent change in the political environment in Malaysia. Currently, the country is experiencing a transition era from an ethnically driven political environment to a political situation defined by social class. This new generation having the voting right has expressed a need for political change, freedom of speech, transparency in political moves, and policies that favour equality. The high percentage of youth population (44.7% aged between 15 and 40 years old; EPU, 2016) presents the Malaysian government with exacerbating challenges in nearly all dimensions including social, economy, and politics.

Members of Generation Z as Consumers in Malaysia: Influential and Independent

Influential and Responsible Consumers

Decision-Making Process.   Generation Z consumers in Malaysia are skilled online researchers and adept at getting any information they deem necessary. They are likely to search for new products, fresh ideas, and experiences that invoke excitement (Ong, 2015). While digital connectivity is important to Generation Z, they are found to be sceptical about information online. Since they are a better educated generation, they do not fall for hoaxes or fake news easily (Advertising & Marketing, 2015).

There has been a decline in birth and fertility rate in Malaysia, from 4.9 children per family in 1970 to 1.9 in 2017 (Department of Statistics, 2018). Due to decreased family size, the family dynamics are slightly different from previous generations, whereby these young Malaysians play an important influencer role in many household purchase contexts. Digitally popular but physically awkward, Malaysian young people are family oriented and enjoy staying at home. Their opinions are certainly valued and trusted by their parents (Curtis, 2016) resulting in high levels of confidence in buying decisions.

For Malaysian Generation Z, the family is not the only source of consumer socialisation. Other sources, such as local and international friends and celebrities, may play an important role in their lives, especially in the formation of attitudes, values, and consumption patterns. However, it is likely that instead of traditional celebrities (i.e. the likes of famous athletes or movie stars), Generation Z admires online influencers, such as YouTubers, bloggers, and social activists. Many of these online idols have become brand ambassadors due to their number of followers (Dhesi, 2018). For instance, 21-year-old Sharifah Rose, a Malaysian model and influencer, has garnered over 500,000 followers and is considered an Instagram star (Famousbirthdays.com). Other young Malaysians, like college students Joey Leong and Naddy Rahman, have 275 and 109 thousand followers, respectively, on Instagram (Pandorabox.com, 2018). These young beauty, travel, and lifestyle bloggers influence the consumption choices of many and are often sought after by brands like Dior, Fave, Dove, and Dah Makan for reviews and endorsements.

Responsible Consumption

Malaysian Generation Z show great concern for social and environmental issues. Nielsen's Global Corporate Sustainability Report (Nielsen, 2015), for instance, found that about 69% of 513 young Malaysians stated that they were willing to pay a premium price for products and services from companies committed to sustainable practices. The same report also shows that more than 40% of 513 young Malaysian respondents claimed that they support products with environmentally friendly packages and that are produced by companies with a good reputation in sustainable practices.

In a recent study on Generation Z and green purchases, Noor, Jumain, Yusof, Ahmat, and Kamaruzaman (2017) reported that attitudes towards green activities, subjective norms, perceived green knowledge, and social visibility are positive influences on green purchase decisions among Malaysian Generation Z. They also found that members of Generation Z in Malaysia are aware of environmental concerns and display a keen willingness to participate in a green lifestyle, which includes the purchase and consumption of environmentally friendly products. Additionally, the young people also hold a positive attitude towards green activities and are influenced by family and peers in the development of green attitudes and potential purchase decisions.

In another study of natural beauty product purchases, Ahmad, Omar, and Hassan (2016) found that environmental consciousness is the key determinant of purchase intentions among Malaysian Generation Z. The influence of environmental consciousness was higher than three other personal values investigated, i.e. health consciousness, appearance consciousness, and need for uniqueness.

Shopping Behaviour

Buying Power and Habits.   As an upper middle-income country (GDP per capita amounted to US$29,100 in 2017; CIA, 2019), Malaysian purchasing power is among the highest in Asia (Santandertrade, 2019). For Malaysian Generation Z alone, monthly disposable income is estimated to reach US$327 million (Tieu, 2015), which has increased by approximately 23% in 2019 (The Star, 2019c). This is attractive for marketers of a wide range of products and services, ranging from fashion, food, and electronics to educational and telecommunication services.

Rising wealth and education levels account for the changing consumer lifestyle in Malaysia. Although Malaysian consumers are price sensitive, they are at the same time brand-conscious, look for quality products, and prefer global brands to local ones (Santandertrade, 2019). One of the most typical Malaysian consumer behaviours, including among Generation Z, is that they like to spend their spare money for holidays or vacations and for buying new technology products (Nielsen, 2018; Santandertrade, 2019). Family trips are very common among Malaysians, especially those from middle- and upper-income families (Lau, 2018). Another consumer behaviour trend to watch is the growing preference for online shopping, especially among those aged under 30 (Santandertrade, 2019).

Social Media and Online Shopping.   By 2017, more than 78% of the Malaysian population used the Internet (CIA, 2019; Santandertrade, 2019). In fact, Malaysia has been considered as one of the Southeast Asian Internet-native countries with huge e-business opportunities (an estimate of US1.1 billion in 2017) (Aditya, 2017). A recent study conducted by Picodi (Tan, 2019) provides four interesting insights about online shopping habits in Malaysia: (1) more women than men make online purchases (58% vs. 42%); (2) the majority of online shoppers are from the young generation, i.e. people aged between 25 and 34 (51%) and between 18 and 24 (24%); (3) the most popular products purchased online by Malaysians include food delivery, travel, clothing, cosmetics, and sports, with the average order value of US$41, and (4) most of the transactions are made on computers (68%), followed by smartphones (31%) and tablets (1%). Online purchases via smartphones are estimated to grow significantly and will be the dominant device in the near future (Free Malaysia Today, 2018; Tan, 2019).

In a global survey of more than 22,000 consumers across 27 countries, PricewaterhouseCoopers (PwC) showed that social media influence more than half of Malaysian consumers in their online and in-store shopping activities (Free Malaysia Today, 2018). Another study by VASE.AI revealed that Malaysians spend an average of 5 hours on social media daily and get the inspiration to buy something when they are surfing social media (Aditya, 2017). They usually consider online reviews and electronic word-of-mouth communications posted on Facebook, Instagram, Pinterest, Twitter, YouTube, Tumblr, and other platforms when making purchases.

In terms of media consumption, Malaysian Generation Z consumes less TV, radio, and print media. As an implication, they are one of the hardest cohorts to impress with advertising according to Kantar Millward Brown's AdReaction study (Digital News Asia, 2017). The same study found several interesting findings about Generation Z in Southeast Asia, including Malaysia: (1) they are not interested in any advertisements longer than ten seconds; (2) a growing number of them have used ad blocking software on their desktops (about 23%) and smartphones (about 18%); (3) they are more receptive towards skippable pre-rolls and mobile rewards videos; (4) they love ads with humour, interesting stories, and music; and (5) they are not impressed with the use of celebrity endorsement in ads. These findings suggest that Malaysian Generation Z needs a sense of control and a more personalised communication from marketers.

The Return of Brick and Mortar Shopping?   Cheung, Glass, Haller, and Wong (2018, p. 1) were right in highlighting that 'Generation Z shoppers are full of surprises'. Despite the fact that Malaysian Generation Z is highly digitally active, they still have a strong interest in bricks and mortar shopping (i.e. shopping at physical stores that offer products and services to customers face-to-face; Chen & Murphy, 2019). Two separate studies by Fluent Commerce (Swain-Wilson, 2018) and PricewaterhouseCoopers (PwC) (Free Malaysia Today, 2018) consistently found this phenomenon, including in Malaysia. Malaysian Generation Z enjoys visiting malls, especially for purchasing fashion, food, and entertainment products, as well as hanging out with their families or friends. With more than 50 big shopping malls (about half of which are located in Kuala Lumpur), Malaysia is one of the shoppers' favourite destinations (Wonderful Malaysia, 2017). In fact, one of the 10 biggest shopping malls in the world is 1 Utama Shopping Centre, situated in Damansara, Petaling Jaya, with a gross leasable area of 4.9 million square feet (World Atlas, 2019).

Generation Z at Work in Malaysia: Curious, Caring, Competent, and Confident

Who are 'They' in the Workplace?

Malaysian Generation Z is open-minded and curious. They are willing to take work challenges as long as they think they are worthwhile. According to a study of the Asian Institute of Finance (February 27, 2018), Generation Z employees are willing to sacrifice immediate pleasures for a greater future reward (Asian Institute of Finance (AIF), 2018). This finding indicates that this new generation may behave differently compared to Generation Y in Malaysia, who is associated with the need for instant gratification.

In another study conducted in Malaysia among 250 Generation Z students between the ages of 11 and 17, and 100 teachers in the country (New Straits Times, 2018), 96% of Generation Z respondents believed that their future careers will need creativity, and the current education focussing on computers and technology may sharpen their creativity and best prepare them for their future careers (New Straits Times, 2018). They feel confident that they possess the technology skills that employers demand (Dell Technology, 2018).

Malaysian Generation Z is not satisfied with just following instructions and completing a to-do list. They like to be involved in innovative tasks and want to feel like they are challenging themselves to develop new solutions to problems (Deep Patel, 2017). In a study among 500 individuals from Generation Z in Malaysia, 42% of respondents reported that they want to do something completely new when making career choices, 37% hope to turn their hobbies into a profession, and 31% want to start their own business (INTI International University, 2015).

Expectations

Generation Z in Malaysia values a work–life balance that allows them to plan time for their personal life and work (AIF, 2018). According to Bresman and Rao (2017), Generation Z may turn away from leadership roles or the entire job if they find there is an imbalance in their work and life.

A global study of 724 Malaysian Generation Z from August to September 2018 (Dell Technology, 2018) found them to be more concerned about whether the organisation that they work at is socially or environmentally responsible compared to those in many other countries in the study. Companies which are more socially or environmentally responsible tend to have more corporate social responsibility (CSR) events or have more concerns about the eco-friendly environment at the work place. Forty-seven per cent of Malaysians as compared to 38%, of all respondents from 17 countries (i.e. United States, Canada, Brazil, United Kingdom, France, Germany, Turkey, Australia or New Zealand, and eight Asian countries including Malaysia), expressed that they would like to work for an organisation that is socially or environmentally responsible (Dell Technology, 2018).

Behaviour in Companies

Communication.   Generation Z in Malaysia prefers talking to co-workers in person rather than texting or e-mailing (Dell Technology, 2018). They would like to consult fellow employees in a fixed physical office when they need to do something at their job for the very first time. This young generation values the opportunities to actually sit and talk with their colleagues and superiors. This gives them a chance to ask questions and voice their opinions. Furthermore, they are concerned that communication via e-mail may not accurately convey the message, there is a lack of interaction and they are not able to get immediate feedback. In addition, Generation Z in Malaysia is aware of missing updates because of insufficient interaction among the peers.

Digitalisation at Workplace.   Many higher learning education institutions in Malaysia are using e-learning portals such as Moodle, Blackboard, and E-learn in education courses; therefore, most of Generation Z have used technology substantially at school, such as online learning, laptops, and smartphones. Generation Z perceives literacy on technology and digitalisation as an important matter in their future career. When Malaysian Generation Z was asked to give their opinion on whether they were interested in working with cutting-edge technology when they enter the workforce, almost all of the Malaysian respondents (94% male; 88% female) replied 'yes' to this question (Dell Technology, 2018).

As Generation Z has a natural affinity with digital technologies, they can adapt themselves in the working environment with digitalisation. In addition, they will be highly adaptable and confident of dealing with change in digital technologies (AIF, 2018). They are also willing to mentor other colleagues who are not used to advanced technology. In the study of Dell Technology (2018), 80% of 724 Malaysian respondents from Generation Z noted that they would be comfortable mentoring an older co-worker who needs help in using the technology. They may call themselves a 'digital ambassador' at their workplace, who is technology-savvy and willing to be responsible for learning and promoting new technology to other co-workers.

Relationships with the Team.   When Generation Z was asked about the work skills that they expect their employers to value most in their employees, close to half of the Malaysian respondents (46%) think that teamwork and collaboration are what they expect (AIF, 2018). Therefore, clear face-to-face communication is important to their future career. As they value relationships with co-workers and participation in discussion at the workplace, it is important that they are invited to participate in project meetings rather than just to communicate via e-mails or messages.

Leadership/Entrepreneurship.   Generation Z in Malaysia inherited many resources and information earlier in life by way of the Internet: this gives them more signs of being more entrepreneurial. However, as they value relationships with co-workers, sometimes as a leader they may feel uncomfortable solving conflict pertaining to ethics and principles at the workplace if these are not clearly defined. They may be worried about the consequences of the failure in their leadership and communication with colleagues (AIF, 2018).

When mentioning entrepreneurship, about 63% of Generation Z in Malaysia shared that they plan to start their own business either on a full-time or part-time basis (The Star, 2018a). The AIF also reported that about two-thirds of the technology savvy Generation Z in Malaysia are interested in starting their own business providing they have gained sufficient work experience and have accumulated enough capital in their current job. These findings indicate that this generation prefers to be an entrepreneur than just an employee in a company over the longer period. They may start their career development by looking for a job with stable income and some professional development opportunities. Once they have obtained sufficient knowledge and skills to start their own business, they may be keen to become their own boss with their own savings as the start-up capital. This shows that these people have a strong sense of self-reliance and are more realistic.

Nevertheless, in Malaysia, the idea of becoming entrepreneurs does not totally contradict employment, meaning that the Generation Z does not need to quit their full-time job to become entrepreneurs. Some Generation Z intend to become an entrepreneur because it can be a good source of additional income to supplement their full-time job (AIF, 2018). Therefore, Generation Z in Malaysia might be both an employee and entrepreneur at the same time with longer working hours. Besides running their own business, Generation Z in Malaysia is also interested in overseas employment, with Singapore, Australia, and the United Kingdom as the top destinations (AIF, 2018).

How to Deal with Generation Z in Malaysia: Let them Lead the World

Dealing with the Future Consumers in Malaysia

Similar to their global peers, members of Generation Z in Malaysia are digitally savvy and have easy access to global information. Being socially conscious consumers implies that marketers must align themselves with social issues and demonstrate their corporate social responsibility. A number of options are available here, from being environmentally friendly to reducing overconsumption of clothes, for instance, or discouraging wastage of food. These would enhance the corporate image of the companies in the long run. Supporting social causes such as the refugee crisis in Malaysia or supporting underprivileged or abused children is also likely to be welcomed by Generation Z. In short, marketers need to stand for a cause. Such support is likely to garner strong brand loyalty and generate favourable e-word of mouth among these young consumers.

To create and retain a loyal customer base, firms need to be digitally savvy and remain accessible. Digital connectivity is important to the target market as they are afraid of losing out. Using the right digital platforms and digital strategy is important to communicate effectively. For example, Hada Labo, a Japanese beauty brand, engaged its most passionate audience (between the ages of 18 and 34) by using YouTube to catch up with their digital customers. In comparison to its competitors, Hada Labo lacked brand awareness in the Malaysian market.

The beauty brand ran a 100% digital campaign to launch a new line of body lotion. Within 4 weeks of launch, the campaign garnered 1.7 million views, recorded a lower cost per view by 40%, increased brand awareness, and recorded a 40% year-on-year sales growth for the brand (Think with Google (thinkwith-google.com), 2018). Additionally, it is imperative that marketers promise and deliver value for money by using promotions such as cash back or larger rewards from loyalty programs and shorter delivery times for online purchases. It is very likely that the use of Artificial Intelligence, robotics, and Virtual Reality will be widespread in the next few years, thus, keeping abreast of changes in the digital era and adapting to such changes are essential to survive in the current and future marketplace.

What Next?

Each new generation has its own uniqueness. Then, how to deal with Generation Z in Malaysia? The answer may refer to a relevant quote from a popular song 'Greatest Love of All' (performed by Whitney Houston): '*I believe the children are our future. Teach them well and let them lead the way*'. If we believe that Generation Z is our future, then we must provide the best possible education to them and provide them a chance to lead the way as future consumers, workers, and entrepreneurs.

References

Aditya. (2017). Report: 2017 *Online shopping trends in Malaysia*. Retrieved from https://vase.ai/resources/2017onlineshoppingtrends/

Advertising & Marketing. (2015, November 6). *What does it mean to be Gen Z in Malaysia?* Retrieved from http://www.marketing-interaction.com/mean-gen-z-Malaysia/

AIF (Asian Institute of Finance). (2018). *Tomorrow's professionals: Generation Z in Malaysia*. Kuala Lumpur: Asian Institute of Finance.

Ahmad, S. N. B., Omar, A., & Hassan, S. H. (2016). Influence of personal values on generation Z's purchase intention toward natural beauty products. *e-Journal of Economics and Management Science*, 2, 1–11.

Bresman. H., & Rao, V. (2017). *What generations X, Y and Z want from leadership*. Retrieved from https://knowledge.insead.edu/leadership-organisations/what-generations-x-y-and-z-want-from-leadership-5716

Chen, J., & Murphy, C. B. (2019). *Brick and mortar*. Retrieved from https://www.investopedia.com/terms/b/brickandmortar.asp

Cheung, J., Glass, S., Haller, K., & Wong, C. K. (2018). *What do Gen Z shoppers really want? Retail essentials and customized experiences top their list*. Armonk, NY: IBM Corporation.

CIA. (2019). *The world factbook: Malaysia*. Retrieved from https://www.cia.gov/library/publications/resources/the-world-factbook/geos/my.html

Curtis, L. (2016). *What brands need to know about Gen Z in Malaysia*. Retrieved from https://www.decisionlab.co/blog/malaysia-what-brands-need-to-know-about-generation-z

Deep Patel. (2017). *Why transparency is the key to integrating Generation Z in the workplace*. Retrieved from https://www.forbes.com/sites/deeppatel/2017/09/22/why-transparency-is-the-key-to-integrating-generation-z-in-the-workplace/#ce7247225fed

Dell Technology. (2018). *Gen Z: The future has arrived*. Retrieved from https://www.delltechnologies.com/en-us/perspectives/gen-z.htm#

Department of Statistics Malaysia. (2018). *Population and demography*. Retrieved from https://www.dosm.gov.my/

Department of Statistics Malaysia. (2019). *Population and demography*. Retrieved from https://www.dosm.gov.my/v1/

Dhesi, D. (2018). *Engaging with Gen Z on digital platforms*. Retrieved from https://www.thestar.com.my/business/business-news/2018/09/08/engaging-generation-z-on-digital-platforms/

Digital News Asia. (2017). *Gen Z in Southeast Asia are growing up and hard to impress: Study*. Retrieved from https://www.digitalnewsasia.com/digital-economy/gen-z-southeast-asia-are-growing-and-hard-impress-study

EPU (Economic Planning Unit). (2016). *Eleventh Malaysia plan (2016–2020)*. Retrieved from http://epu.gov.my/en/rmk/eleventh-malaysia-plan-2016-2020

Emran, M. N., & Rahim, A. (2016). *Gen Z defined*. Retrieved from https://www.delltechnologies.com/en-us/perspectives/gen-z.htm/

Focus Malaysia. (2019). *Gen Z expect a digital workplace, but value...* Retrieved from http://www.focusmalaysia.my/All/gen-z-expect-a-digital-workplace-but-value

Free Malaysia Today. (2018). *More than half of Malaysians guided by social media when shopping*. Retrieved from https://www.freemalaysiatoday.com/category/nation/2018/03/13/more-than-half-of-malaysians-guided-by-social-media-when-shopping/

Hirschmann, R. (2019). *Average household size in Malaysia from 2016 to 2019*. Retrieved from https://www.statista.com/statistics/1047856/malaysia-average-household-size/

Hoyt, E. (2019). *The 5 key components of financial literacy*. Retrieved from https://www.fastweb.com/student-life/articles/the-5-key-components-of-financial-literacy

INTI International University. (2015). *INTI International University conducts survey on Gen Z in Malaysia*. Retrieved from https://www.laureate.net/ournetwork/asiapacific/malaysia/intiinternationaluniversitycolleges/content/public/announcement contentfolder/2015/03/inti-international-university-conducts-survey-on-gen-z-in-malaysia

Knoema. (2020). *Malaysia – GINI index*. Retrieved from https://knoema.com/atlas/Malaysia/topics/Poverty/Income-Inequality/GINI-index

Lau, L. (2018). *A closer look at Gen Y and Z in Malaysia*. Retrieved from https://leadero-nomics.com/career/gen-y-z-malaysia

Lusardi, A. (2015). Financial literacy skills for the 21st century: Evidence from PISA. *Journal of Consumer Affairs, 49*(3), 639–659.

Malay Mail. (2019). *Malaysia faces youth unemployment crisis*. Retrieved from https://www.malaymail.com/news/what-you-think/2019/09/10/malaysia-faces-youth-unemployment-crisis-murray-hunter/1789238

Manimaharan, K. (2019). *Young Malaysians lack financial knowledge: How true is that?* Retrieved from https://wma.my/business/finance/young-malaysians-lack-financial-knowledge-how-true-is-that/

Mariappan, T. (2015). *55 per cent of Malaysia's Gen Z addicted to gadgets*. Retrieved from http://english.astroawani.com/malaysia-news/55-cent-malaysias-gen-z-addicted-gadgets-57746

Ministry of Economic Affairs. (2019). *Summary: Shared Prosperity Vision 2030*. Retrieved from https://www.pmo.gov.my/wp-content/uploads/2019/10/SPV2030-summary-en.pdf

Ministry of Education Malaysia. (2015). *Malaysian education blueprint 2015–2025 (Higher Education*. Retrieved from https://www.um.edu.my/docs/default-source/

about-um_document/media-centre/um-magazine/4-executive-summary-pppm-2015-2025.pdf?sfvrsn=4

New Straits Times. (2018a). *Gen Z sees creativity as key to success.* Retrieved from https//www.nst.com.my/education/2018/01/323612/gen-z-sees-creativity-key-success

New Straits Times. (2018). *M'sia's fertility rate drops to lowest level ever recorded.* Retrieved from https://www.nst.com.my/news/nation/2018/08/401862/msias-fertility-rate-drops-lowest-level-ever-recorded

Nielsen. (2015). *Sustainability continues to gain momentum among Malaysian consumers.* Retrieved from https://www.nielsen.com/my/en/insights/news/2015/sustainability-continues-gaining-momentum-among-malaysians.html

Nielsen. (2018). *Malaysian consumers among the world's most confident in Q2 2018.* Retrieved from https://www.nielsen.com/my/en/insights/news/2018/malaysian-consumers-among-the-worlds-most-confident-in-q2-2018.html

Nielsen. (2019). *Understanding Malaysia's Gen Z… and how to reach them.* Retrieved from https://www.nielsen.com/my/en/insights/article/2019/understanding-malaysias-gen-z/

Ng, A., & Tan, K. M. (2018). *Improving income inequality: fact or fiction?* Retrieved from http://www.krinstitute.org/Views-@-Improving_Income_Inequality-;_Fact_or_Fiction%5E.aspx

Noor, M. N. M., Jumain, R. S. A., Yusof, A., Ahmat, M. A., & Kamaruzaman, F. (2017). Determinants of generation Z green purchase decisions: A SEM-PLS approach. *International Journal of Advanced and Applied Sciences, 4*(11), 143–147.

Ong, A. (2015). *7 fun facts you weren't sure about Malaysian Gen Z youth, until now.* Retrieved from https://says.com/my/fun/gen-z-the-age-of-giving-back-and-oversharing-in-a-research-by-inti

Pandorabox.com (2018). *Top 10 most gorgeous sexy Malaysian students.* Retrieved from https://pandorabox.com.my/2018/12/07/top-10-most-gorgeous-sexy-malaysian-students/

Paul, S. (2019). *From baby boomers to Gen Z: Here's a breakdown of when each generation begins and ends.* Retrieved from https://says.com/my/lifestyle/the-differences-between-generations-in-malaysia

Prime Minister's Office of Malaysia. (2019). *Economic development.* Retrieved from https://www.pmo.gov.my/2019/07/economic-developments/

Rao, M. (2019). *Tackling income disparities in Malaysia.* Retrieved from https://themalaysianreserve.com/2019/10/24/tackling-income-disparities-in-malaysia/

Santandertrade. (2019). *Malaysia: Reaching the consumer.* Retrieved from https://en.portal.santandertrade.com/analyse-markets/malaysia/reaching-the-consumers

Statcounter. (2020). *Social media stats Malaysia.* Retrieved from https://gs.statcounter.com/social-media-stats/all/malaysia

Swain-Wilson, S. (2018). *10 ways Gen Zs spend money differently than their Gen X parents.* Retrieved from https://www.thisisinsider.com/gen-z-vs-gen-x-spending-habits-2018-11

Tan, H. H. (2019). *Interesting facts about the shopping habits of Malaysian internet users.* Retrieved from https://www.minimeinsights.com/2019/03/20/interesting-facts-about-the-shopping-habits-of-malaysian-internet-users/

The Star. (2015). *OMD and partners unveil study on Gen Z.* Retrieved from https://www.thestar.com.my/business/business-news/2015/07/11/omd-and-partners-unveil-study-on-gen-z/

The Star. (2018a). *Two-thirds of Gen Z in Malaysia want to start own business.* Retrieved from https://www.thestar.com.my/business/business-news/2018/03/06/two-thirds-of-gen-z-in-malaysia-want-to-start-own-business/#ItGhKOfSE64PSK8Z.99

The Star. (2018b). *Study: Malaysia's income gap doubled in two decades*. Retrieved from https://www.thestar.com.my/news/nation/2018/10/15/study-malaysias-income-gap-doubled-in-two-decades/#V2t4mGe1mY70BLL7.99

The Star. (2019a). *Report: Gen Z to be a game changer*. Retrieved from https://www.thestar.com.my/news/nation/2019/07/10/report-gen-z-to-be-a-game-changer

The Star. (2019b). *Giving Malaysian youth movement new energy*. Retrieved from https://www.thestar.com.my/opinion/letters/2019/07/12/giving-malaysian-youth-movement-new-energy

The Star. (2019c). *Cryptic lives of Malaysia's Gen Z decoded*. Retrieved from https://www.thestar.com.my/business/business-news/2019/12/02/cryptic-lives-of-malaysias-gen-z-decoded

The Sun Daily. (2019). *Trailblazers of the future*. Retrieved from https://www.thesundaily.my/supplement/graduate/trailblazers-of-the-future-DF601555

Think with Google. (2018). *Malaysia's traditional businesses use YouTube to catch up to their digital customers*. Retrieved from https://www.thinkwithgoogle.com/intl/en-apac/ad-channel/video/malaysias-traditional-businesses-use-youtube-catch-their-digital-customers/

Tieu, B. (2015). *Reaching out to Malaysia's digitally savvy Gen Z*. Retrieved from http://digitalmarket.asia/reaching-out-to-malaysias-digitally-savvy-gen-z/

Tourism Malaysia. (2019). *Malaysia truly Asia*. Retrieved from https://www.tourism.gov.my/campaigns/view/malaysia-truly-asia

UNESCO. (2016). Malaysia. Retrieved from http://uis.unesco.org/en/country/my

Wonderful Malaysia. (2017). *Shopping in Malaysia*. Retrieved from http://www.wonderfulmalaysia.com/shopping-malls-malaysia.htm

World Atlas. (2019). *The biggest shopping malls in the world*. Retrieved from https://www.worldatlas.com/articles/the-biggest-shopping-malls-in-the-world.html

Worldometers. (2020). *Malaysia demographics*. Retrieved from https://www.worldometers.info/demographics/malaysia-demographics/

Part V

What the Experts Tell Us about Western Asia

Chapter 11

Generation Z in Turkey: A Generation with High Hopes and Big Fears

Berna Tarı-Kasnakoğlu, Meltem Türe and Yunus Kalender

Abstract

This chapter provides fresh insight into the lives of Generation Z in Turkey, who are described as the generation born after 1995. The chapter uses secondary information harvested from academic and popular literature, and national statistics. In addition, results from a quantitative survey conducted among 237 Generation Z members in Turkey and insights gathered from a qualitative study based on semi-structured interviews performed with 12 individuals from Generation Z have been utilised. Understanding Generation Z in Turkey is challenging because the effects of fast digitalisation, cultural globalisation, and new challenges in attaining high-quality education and finding good jobs are not yet fully known. This chapter offers insights on Turkish Generation Z, including but not limited to their (1) future-orientation, (2) multipolarity of selves, (3) identity as consumers, and (4) perceived challenges regarding future work life.

Keywords: Generation Z; Turkey; digitalisation; globalisation; consumers; work

Introduction: A Future-oriented Generation

By 2018, more than 32 million of the Turkish population was under 25-years old, with a little more than 19 million in the 10 to 24-year-old age group. In Turkey, young people born after 1995 (Generation Z) are different in attitudes and behaviour compared to other generations (Kuyucu, 2017; Tuna, 2002). However, there is only scant knowledge on Generation Z in the country (Kavalcı & Ünal, 2016; Özkan & Solmaz, 2015). Located between Europe and Asia, Turkey is a diverse

The New Generation Z in Asia: Dynamics, Differences, Digitalisation
The Changing Context of Managing People, 167–179
Copyright © 2020 by Emerald Publishing Limited
All rights of reproduction in any form reserved
doi:10.1108/978-1-80043-220-820201017

society with a rich history, currently hosting more than 82 million people. The country's ceaseless quest for modernisation and yearnings for tradition accompanied by rapid industrialisation and recent waves of immigration have shifted Turkish socio-cultural, economic, and consumption scenes. Below we provide a brief glance at these domains.

Economy and General Outlook

According to the General Directorate of Budget and Fiscal Control, in 2017, the country's GDP is more than three trillion Turkish Liras with per capita income of 38,680 TL (10,602 Dollars). Turkey is considered as an emergent economy facing rapid changes and an uncertain geo-political situation. Thus, Turkey is consistently in the league of the 'Fragile Five' – a group of countries whose emerging economies are too dependent on foreign investment for growth (Kuepper, 2018).

Yet, Turkey has a high potential for economic growth. According to the Turkish Statistical Institute (Turkish Statistical Institute (TurkStat), 2019), the majority of Turkish people, including 59.85% of the younger population (i.e. TurkStat surveys usually focus on young people from 18 to 24-year-olds, which covers some but not all Generation Z in Turkey), expect the economy to be stable or change for the positive in the next 5 years, revealing a hopeful outlook for the future.

General Values and Norms

The modern/traditional dichotomy has prominently shaped Turkish society's collective consciousness, nurturing its values and norms, and unfurling other dichotomies of urban/rural, religious/secular, and global/local (Kandiyoti, 2002). According to recent research by Konda, Research and Consultancy (2017), among Turkish people older than 18 years old, 26% define themselves as modern, 46% as traditional conservative, and 28% as religious conservative.

Traditions, religion, and family life are still central to Turkish identities (Keyman, 2007). According to life satisfaction and social prestige surveys, more than 74% of the Turkish population regards family as the main sources of happiness while, for more than 35%, having a good family life is the main indicator of social prestige (TurkStat, 2019). Following a similar pattern, young people believe that having a good family life (nearly 40%) and a moral life code (26%) are the main reasons for gaining social acceptability and prestige in Turkey (TurkStat, 2019). While the recent political developments seem to nurture a conservative social and political stance for Turkish people – especially for upper and middle classes living in urban centres – economic modernism reflected by access to modern consumption goods is also very important (Kandiyoti, 2002). By 2018, nearly 92% of the population in the 10–24-year-old age group (nearly 18 million) was registered in the urban city centres while only 8% of this young population lived in rural areas (TurkStat, 2019) with less access to shopping centres, other consumption venues and socio-cultural activities as we will discuss below.

Basics of Generation Z in Turkey: Multipolarity of Selves

A Need to Understand Generation Z in Turkey: Two New Studies

To obtain more insights on Generation Z in Turkey, we conducted two new studies. In our qualitative study, we interviewed 12 high-school and junior university students, whose age ranged between 16 and 24. Seven participants were female, three of them were from a lower socio-economic background, and four of them were high school students. All interviews are conducted and analysed in anonymity, where all names are kept confidential.

We also conducted a quantitative survey among a sample of 237 young people from Generation Z in Turkey. The quantitative sample consisted of 60% female and 40% male participants with an average monthly household income of 7,634 Turkish Liras (1,204 Euros). Their ages ranged from 15 to 23, with a mean of 19.32. Forty-one per cent of them were still going to high school and 20% were high-school graduates, while 39% were mostly the first- or second-year college students.

While the survey provided us with diverse perspectives about Generation Z, the interviews helped us comprehend their deeper motivations, thoughts, and feelings, enriching the survey results. All findings are presented in an integrated way as suggested for a mixed-method research approach (Bazeley, 2018). The data from our survey, interviews, and/or secondary sources are presented without following a pre-defined order and, instead, to best illustrate each argument or explanation in each section.

Consumption Patterns

Our survey and interviews reveal that Generation Z has an intense desire for a high-paying job and is willing to invest in a professional career path, as represented by an increased demand for higher education. For example:

> [...]*I can spend money for more education whatsoever. I also want a good job providing me with the good life that I believe I deserve. I would be willing to spend my own money for good education for a future job that pays well.* [M24, university student, interview]

This result aligns with the findings of the TurkStat's (2019) household budget survey, which shows that the individual households' expenditure for education has increased over the last decade. Young people are increasingly attending graduate schools to receive Masters or PhD degrees, probably to put themselves ahead of the competition in the job market and enhance their chances of going abroad for or after their studies.

Aside from education, Turkish consumption has been nurtured by the government's neo-liberal policies since the 1980s and has experienced a global flow of consumption goods (Özman & Coşar, 2007). Turkish people are usually fast to adopt personal electronics and communication technologies. A recent study further shows that compared to older people, Turkish youth attribute more positive meanings to smart phones and, therefore, are more dependent on these tools (Kuyucu, 2017). Members of Turkish Generation Z show an increasing interest in fashion and culture domains. According to the TurkStat (2019), young people (aged 18–24) report more interest (about 49%) in fashion and relevant domains compared to the whole population, which has a low level of interest in these domains.

Internet and Social Media Usage

As of January 2019, Turkey is the fourth country in the world with nine million active Twitter users (Statista, 2019). Specifically, 65% of young Turkish people (18–29) stated that they use the social networking sites for daily news (Pew Research Center, 2018). In line with the general statistics, the results from our quantitative study among 237 Turkish young people reveal that Generation Z in Turkey uses social media very frequently. About 64.1% of the respondents stated that they follow people on social media (with a mean score above 3 out of 5 points), and 75.3% stated that they like looking at photos on social media. For the members of Generation Z in our survey, social media is the third 'place' they spend their time after home and school. They seem to like a variety of social media platforms, with almost 80% of our respondents naming Instagram, Twitter, and YouTube as the most frequently used ones, followed by Reddit, Facebook, Pinterest, and LinkedIn.

A recent study conducted by Sarıtaş and Barutçu (2016) found that Generation X and Generation Y in Turkey use social media mostly for research, collaboration, and fun, while Generation Z uses it mainly for establishing and maintaining social relationships. Our survey expands this insight by revealing that Generation Z in Turkey heavily uses Instagram and Twitter to mostly follow comments and photos on social media, while restraining from making comments personally. These insights hint that Generation Z in Turkey relies on social media platforms that allow them to, probably more visually than verbally, build relationships and communicate within their networks.

Spare Time and Values

Our survey reveals that Generation Z spends a lot time with friends and family (63 points in total out of 100), mostly chatting (29 points) and sharing their day. Generation Z also spends a lot of time studying (24 points), which is not surprising since they spend most of their time at school and training with tutors or in private classes to enhance their chance of getting into a good college. For the participants in our survey, entertainment is another major part of their daily time (21 points), which also aligns with TurkStat's (2019) findings that the 10–25-year-old group spends a lot of time watching TV and listening to music.

It is worth emphasising that after school and home, members of Generation Z in Turkey spend most of their time on social media, and less time in shopping malls, outdoors, or at friends' houses. This could indicate a virtualisation of social life and entertainment for Turkish Generation Z, probably in line with their global counterparts. Different from a decade ago, for today's Turkish youth, Internet cafes and game centres are losing their popularity. After they first appeared in Turkey in 1995, Internet cafes had been very popular among young and middle-aged Turkish people. The strict regulation of Internet cafes, increase of cheaper Internet access to households, and proliferation of smart phones and other mobile devices for on-the-go connection have made Internet cafes relatively obsolete for young people in Turkey. Moreover, regular cafes, restaurants, and shopping malls usually provide WiFi service, replacing Internet cafes with more interesting and convenient alternatives.

When it comes to the life values most important for Generation Z, our survey reveals a hierarchy as follows: freedom, followed by success, respect, justice, knowledge, happiness, love, courage, and inner peace. Fame, courtesy, rank, adventure, loyalty, society, and spirituality are the least valued for Generation Z. That is, values such as courtesy or spirituality are not perceived as important to Generation Z in Turkey. One potential explanation of this result is that in a country where religion is considered by many as an important identity marker and a basic regulator of private life (Keyman, 2007), such values might be perceived as secondary. Instead, Generation Z prioritises more the values that can be directly 'applied' in their lives, such as success and knowledge, which will more concretely help them get a good job as they desire.

To see whether and how these values interact with each other, we ran a factor analysis on our quantitative data with all 40 values. Results indicate that success and power are combined together as the so-called 'potency' factor, implying that Generation Z in Turkey sees success as an important condition for achieving power. Religion and love are combined negatively with freedom, indicating that Generation Z perceives both religion and love as restrictive forces that would prevent them from fully experiencing their freedom. Love is also negatively loaded onto success and power factors, indicating that Turkish Generation Z might see career/success and love as different domains with conflicting requirements. The third main factor includes happiness as negatively correlated with wisdom, constituting a possible 'ignorance is bliss' component for Turkish Generation Z.

Dreams and Fears

Our survey reveals that for Generation Z in Turkey, success at school could only partially determine their success in life (mean=2.41 out of 5), while success at work will influence more their life-long achievements (mean=3.02). This seems to contradict Generation Z's quest for better education. High schoolers in Turkey, however, are required to take the higher education exam to go to university (Council of Higher Education, 2019), which is perceived as *the* obstacle they need to overcome before they can start their 'real' education (Ekici, 2005). In Turkey, children start school at the age of 6 and preschool at 5, leading to a 12-year education marathon before the higher education entry exam (Ministry of National Education, 2019). This process creates anxiety and cynicism among young people who are anxious to beat the competition for the limited university quotas and need to 'rush to find a job'. Consider this script from a university student who is preparing to take the exam a second time:

> *For me, this exam is like a nightmare. It is like this "level boss" [a gaming term that refers to a computer-controlled enemy the gamers need to beat to finalize the stage] at the end of [high] school. You think it's over, but it's not ... At high school, you just go to the school and go back home and it goes on like this until you enter the university entrance exam. Your destiny is squeezed in those 3–4 hours during the exam.* [F20, university student, interview].

Competition for higher education and the exam labelled as 'winning the university' is severe. Moreover, in Turkey, the annual unemployment rate has been declared as 11% in 2018 (TurkStat, 2019). In line with this, more than 47% of the 18–24-year-olds are pessimistic about the prospects of finding a good job in the upcoming years.

Political Attitudes and Social Opinions

According to Saktanber and Beşpınar (2012), since the 1990s, Turkish youth has been considered as the most important party for the wellbeing of the country. Yet, in Turkey, where half of the whole population reports low or no interest in political issues, only 46% of the politically active Generation Z (the 18–24-year-old group) report any real interest in politics (TurkStat, 2019).The analysis of our survey data regarding political attitudes, however, presents a slightly different picture as almost 55% of our respondents stated that they are highly attentive to political developments in Turkey, with 52% being attentive to global political issues. Moreover, 42% stated that they feel personally close to one political ideology. While only 7% of our survey respondents declare that there is not much to criticise in Turkey, the rest is more critical.

Some background information on the recent Turkish political scene might be helpful to explain these differing results. As of 2019, Turkey has been ruled by the same government (Justice and Development Party [AK Parti]) for the last 17 years. Among the important political developments during this time were: the 2008 movement when the alleged members of a clandestine group were detained as part of a long and complex trial; civil protests as a response against the removal of Gezi Park in Taksim, Istanbul, in 2013; an attempted coup in 2016 designed by an oppositional group led by a US-based Muslim cleric; and the constitutional referendum in 2017, where the public was almost half-way divided between those who wanted a presidential system and those who wanted to keep the parliamentary system. Eventually, Turkey switched to the presidential system with 51.41% of the population voting 'yes'.

Starting from an early age, Generation Z in Turkey witnessed all these developments through the news on TV, word of mouth on the street, and the social media, especially Twitter. Such intensive exposure to political issues through digital and traditional media has made these issues a prevalent part of everyday life for Generation Z in Turkey, hinting that, their personal interest in politics have not always been voluntary. Unable to escape the reality and occasionally frustrated, the youth turn to humour to negotiate what they believe they cannot change. Consider the following comment from a university student we interviewed:

> *I can't believe some people call the new generation apolitical. Tell me, how can you stay apolitical in Turkey? Everything is on the news, and there are rumours, jokes, and conspiracy theories about everything, everywhere. According to one half, everything is super great while the other half thinks Turkey is going down. Which one do you believe? I believe none of them. I believe in cartoons which make fun of this political conflict.* [M20, university student, interview]

Multiple Contradicting Selves Living Peacefully

These results seem to point to a generation highly paradoxical in nature. The identity of Generation Z in Turkey can be best described as a multipolarity of selves. Having changing perspectives about life, education, and work, these young people try to blend different views to create a coherent, happy life. To explain more analytically if and how these perspectives merge into different identity dimensions, we ran an exploratory factor analysis on all Likert questions in our quantitative study (42 questions, Cronbach's alpha=0.789). The analysis revealed 11 different identity dimensions, which can be interpreted as representing the different selves of Generation Z in Turkey: (1) Current Self, (2) Steady Self, (3) Fearful Self, (4) Consuming Self, (5) Political Self, (6) Materialist Self, (7) Coder Self, (8) Digitally Social Self, (9) Plain Self, (10) Ethnocentric Self, and (11) Patriarchal Self. Below, we explain the first three most prominent identity dimensions:

1. The current self represents the young person in the present. It consists of seven statements about how young people organise their present life, including talking and doing online tasks. The current self also includes Generation Z's reflections on and predictions about their future life such as their dreams, career views, and cultural adventures. The mean for this self was 4.05 (5 being the maximum score), showing that our respondents are highly engaged with mundane matters (e.g. 'I like talking to people' or 'I use my mobile phone for online tasks') but they also relate these matters to their futures (e.g. 'I have a dream' or 'I want to be the boss of my own job').
2. The steady self conveys stability and contentment. In line with country-level life satisfaction statistics mentioned earlier, most participants feel that they are calm and happy with their lives, in harmony with their families.
3. The fearful self reflects that, although members of Generation Z focus on the present and are content in general, they are also very fearful about their future professional life. The existence of this fearful self aligns with TurkStat's (2019) national survey on young people's pessimism about employment expectation presented above.

Generation Z as Consumers in Turkey: Consumption for Selves

The Digital Generation

Technology is a crucial part of the digitally competent Generation Z's everyday lives (Şenbir, 2004). Latif, Uçkun, and Demir (2015) argue that the proliferation of the Internet and mobile phones has created a different language in Turkey, isolating those who frequently use social networks. Although some studies have found that Generation Z in Turkey cannot be described as 'addicts' to electronic communication (Özkan & Solmaz, 2015), other studies conclude that they are relying on social media significantly more compared to other generations for building and maintaining social relations (Sarıtaş & Barutçu, 2016). Marketers have been advised that the best way to reach Generation Z is through mobile applications (Tuncer & Tuncer, 2016).

Expanding these insights, participants of our quantitative study like to look for and purchase new things (mean=3.96 out of 5), shop in general (mean=3.38), window shop (mean=2.99), and shop online (mean=3.44). Their brand loyalty is quite low (mean=2.49). Although the second-hand consumption is not appreciated in Turkish culture, Generation Z consumers seem more positive towards the second-hand items (mean=3.08). Based on our survey, Generation Z in Turkey is open to different and new consumption items and ways of consuming.

Shopping Criteria

Based on our quantitative study, Generation Z in Turkey seeks functional effectiveness (30%), followed by aesthetic or artistic features (15%) and high brand image (15%). Self-image (8%), status (3%), and spiritual satisfaction (5%) are more secondary in determining their shopping choice. In-depth interviews revealed further insights in relation to shopping criteria. For instance, for Generation Z, functionality is:

> *I am buying clothes, for example. I of course consider if the clothing item is comfortable or not. But probably more than I value whether it looks good or not. For me, it doesn't matter, really. As long as it looks fashionable, or else to put it, if my friend would find it chic and cool, then it is OK for me, too ... Even though there is a more comfortable option, and there is always a more comfortable option, I would still buy the cool one. You ask me about the functionality, well ... If it makes me look good, then it would fulfil its function.* [M20, university student, interview]

The first three criteria for shopping, namely, functional effectiveness, aesthetics, and the brand image, combine together to highlight the 'cool' effect of products. The brands, rather than being valued for their attributes, are used by Generation Z in Turkey to decide whether the purchase is good enough for their social circle.

Generation Z at Work in Turkey: An Imaginary Future

Plans and Worries

The life of Turkish Generation Z revolves around three big 'spaces': family (home), school, and work, the last one creating the most concern for the future and leaving young people uncertain about their education. Our interviews reveal anxieties about finding a good job and choosing the right university–department combination required for it:

> [...]*I will probably choose the best universities and departments with the highest scores. I will assume that those departments are the best. Best for what? The education system in Turkey does not allow me to have dreams but still I sometimes find myself dreaming about curing people and finding medical treatments that would change everything. But I am a "social [sciences]" student so I can't be a doctor, see? No guarantee that the profession that I choose is going to make me happy or productive.* [F18, high school student, interview]

For Generation Z in Turkey, everything about their future boils down to the university entrance exam, only after which they can choose their universities and departments Universities hold 'publicity days' during this period, where students can attend and learn about different options. We have observed over the years that the first and most frequent question asked by students is 'what job do I get when I graduate?'

Considering the high unemployment rates in Turkey, which hit 14.7% for January 2019 (TurkStat, 2019), it is not surprising that Generation Z, albeit having a dream job, is fearful for not being able to find a job they like.

Work–Life Blending

The young people in our quantitative study mostly agreed with the statement 'I believe I will successfully find a balance between home and work' (mean score= 3.97 out of 5), revealing their high hopes of reaching harmony in life. To obtain a clearer picture of school–work–home balance for Generation Z in Turkey, we questioned their plans for work and marriage. A major part of our respondents (83%) plan to get married between age 25 and 32, which corresponds to a period after graduation and probably finding a job. This finding corresponds to TurkStat's report that the average marriage age is 30.2 for men and 26.5 for women in 2018.

Regarding their attitudes at work, young members of Generation Z in Turkey are anxious about their office life as our survey participants mostly agreed with 'Relations at work make me anxious' (mean score= 3.13 out of 5). One explanation is it is too early and difficult for the majority of Generation Z members in Turkey to predict what they will do or encounter at work. While imagining about work makes them worry, studies on Generation Z in Turkey reveal that they quickly adapt to new situations, are better at coming up with new ideas and solutions, and capable of enunciating themselves at work (Büyük, 2019). To solve this tension, many of them postpone worrying about work until after they find a job:

> [...] *During my internships, some people have their backers … they don't even come to work. But some others work very hard. So yes, I am worried. But I am not very much worried about it right now, because I need to find a job first, right?* [F21, university student, interview]

Entrepreneurship

Generation Z in Turkey was called the best candidates for today's creators of entrepreneurial success because of their individualistic tendencies and their acceptance for change (Yelkikalan, Akatay, & Altın, 2010). Our survey data reveal similar tendencies among Generation Z in Turkey, who are eager to establish their own businesses, agreeing with 'I would consider being an entrepreneur myself' (mean score= 3.56 out of 5) and 'I would like to be my own boss'(mean score= 3.95).

To further our understanding of what might be leading their entrepreneurial desires, we ran a hierarchical regression analysis. According to our regression model, Generation Z in Turkey who aspire to be their own bosses and closely follow the developments in the digital world are more likely to possess a desire for entrepreneurship. One explanation is that digital developments might be inspiring Generation Z to have entrepreneurial ideas. The desire for entrepreneurship is also positively influenced by Generation Z's openness to talk to people and try out new brands. Talking to people might help Generation Z in accumulating the social skills and networking to realise their entrepreneurship ideas. Similarly, trying out new brands might indicate openness to new things and ideas that stimulate entrepreneurship tendencies. Alternatively, Generation Z might be predicting that they would be free and well off to try new brands if they have a business of their own. Yet, most of the participants had a desire for entrepreneurship without an actual, concrete entrepreneurial idea. For example:

> *I do dream about a firm of my own. And I really would like to pursue that dream. I think my school trained me well to measure things, and go after risks and opportunities. I think the digital world is changing everything, and I see a lot of opportunities out there. Maybe I would develop and sell a mobile phone game or sell stuff online, I don't know…* [M20, university student, interview]

How to Deal with Generation Z in Turkey: They are Different, and They Know it

Our quantitative research revealed three segments among Generation Z consumers in Turkey: the aesthetically sensitive, the ethical consumer, and the status-seeker. To communicate with the first two segments, marketers should highlight the functional effectiveness of their offerings but use different messages as the definition of functionality differs across these segments (e.g., hedonic experiences vs. spiritual enhancement). Status-seeking Generation Z consumers might be more responsive to offerings and communication strategies with status-enhancement potential.

Generation Z in Turkey appears to make seemingly contradictory consumption choices. While they desire the new, in line with Turkish culture's historical quest for progress and modernity, they are more open to second-hand items than their parents. This hints that Generation Z in Turkey commits to a global consumer culture that elevates retro/vintage objects as sophisticated taste and celebrates cyclical consumption to circulate and reuse objects. This provides many opportunities for policy-makers as well as marketers. For instance, managers and government administrators in Turkey can adopt more sustainable business practices by encouraging young people to circulate their used items and collaborating in the assortment and handling of the second-hand materials. They can also promote to Generation Z the job opportunities more related to the environment and social responsibility.

How to Deal with Generation Z in Turkey for Managers?

In his analysis of Turkish education system, Seymen (2017) discusses the importance of providing more courses on coding and other computer skills in schools, customised for the local peculiarities. Our conclusions support this point. Generation Z in Turkey is tech-innate and willing to pay for the training to improve these skills.

In line with the broader research on Generation Z, our own study shows that Generation Z in Turkey converges with their global counterparts in relation to increasing use of social media and the diversity of online platforms used. It is important to emphasise that social media is a major venue for networking and relationship management for this generation. These sites could enrich themselves along these dimensions, creating applications to provide alternative communication forms or using AI-based technologies to help Generation Z to spot potential social network members.

Regarding the identity of Generation Z in Turkey, we highlight the strong presence of the 'current self'. This identity dimension allows Generation Z to concentrate on daily activities to help them navigate their future, such as maintaining work–home balance. Innovations that assist their current self will be valued by these young people. For instance, services and innovations to decrease the time spent in traffic or driving would help those young people living in big cities. Members of Generation Z in Turkey are both happy and scared at the same time: consuming helps them keep up-to-date and cope with the transition from home to 'real life', and provide some form of relief from concerns about exams and work. Business ideas that help Generation Z with easing these tensions could appeal to these consumers. Similarly, managers could create hybrid atmospheres in work and office design, where Generation Z employees 'feel at home' but are encouraged to work productively.

Conclusions

We conclude our chapter with a direct quote from one of our interview partici-pants. As both a member and criticiser of Generation Z in Turkey, her narrative summarises the main characteristics of her own generation – continuous connec-tivity via online platforms and the paradoxical identity dimensions:

> *I cannot believe how fast things are changing. I remember my sister playing with her doll all the time. Just one toy. She used to dress her, bath her, and do everything with one toy only. I remember myself growing up with a lot of toys. My parents used to give their cell phones to me all the time. And I was playing with my dad's computer. I was born into these electronic devices. They were my toys. Today they are still my toys. I am using probably around 30 or 35 different applica-tions. I get up in the morning, come to school, listen to lectures, hang out with my friends, and go back home, and eat, and sleep. Why do I need those applications and all these gadgets and everything? My lifestyle and the way my friends live force me to use those apps. If I stop using Instagram, I would lose contact with my friends although I see them every day. I see them with my eyes, but we don't commu-nicate. I am both scared by these developments, and I also like them. I have to like them.* [F20, university student, interview]

References

Bazeley, P. (2018). *Integrating analyses in mixed methods research*. Los Angeles, CA: Sage.

Büyük, S. S. (2019). Daha genç ama daha dinamik mi? [Younger but more dynamic?]. *Popüler Yönetim Dergisi, 35*, 28–39.

Council of Higher Education (YÖK). (2019, September 22). *Student Statistics*. Retrieved form https://www.yok.gov.tr/

Ekici, G. (2005). Lise öğrencilerinin öğrenci seçme sınavına (ÖSS) yönelik tutumlarının bazı değişkenler açısından incelenmesi. [An investigation of student attitudes toward the student selection examination (SSE) through a number of variables]. *Hacettepe University Journal of Education, 28*(28), 82–90.

Kandiyoti, D. (2002). Introduction: Reading the fragments. In D. Kandiyoti & A. Saktanber (Eds.), *Fragments of culture: The everyday of modern Turkey* (pp. 1–33). London: I.B. Tauris.

Kavalcı, K., & Ünal, S. (2016). Y ve Z Kuşaklarının Öğrenme Stilleri ve Tüketici Karar Verme Tarzları Açısından Karşılaştırılması [A research on comparing consumer decision- making styles and learning styles in terms of the generation Y and Z]. *Atatürk Üniversitesi Sosyal Bilimler Enstitüsü Dergisi, 20*(3), 1033–1050.

Keyman, E. F. (2007). Introduction: Modernity and democracy in Turkey. In E. F. Keyman (Ed.), *Remaking Turkey* (pp. 15–27). Plymouth: Lexington Books.

Konda, Research and Consultancy. (2017, July 25). If there were 100 people in Turkey.

Kuepper, J. (2018, September 30). What are the fragile five? Five emerging markets overly dependent on foreign investment. Retrieved from https://www.thebalance.com/what-are-the-fragile-five-1978880

Kuyucu, M. (2017). Gençlerde akıllı telefon kullanımı ve akıllı telefon bağımlılığı sorunsalı: "Akıllı telefon(kolik)" üniversite gençliği. [Smart phone usage and problematization of smart phone addiction among young people: "Smart phone (colic)" university youth]. *Global Media Journal TR Edition, 7*(14), 328–359. Retrieved from https://www.guvenliweb.org.tr/dosya/6OV1q.pdf

Latif, H., Uçkun, C. G., & Demir, B. (2015). Examining the relationship between e-social networks and the communication behaviours of generation 2000 (millennials) in Turkey. *Social Science Computer Review, 33*(1), 43–60.

Ministry of National Education, Republic of Turkey. (2019, May 12). *Eğitim Sisteminin Temel Özellikleri [Main Characteristics of the Education System]*. Retrieved from http://www.meb.gov.tr/en/

Özkan, M., & Solmaz, B. (2015). Mobile addiction of generation Z and its effects on their social lives: An application among university students in the 18–23 age group. *Procedia-Social and Behavioral Sciences, 205,* 92–98.

Özman, A., & Coşar, S. (2007). Reconceptualizing center politics in post-1980 Turkey: Transformation or continuity? In F. Keyman (Ed.), *Remaking Turkey: Globalization, alternative modernities, and democracies* (pp. 201–226). UK: Lexington Books.

Pew Research Center. (2018). Social Media Use. Retrieved from https://www.pewglobal.org/interactives/media-habits-table/. Accessed on January 27, 2018.

Saktanber, A., & Beşpınar, F. U. (2012). Youth. In M. Heper & S. Sayarı (Eds.), *The Routledge handbook of modern Turkey* (pp. 271–281). London: Routledge.

Sarıtaş, E., & Barutçu, S. (2016). Tüketici davranışlarının analizinde kuşaklar: Sosyal medya kullanımı üzerine bir araştırma. [Generations in analysis of consumer behavior: A study on social media usage]. *Pamukkale Journal of Eurasian Socioeconomic Studies, 3*(2), 1–15.

Şenbir, H. (2004). *Z Son İnsan mı? Z kuşağı ve sonrasına dair düşünceler.* [Is Z the last human? Thoughts on Generation Z and Beyond]. İstanbul: Okuyan Us Yayınları.

Seymen, A. F. (2017). Y ve Z kuşak insanı özelliklerinin Milli Eğitim Bakanlığı 2014–2019 Stratejik Programı ve TÜBİTAK Vizyon 2023 öngörüleri ile ilişkilendirilmesi. [The association of the characteristics of Y and Z generation people with the 2014–2019 Strategic Program of The Ministry of Education and the foresights of TÜBİTAK Vision 2023]. *Kent Akademisi, 10*(4), 467–489. Retrieved from https://dergipark.org.tr/en/pub/kent/issue/34454/346427

Statista. (2019). Leading Countries based on a number of Twitter Users as of January 2019. Retrieved from https://www.statista.com/. Accessed on May 19, 2019.

Tuna, B. (2002, October 5). Sadakatsiz Z kuşağı geliyor. [Here comes the disloyal Generation Z]. *Hürriyet Pazar.* Retrieved from http://hurriyet.com.tr

Tuncer, A. İ., & Tuncer, M. U. (2016). Eğlence reklamlarının viral uygulamaları ve Z kuşağı üzerinden bir değerlendirme. [An assessment of viral applications of entertainment advertisements and their effects on Z Generation]. *TRT Akademi, 1*(1), 210–229. Retrieved from https://dergipark.org.tr/en/download/article-file/204864#page=210

Turkish Statistical Institute (TurkStat). (2019). Retrieved from http://www.turkstat.gov.tr/

Yelkikalan, N., Akatay, A., & Altın, E. (2010). Yeni girişimcilik modeli ve yeni nesil girişimci profili: Internet girişimciliği ve Y, M, Z kuşağı girişimci. [The new entrepreneurship model and the profile of the new generation entrepreneur: Internet entrepreneurship and generation Y, M, Z entrepreneurs]. *Sosyal Ekonomik Araştırmalar Dergisi, 10*(20), 489–506. Retrieved from https://dergipark.org.tr/en/pub/susead/issue/28415/302481?publisher=selcuk

Chapter 12

Generation Z in the United Arab Emirates: A Smart-Tech-Driven iGeneration

Nisreen Ameen and Amitabh Anand

Abstract

Generation Z is deemed to be digital native and has been attracting the attention of many companies when developing digital strategies to understand their consumption behaviour and their expectations in the workplace. Although research is progressing in relation to understanding Generation Z's attributes, very little is known in the context of the United Arab Emirates (UAE) where a total of 1.4 million individuals who are part of this generation are located. This chapter aims to provide an overview of Generation Z in the UAE, their needs, characteristics, and preferences to enable companies to offer them targeted products and services and a suitable workplace which in turn will positively impact organisational performance. The findings suggest that Generation Z in the UAE has five main characteristics. They are (1) digital natives; (2) highly influenced by social influencers; (3) risk averse; (4) emotionally mature; and (5) highly involved in political debates. Accordingly, we outline directions for future research on Generation Z consumers and managerial implications for employers, retailers, and shopping malls operating in the UAE.

Keywords: Generation Z; consumption; United Arab Emirates; Middle East; smart technology; artificial intelligence; political debates; risk aversion

Introduction to the United Arab Emirates

The United Arab Emirates (UAE) is considered one of the most advanced digital economies in the world, being ranked top 20 globally and the first in the

The New Generation Z in Asia: Dynamics, Differences, Digitalisation
The Changing Context of Managing People, 181–192
Copyright © 2020 by Emerald Publishing Limited
All rights of reproduction in any form reserved
doi:10.1108/978-1-80043-220-820201018

Arab world in relation to digital competitiveness (Gulf News, 2018a). The Gross Domestic Product (GDP) per capita in the country was 43,005 US Dollars in 2018 (World Bank, 2019). Furthermore, the combination of high economic growth, and a population of 9.39 million internet users (The Media Lab, 2019), out of 9.77 million total population in 2019 (World Population Review, 2020), have further created new and exciting opportunities for businesses to serve the needs of consumers in the UAE. The country has 400,000 small and medium enterprises (SMEs), which contribute over 60% of the UAE non-oil economy and provide 86% of the private workforce (NBF, 2019). They make up 73% of the wholesale and retail trade sector, 16% of the services sector, and 11% of the industrial sector (NBF, 2019).

Generation Z is an important target group for retailers and marketers (Geronimo, 2018). While 66% of the UAE population falls in the age group of 25–54 years (Global Media Insight, 2020), Generation Z has a population of around 1.4 million in the UAE. (Gulf News, 2019a). The UAE is one of the top destinations for tourists from all around the world, with over 12 million visitors in Dubai alone in 2019 (Gulf News, 2019b). This makes Generation Z in the UAE more open to other cultures and tastes than previous generations.

There is a requirement from companies, retailers, and policymakers to gain a deeper understanding of this generation to ensure sustainability. Therefore, in this chapter, we aim to provide an overview of Generation Z in the UAE. Specifically, we aim to understand their needs and their preferences, provide directions for future research and practical implications for retailers and employers to gain a better understanding of this generation.

Digitisation in the United Arab Emirates

The UAE has one of the highest smartphone adoption rates in the world (Ameen, 2017; Ameen, Willis, & Shah, 2018). Individuals in Generation Z in the UAE are heavy users of technology and they possess unique characteristics compared to other generations in relation to needs, preferences, and consumption patterns (Priporas, Stylos, & Fotiadis, 2017; Schlossberg, 2016). Generation Z spends more time on their mobile devices than any other generation (Criteo, 2018). This generation has never experienced a world with no digital technology. They have lived in a digitised environment in the UAE for their entire lives and they are technology natives (Gulf News, 2020).

Smartphones in the UAE are used by 96% of the population, while tablet devices are used across 28% of individuals (The Media Lab, 2019). This applies to Generation Z in the country as their use of smartphones exceeds the use of other devices such as laptops and tablets (Mesmar, 2019). Generation Z in the UAE uses their smartphones for an average of 3 hours a day to consume media (Al Hinai, 2017). The country is pioneering the use of emerging and innovative technologies such as artificial intelligence, machine learning and biometrics as part of the services offered to its citizens. Hence, Generation Z in the UAE is exposed to some of the most advanced technologies which play a key role in shaping their behaviour. In addition, post-adoption issues such as smartphone security are becoming some of the main concerns for the young generation in the UAE (Ameen, Tarhini, Shah, & Madichie, 2019). This is largely due to the significant and positive role of the cybersecurity awareness programmes in UAE which are targeted towards the younger generations (Chandra, Sharma, & Liaqat, 2019).

The government of the UAE has developed a strategy for building the infrastructure required to develop smart cities and services (Smart Dubai, 2020). For instance, the IMD Smart City 2019 Index placed Dubai in the 45th spot out of the 102 cities ranked while Abu Dhabi took the 56th spot (IMD Smart City Index, 2019). This has made the UAE the most desirable nation for the Arab youth to live in (Sanderson, 2019). The Smart Dubai initiative structures its end-goals across a carefully crafted set of strategic pillars. These pillars are to provide efficient, seamless, safe, and personalised services to the UAE's citizens. The pillars of this initiative provide a distinct view of the impact the city needs to create, in tandem with all public and private stakeholders (Smart Dubai, 2020). This subsequently has made UAE to be one of the pioneering countries in terms of the digitisation of services offered to its citizens (Rodrigues, Sarabdeen, & Balasubramanian, 2016). This digitisation of services and the introduction of smart services in the country increases Generation Z's dependency on technology and digital platforms such as Google, Facebook, and Twitter, making them even more tech-savvy and decreases their interest in other activities such as reading and shopping in physical stores (Khamis & Zaatarti, 2019). Furthermore, they are the primary drivers of the country's future digital economy (Gulf News, 2020). In addition, the vast amounts of digital information at their disposal also enable Generation Z in the UAE to be more analytical in their decision-making than previous generations (Gulf News, 2020).

Basics of Generation Z in the UAE

Generation Z in the UAE is risk averse in relation to both their attitude and behaviour as they like to play it safe and they have the ability to detect whether or not something is relevant to them (Gulf News, 2020; Khamis & Zaatarti, 2019). In addition, Generation Z in the UAE tends to be more responsible and pragmatic than Millennials (Gulf News, 2020).

Generation Z believes that music allows people to connect with one another and with different cultures. They listen to more international music than any other generation (Gulf News, 2019b). This generation may appear to be obsessed with their screens, but they value audio as an escape from visual stimulation overload (Gulf News, 2019b). This is applicable to Generation Z in the UAE who are aware of their emotional status and are open to other cultures since the country is open to other cultures with a high number of tourists visiting every year and the absence of boundaries on travelling.

Family ties and social relationships play a significant role in people's decision making and the way they interact with brands (Ameen, 2017; Ameen, Willis, & Shah, 2018). This is also applicable to the young of the Middle East in general and the UAE's population in particular. Within the cultural norms of the UAE, there are obstacles with respect to Emirati women's actions, activities, and interactions (Erogul, Rod, & Barragan, 2019). For example, male family members limit the ability of Arab women to access their proximal social network including the wider social network structure to facilitate their business operations (Ameen & Willis, 2019; Erogul et al., 2019; Goby & Erogul 2011). This also affects how people socialise and interact in the country.

It can be concluded that Generation Z in the UAE is the first real global generation. High-tech is in their blood and they have grown up in an uncertain and complex environment, which determines their viewpoint about work, studying, and the world. Arising from their habitat, they have different expectations in their workplaces (Dill, 2015). This is a careerist, professionally ambitious generation, but their technical and language knowledge are on a high level.

Members of Generation Z as Consumers in the UAE

The existing literature is rich with studies focussing on consumer behaviour in smart retailing (e.g. Dacko, 2017; Kim, Lee, Mun, & Johnson, 2016; Priporas et al., 2017; Roy, Balaji, Sadeque, Nguyen, & Melewar, 2016; Vrontis, Thrassou, & Amirkhanpour, 2016). Nevertheless, we report a lack of research on Generation Z's behaviour as consumers in omnichannel retailing in the UAE, despite the importance of this market.

Individuals who are part of Generation Z in UAE have constant access to search engines which makes them more informed consumers. They also read reviews, share their views, and have access to more online resources than the previous generations (Mesmar, 2019). Moreover, they expect personalised services and products and they expect companies to be able to identify their needs and understand their importance as consumers. For example, they would pay a premium for products that highlight their individuality or embrace causes they feel they relate to (Mesmar, 2019). Given the high spending power in the UAE and that it is a hub for global luxury brands such as Cartier, Chanel, and Gucci, Generation Z in this country is expected to place further emphasis on personalisation and high-quality products. This new breed of consumers expects more than ever to be able to consume products and services at any time and place and they need access 24/7. This means omnichannel marketing and sales must reach a new level of efficiency (Geronimo, 2018).

The rise of influencer marketing proves that word of mouth plays a huge part in shaping the preferences of these young consumers. Influencer marketing has become extremely popular for targeting younger demographics in the UAE. Influencers appear more genuine as they carry their own loyal audiences and the content they produce tends to outperform the content most brands create internally (Patel, 2017). They are role models, movement leaders, and even educators. It is common for Generation Z to turn to YouTube when they want to learn something or when deciding whether to buy a product (Patel, 2017). The UAE has made licenses for commercialised influencers mandatory, hence, the country has been able to regulate social media players (Duncan, 2018; Euro News, 2019). In 2019, more than 1,700 licenses for social influencers were issued in the UAE (Euro News, 2019). They are priced at around $4,000 dollars a year and require applicants to be a minimum of 21 years old and to hold a bachelor's degree (Euro News, 2019). Some leading brands in the UAE such as Sephora work extensively with influencers. The influence of Generation Z, which is the first truly digitally native generation, means that businesses in the UAE must understand the changing consumer needs, trends, and preferences. This is particularly true when it comes to communication, transparency, and ethics. Generation Z consumers in the UAE are known for their preference towards saving for the future rather than overspending on products and services (Khamis & Zaatarti, 2019). In addition, they need continuous updates and stimulation, reportedly having an attention span of *eight* seconds (Patel, 2017). Today, more than ever, marketers have to focus on the quality of the content. For companies in the UAE, it is important to add value to the conversation and make their content as memorable and creative as possible.

Recent research found that Generation Z in the UAE prefers the real-world smart retailing experience, augmented by technology (Geronimo, 2018). It embraces physical shopping again, supported by the use of technology. Therefore, retailers must target this mobile-focussed generation with a highly personalised ad experience and take a powerful omnichannel approach to address the evolving consumer behaviour and needs (Geronimo, 2018). This Instagram generation lives by visuals and expects their retailers to make experiences enjoyable and aesthetic, show how products are used, and feature them in their best light. To achieve this, retailers should enhance the online experience and improve store display and design. Generation Z in the UAE craves the tactile nature of the in-store experience but gravitates to the convenience of online shopping.

Due to Generation Z's need to be unique and unpredictable, it has a tendency to stray away from traditions. This makes it a difficult group to please. They can be quite cynical, yet have aspirations to make a difference in the world. They also love to hear a good story. With these factors in mind, it seems that this generation will enjoy a brand story that inspires some change in the world to capture their attention (Rauser, 2016). There are also opportunities to bring on Generation Z'ers in the UAE to become brand ambassadors for brands from an early age, securing their loyalty and offering them an opportunity to grow brands. Including them in organisational decision making through blogging opportunities will make them feel dedicated to the brand's mission, and that is a statement that can last a long time. This generation expects brands in the UAE to be transparent and authentic. To attract this generation and build loyalty, brands in the UAE must provide opportunities for engagement and co-creation, and demonstrate they are trustworthy as well as relevant (Toronto, 2017). In addition, they want to contribute and have an active role in brand engagement to feel a higher sense of involvement.

The UAE has some of the most advanced shopping malls in the world in which physical and virtual environments are integrated (Gulf News, 2018b). For example, Emaar launched a new 'tech-driven' mall and it will promote 'omnichannel retailing', to offer Generation Z customers options to shop via desktop, mobile, or in a retail store (Nagraj, 2018). In 2019, the Dubai Mall won two top honours at the Dubai service excellence scheme for its exceptional customer service and is one of the most visited shopping malls by young consumers around the world (Al Bawaba, 2019).

Technology is integrated in nearly every aspect of Generation Z's shopping experience in the mall such as Wifi, smart parking, and mobile applications in which shoppers are provided with the latest offers from their favourite stores. In addition, e-mails are sent to these shoppers after they leave the mall to request their evaluation of their shopping experience as a whole, for example: the retail stores they visited, cleanliness, convenience, Wifi, security inside the mall, customer service, navigation, restaurants, car parking, and entertainment outlets and events in the mall. In addition, retailers in the mall use new advanced technologies to improve customer service for Generation Z. For example, Lululab started one of the first artificial intelligence beauty stores in the world to provide a better customer service (PR News Wire, 2019) and the Asian restaurant Tanuki greets customers with a state-of-the-art robot (Prideaux, 2019). Generation Z customers show a high interest in these technologies as they act as motivators to shop in these stores.

The sharing economy in the UAE is the epitome of convenience for this generation (Sadaqat, 2017). It is easy, fast, and it provides cost-effective services (Patel, 2017; Sadaqat, 2017). This type of economy was birthed from the digital revolution in the UAE and the obsession with decentralisation that Generation Z and Millennials crave (Bohsali, Papazian, & Samad, 2017). If the sharing economy grows as it is predicted to, not only will safety, security, and privacy management be important but innovation in business will also need to digitally transform to keep up with the pace of this demographic segment.

Generation Z at Work in the UAE

Lim (2012) emphasises that companies in the UAE need to attract and retain talented employees as this may have implications for the country's continued economic growth. Furthermore, the population distributions of the UAE labour force by nationality are often skewed towards expatriate residents, for instance in 2017, immigrants accounted for 88% of the total population (McCarthy, 2019). This presents a diverse distribution that poses challenges to understanding the motivations of Generation Z. This generation views companies' culture as a more important factor than salary (Talhouk, 2019). In addition, for this segment of employees, companies' ethical goals and values play an important role in determining whether they join them or not. The use of bring your own devices (BYODs) for work-related tasks is more common among this generation in the UAE (Ameen et al., 2019). For example, Masafi, the leading producer and distributor of pure, natural mineral water, and premium products in the UAE, started a company-wide mobility initiative where employees can use their own devices for work purposes (Soti, 2020).

According to Talhouk (2019), in the UAE, Generation Z members may not be great collaborators with colleagues as they prefer to work on their own and have a higher tendency to be independent and competitive. Thus, managers need to understand their priorities and give them tasks that can match their characteristics for better performance. It is anticipated that managers in the UAE will have a challenge in handling these newer generations and integrating them with the other generations, thus, managerial training is essential to create strong interpersonal communication and build a long-lasting relationship with Generation Z.

Males account for 72% of the UAE population and females for 28% of this population (Global Media Insight, 2020). Previous studies have reported significant gender issues and differences in the use of mobile applications in the UAE and acknowledged the effects of cultural factors on women's use of these applications (Ameen et al., 2019). Furthermore, these gender issues extend to other aspects of life, for example, starting and running a business which often relies on the use of technology. The existing literature concerning Arab women's entrepreneurship in the UAE explains that many Arab and Emirati women are restricted by gender-based barriers, for example, due to a number of unique socio-cultural norms, family members deter women from becoming entrepreneurs (Ameen & Willis, 2016). This is due to the UAE being classified as a collectivistic society in which social norms and values are different from the west and it is apparent that gender issues still exist in the society in the country.

How to Deal with Generation Z in the UAE

Implications for Retailers and Shopping Malls Operating in the UAE

Retailers and shopping mall management teams in the UAE should take advantage of real-world retail that interests this generation, improve these consumers' online experience by providing accurate product descriptions with dynamic content, aesthetically pleasing images, 360° rotations, video demonstrations geared to their age group, and reviews optimised for their sceptical minds. In addition, stores and shopping mall displays should be creative and desirable. Furthermore, retailers should make the best use of YouTube and social media as these are a window to millions of influencers who have a strong influence on the opinions and behaviour of Generation Z consumers (Criteo, 2018). More importantly, this generation in UAE desires to have their shopping experiences tailored to them delivered by technology and they desire customised products as well as a customised marketing experience.

As members of Generation Z in UAE use their smartphones and other technologies very extensively for shopping, retailers should be prepared to deal with their demands such as ease and speed of transactions, information, convenience, and assurance of providing safety with digital communication (Priporas et al. 2017; Wood, 2013). Generation Z is frequently labelled as the 'sensible, stay at-home generation' and a generation that socialises less outside and more inside their family circle and online. This implies that they are more likely to be influenced by friends and celebrities, follow brands and make transactions. Hence, companies and retailers in UAE should be building online communities, such as using social media to engage, interact, share knowledge, get feedback, and eventually understand the changing needs of this generation. Beauty brands in the UAE have been pioneering in relation to using social media to reach out to their young customers, for example, Sephora has been building a strong online community to build better customer relationships and a sense of involvement (Clarke, 2016).

Generation Z in the UAE is believed to value individual expression and avoid labels. For instance, they believe profoundly in the efficacy of dialogue to solve conflicts and improve the world, in a more analytical, pro-social, and pragmatic way (Khamis & Zaatarti, 2019). Generation Z in the UAE is very much concerned with environmental issues, conscious of looming shortages, and water shortages which indicates that they have a high sense of responsibility towards natural resources (Baldwin, 2016). In fact, a global UAE-sponsored survey shows that young people aged 18–25 in the UAE are more concerned about climate change than a raft of other pressing issues including the economy, terrorism, and unemployment (Baldwin, 2016). Hence, it is critical for both local and international companies in the UAE to be more socially and environmentally conscious in promoting products and not just being smart. Sustainable oriented practices and operations such as recycling, contribution towards climate change, and adopting policies to reduce the damage to the environment may also help in attracting Generation Z consumers in the UAE (Masdar, 2016).

Implications for Employers

Generation Z in the UAE represents the greatest generational shift, and, as such, will pose a significant challenge to organisations and managers in the long run. Studies suggest that they have more power than any previous generation to redefine production and consumption.

While both Generation Z and Millennials in the UAE search for jobs that offer a sense of purpose, the former demographic has a higher tendency to lose focus and become impatient. If they are not impressed with their current jobs, Generation Z will most likely leave (Talhouk, 2019). Hence, employers in the country should prove they are worth their time by providing a tangible vision they can implement and evaluate (Mesmar, 2019). In addition, setting flexible hours will maintain focus and guarantee productivity. Including flexible hours as part of the job description will spark the UAE's Generation Z's interest and appeal to a wider pool of applicants (Talhouk, 2019).

Generation Z in the UAE embraces multiculturalism as the foundation for who they are as a generation, and this influences many of their decisions, and how they view society. Hence, employers should work towards ethical goals as Generation Z believes that the success of a business is measured in its focus on improving society above its financial results (Mesmar, 2019). Furthermore, despite the fact that Generation Z is concerned with savings, salary and raises are far less important to this generation than a work culture with a high degree of autonomy as they seek independence (Scott, 2018). Hence, it will be critical for employers in the UAE to demonstrate that they can and will help these new employees reach their career goals and ambitions as well as a sense of purpose rather than focussing mainly on offering them an increase in salary (Talhouk, 2019).

Since Generation Z employees are tech-natives, employers should embrace the use of technology for this generation of employees. To gain and sustain the attention of this generation, employers need a multiplatform approach that incorporates the sophisticated use of various social channels. Nevertheless, as their devices are used for personal and work purposes, companies should develop more effective cybersecurity policies to ensure the safety and security of their data and their customers' data.

Conclusions

This chapter showcased an overview of the UAE's Generation Z's characteristics in relation to their consumption and behaviour. This may have an impact on retailers' operations as well as workplace consequences. Our findings highlight new areas for research on Generation Z in the UAE. First, there is a gap in the existing literature in relation to focussing on Generation Z's behaviour and attitudes as consumers in the UAE. Further research can focus on this generation's preferences in relation to building relationships with luxury brands in the UAE, having a personalised shopping experience and their views on privacy and security of their data. Second, while the existing body of literature is rich with studies on users' pre-adoption and post adoption of smart technologies (e.g. Ameen et al., 2018, 2019; Sela, Zach, Amichai-Hamburger, Mishali, & Omer, 2020; Wang, 2020), there is a lack of research studying how these technologies are embedded in Generation Z's lifestyle and decision making in the context of the UAE. Third, as Generation Z in the UAE is tech-native, further research is required on post-technology adoption issues in the workplace such as security and protective behaviour of the technologies they use as employees.

References

Al Bawaba. (2019). The Dubai mall wins two top honours at the Dubai service excellence scheme for its exceptional customer service. Retrieved from https://www.albawaba.com/business/pr/dubai-mall-wins-two-top-honours-dubai-service-excellence-scheme-its-exceptional-customer

Al Hinai, M. (2017). Forget millennials: Brands need to be targeting Generation Z. Retrieved from https://www.thenational.ae/business/comment/forget-millennials-brands-need-to-be-targetting-generation-z-1.664913

Ameen, N. (2017). *Arab users' acceptance and use of mobile phones: A case of young users in Iraq, Jordan and UAE* (Unpublished doctoral dissertation). United Kingdom: Anglia Ruskin University.

Ameen, N., Tarhini, A., Shah, M. H., & Madichie, N.O. (2019). Employees' behavioural intention to smartphone security: A gender-based, cross-national study. *Computers in Human Behavior, 104*, 106184.

Ameen, N., & Willis, R. (2019). Towards closing the gender gap in Iraq: Understanding gender differences in smartphone adoption and use. *Information Technology for Development, 25*(4), 1–26.

Ameen, N., Willis, R., & Shah, M. H. (2018). An examination of the gender gap in smart-phone adoption and use in Arab countries: A cross-national study. *Computers in Human Behavior, 89*, 148–162.

Ameen, N. A., & Willis, R. (2016). The use of mobile phones to support women's entrepreneurship in the Arab countries. *International Journal of Gender and Entrepreneurship, 8*(4), 424–445.

Baldwin, D. (2016). Young people say they are more concerned about climate change. Retrieved from https://gulfnews.com/uae/environment/young-people-say-they-are-more-concerned-about-climate-change-1.1931413

Bohsali, S., Papazian, S., & Samad, R. (2017). How we can all get the most out of the sharing economy. Retrieved from https://www.thenational.ae/world/comment/how-we-can-all-get-the-most-out-of-the-sharing-economy-1.630666

Chandra, G. R., Sharma, B. K., & Liaqat, I. A. (2019). UAE's strategy towards most cyber resilient nation. *International Journal of Innovative Technology and Exploring Engineering, 8*(12), 2803–2809.

Clarke, L. (2016). The UAE beauty explosion. Retrieved from https://fridaymagazine.ae/beauty/the-uae-beauty-explosion-1.1677678

Criteo. (2018). The Generation z Report. Retrieved from https://www2.criteo.com/gen-z-report-download

Dacko, S. G. (2017). Enabling smart retail settings via mobile augmented reality shopping apps. *Technological Forecasting and Social Change, 124*, 243–256.

Dill, K. (2015). 7 Things Employers Should Know About the Generation z Workforce. Retrieved from http://www.forbes.com/sites/kathryndill/2015/11/06/7-things-employers-should-know-about-the-gen-z-workforce/print/

Duncan, G. (2018). UAE social media influencer law: Two licences costing Dh30,000 now needed. Retrieved from https://www.thenational.ae/uae/uae-social-media-influencer-law-two-licences-costing-dh30-000-now-needed-1.729355

Erogul, M. S., Rod, M., & Barragan, S. (2019). Contextualizing Arab female entrepreneurship in the United Arab Emirates. *Culture and Organization, 25*(5), 317–331.

Euro News. (2019). License to influence: UAE law regulates social media players. Retrieved from https://www.euronews.com/2019/07/19/license-to-influence-uae-law-regulates-social-media-players

Geronimo, A. (2018). Generation z prefer "real-world retail" over online shopping. Retrieved from https://www.tahawultech.com/industry/retail/gen-z-real-world-retail-over-online-shopping/

Global Media Insights. (2020). United Arab Emirates Population Statistics (2020). Retrieved from https://www.globalmediainsight.com/blog/uae-population-statistics/

Goby, V., & Erogul, M. (2011). Female entrepreneurship in the UAE: Legislative encouragements and cultural constraints. *Women's Studies International Forum, 34*(4), 329–334.

Gulf News. (2018a). UAE most digitally advanced in Arab world. Retrieved from https://gulfnews.com/technology/uae-most-digitally-advanced-in-arab-world-1.2239034

Gulf News. (2018b). A virtual mall promoted by Dubai tech firm is in the works. Retrieved from https://gulfnews.com/business/retail/a-virtual-mall-promoted-by-dubai-tech-firm-is-in-the-works-1.2245306

Gulf News. (2019a). Generation Z in the UAE: Future forward. Retrieved from https://gulfnews.com/uae/education/gen-z-in-the-uae-future-forward-1.61728309

Gulf News. (2019b). Dubai sees over 12 million visitors in 2019. Retrieved from https://gulfnews.com/uae/dubai-sees-over-12-million-visitors-in-2019-1.1574512587178

Gulf News. (2020). UAE's Gen Z switches to 21st century education. Retrieved from https://gulfnews.com/opinion/op-eds/uaes-gen-z-switches-to-21st-century-education-1.69765790

IMD Smart City Index. (2019). Smart city Index. Retrieved from https://www.imd.org/research-knowledge/reports/imd-smart-city-index-2019/

Khamis, J., & Zaatarti, S. (2019). Listen to what Gen Z says. Gulf News asks Gen Zers in UAE about what they believe in and how they view their future. Retrieved from https://gulfnews.com/uae/education/gen-z-in-the-uae-future-forward-1.61728309

Kim, H. Y., Lee, J. Y., Mun, J. M., & Johnson, K. K. (2016). Consumer adoption of smart in-store technology: Assessing the predictive value of attitude versus beliefs in the technology acceptance model. *International Journal of Fashion Design, Technology and Education, 10*(1), 26–36.

Lim, H. L. (2012). Generation Y workforce expectations: Implications for the UAE. *Education, Business and Society: Contemporary Middle Eastern Issues, 5*(4), 282–293.

Masdar. (2016). Gen Z Survey. Retrieved from https://masdar.ae/en/strategic-platforms/youth-4-sustainability/gen-z-survey

McCarthy, N. (2019). Immigrants Account For 88% Of The UAE's Population. Retrieved from https://www.statista.com/chart/16865/estimated-percentage-of-the-population-that-was-foreign-born/

Mesmar, F. (2019). The business of connecting to Generation Z. Retrieved from https://gulfnews.com/business/analysis/the-business-of-connecting-to-gen-z-1.66473506

Nagraj, A. (2018). Dubai Holding, Emaar launch new 'tech-driven' mall, nearly double the size of Dubai Mall. Retrieved from https://gulfbusiness.com/dubai-holding-emaar-launch-new-tech-driven-mall-nearly-double-size-dubai-mall/

NBF. (2019). SME in depth. Retrieved from https://nbf.ae/media/114007/sme-in-depth.pdf

Patel, D. (2017). Five differences between marketing to millennials Vs. Generation Z. Retrieved from shorturl.at/ghoGX

PR News Wire. (2019). Samsung Spin-off lululab to Unveil "AI Beauty Store: A Decision Maker of Cosmetic Products, in Dubai Mall. Retrieved from https://www.prnewswire.com/ae/news-releases/samsung-spin-off-lululab-to-unveil-ai-beauty-store-a-decision-maker-of-cosmetic-products-in-dubai-mall-881452944.html

Prideaux, S. (2019). Robot host welcomes guests at new Dubai Mall restaurant. Retrieved from https://www.thenational.ae/lifestyle/food/robot-host-welcomes-guests-at-new-dubai-mall-restaurant-1.813177

Priporas, C. V., Stylos, N., & Fotiadis, A. K. (2017). Generation Z consumers' expectations of interactions in smart retailing: A future agenda. *Computers in Human Behavior, 77*, 374–381.

Rauser, A. (2016). Marketing to Generation Z: Why your business will need to re-evaluate strategy for the post-Internet generation. Retrieved from https://cxm.world/marketing-to-generation-z-why-your-business-will-need-to-re-evaluate-strategy-for-the-post-internet-generation/

Rodrigues, G., Sarabdeen, J., & Balasubramanian, S. (2016). Factors that influence consumer adoption of e-government services in the UAE: A UTAUT model perspective. *Journal of Internet Commerce, 15*(1), 18–39.

Roy, S. K., Balaji, M. S., Sadeque, S., Nguyen, B., & Melewar, T. C. (2017). Constituents and consequences of smart customer experience in retailing. *Technological Forecasting and Social Change, 124*(C), 257–270.

Sadaqat, R. (2017). Who'll drive the UAE's sharing economy? Retrieved from https://www.khaleejtimes.com/business/local/wholl-drive-the-uaes-sharing-economy

Schlossberg, M. (2016). Teen Generation Z is being called 'millennials on steroids,' and that could be terrifying for retailers. Retrieved from http://uk.businessinsider.com/millennials-vs-gen-z-2016-2

Scott, J. (2018). What Gen Z wants from work is different than you might think. Retrieved from https://www.tlnt.com/what-gen-z-wants-from-work-is-different-than-you-might-think/

Sela, Y., Zach, M., Amichai-Hamburger, Y., Mishali, M., & Omer, H. (2020). Family environment and problematic internet use among adolescents: The mediating roles of depression and fear of missing out. *Computers in Human Behavior, 106*, 106226.

Sanderson, D. (2019). Arab Youth Survey 2019: The UAE is seen as the most desirable nation to live in. Retrieved from https://www.thenational.ae/uae/arab-youth-survey-2019-the-uae-is-seen-as-the-most-desirable-nation-to-live-in-1.855344

Smart Dubai. (2020). Preparing Dubai to embrace the future, now. Retrieved from https://2021.smartdubai.ae/

Soti. (2020). Masafi Case Study. Retrieved from https://www.soti.net/PDF/Masafi_CaseStudy.pdf

Talhouk, G. (2019). Hiring approaches for Generation z differs from millennials. Retrieved from https://www.thenational.ae/business/comment/hiring-approaches-for-gen-z-differs-from-millennials-1.923302

The Media Lab. (2019). UAE Digital Media Statistics 2019 (Infographics). Retrieved from https://www.themedialab.me/uae-digital-media-statistics-2019/

Toronto. (2017). Generation zers are redefining brand loyalty. Retrieved from https://www.ama-toronto.com/blog/gen-zers-are-redefining-brand-loyalty

Vrontis, D., Thrassou, A., & Amirkhanpour, M. (2017). B2C smart retailing: A consumer-focused value-based analysis of interactions and synergies. *Technological Forecasting and Social Change, 124,* 271–282.

Wang, R. J. H. (2020). Branded mobile application adoption and customer engagement behavior. *Computers in Human Behavior, 106,* 106245.

Wood, S. (2013). *Generation Z as consumers: Trends and innovation.* North Carolina: Institute for Emerging Issues: NC State University.

World Bank. (2019). GDP per capita (current US$) – United Arab Emirates. Retrieved from https://data.worldbank.org/indicator/NY.GDP.PCAP.CD?locations=AE

World Population Review. (2020). United Arab Emirates Population. Retrieved from http://worldpopulationreview.com/countries/united-arab-emirates-population/

Part VI

Generation Z in Asia: Patterns and Predictions

Chapter 13

Generation Z in Asia: Patterns and Predictions

Emma Parry

Abstract

This chapter draws the book 'Generation Z in Asia' to a close. It first considers the value of the notion of generations before explaining the contribution of this text. The chapter then reflects on the trends that appear to be common across Asian counties while recognising the differences between them. Finally, the chapter questions whether the positive outlook for Generation Z in Asia will continue into the future.

Keywords: Generation Z; Asia; differences; technology; activism; COVID-19

Introduction

In this book, we have focussed on the youngest generation who are entering the workforce – known as Generation Z and born from the mid-1990s onwards. We have gathered together a range of evidence regarding the characteristics of Generation Z in Asia, both as consumers and employees. Rather than treating Asia as a homogenous region, we have sought to highlight both commonalities and diversity in the characteristics of this age cohort across Asia by sourcing chapters from different countries across the continent – in East, South, South East, and Western Asia. In doing so, we have been able to explore the similarities and differences in the attitudes, preferences, and expectations of members of this generation across different regions. These chapters speak for themselves, and readers will draw their own conclusions about whether there are trends in relation to what is important to this younger age cohort within the region. It is not my job here, therefore, to provide a detailed summary of what has already been covered. Thus, the purpose

The New Generation Z in Asia: Dynamics, Differences, Digitalisation
The Changing Context of Managing People, 195–200
doi:10.1108/978-1-80043-220-820201021

of this chapter is not to analyse the content of these chapters in depth or to present conclusions in the traditional sense. Rather, I have a number of reflections and observations that I would like to make in the form of concluding remarks, to encourage our readers to consider the nature of this youngest generation in Asia and their likely contribution to the world.

The Value of 'Generation' as an Organising Framework

It is worth commenting at this point on the value of the notion of 'generation' in understanding the attitudes and characteristics of the workforce and consumer population in general. Regardless of geographical location, employers, marketers, and policy makers have relied heavily on the idea of generational change over recent years, with many consultants and commentators promoting the idea that new cohorts of individuals are entering the population who are dramatically different to the last age group. Indeed, this fits with theoretical discussions as far back as the 1950s when sociologists such as Mannheim (1952) presented the idea of a constant progression of cohorts of individuals entering and leaving the population, whose attitudes and behaviours were shaped by their experiences during their formative years. For the past 10 years, efforts to understand Millennials have attracted significant attention and investment with the implicit expectation that being able to understand this group of individuals will provide an almost magical solution to the challenges of selling to, and recruiting, young people. More recently, this attention has moved to Generation Z.

We have also seen over this time increased criticism within academic circles of the evidence behind generational differences, with studies failing to agree on the boundaries, and characteristics, of any particular generation and the flaws in methodological approaches to investigating generational differences being highlighted (Parry & Urwin, 2011, 2017). While attempts to provide more valid and rigorous evidence of the existence and nature of generations is underway, it is fair to say that the jury is still out in relation to the value of this notion from an academic sense as a more robust evidence base needs to be developed.

That said, nobody is arguing with the idea that attitudes are changing over time, as the context arounds us changes in relation to the economy, education, technological advancement, and demographic trends, to name but a few. It is apparent that young people entering adulthood today are not the same in their attitudes, preferences and expectations to those who were in this position ten or 20 years ago. Some of these differences are apparent in the chapters within this book, as we see this youngest generation display different preferences to those who are older, driven by contextual influences such as the economy, technological advancement and education. Thus, while we cannot still be convinced whether the demarcation between generational groups is any more than arbitrary, we can suggest that the characteristics of those in the youngest age group are changing over time and that it is, therefore, important for employers, marketers, and politicians to understand these changes in order to be able to attract and retain them to their organisations, products, or political parties. It is with this motivation in mind that we have put together this edited text.

A Contextual Approach to Studying Generations

One criticism that has been made of the current body of research into generational differences is its assumption that the characteristics of generations are universal, so that we would expect a young person in Europe to have similar characteristics to a young person in Asia. Indeed, the North American (particularly the United States) depiction of Millennials and more recently Generation Z has been widely adopted worldwide. However, given that people's attitudes and preferences are said to be influenced by their experiences while growing up, this assumption actually makes no sense as we would not expect the formative experiences of someone growing up in Asia to be the same as someone growing up in Europe or the United States. Most evidence on the characteristics of generations – including Generation Z – is based in the United States, or at least in Anglo Saxon nations such as the United Kingdom, Canada, and Australia. We, therefore, greatly need evidence about Generation Z in other countries so that we can understand the consistencies – and contradictions – between the characteristics of this age cohort in different countries. An earlier text 'Generations Z in Europe' (Scholtz & Renning, 2019), clearly demonstrated both similarities and differences between the younger generation in different countries in the European continent. This current text, focussing on Generation Z in Asia, has further addressed the lack of understanding of the younger generation outside of the United States through our analysis of the characteristics of this generation in different Asian countries. This was our objective when developing this text. Therefore, we have taken a contextual approach by examining the characteristics of Generation Z, not only in an under-explored continent but also by comparing regions and countries within Asia.

Is there an Asian Generation Z?

One objective of this book was, therefore, to explore the idea of an Asian Generation Z, by investigating whether there were commonalities between countries in relation to the attitudes and behaviours of this younger generation. The answer to the question of whether such a thing as an Asian Generation Z exists is mixed. On the one hand, it is clear that the characteristics of young people in each of the Asian countries discussed in this book, are driven by the unique history and context within that nation. The impact of distinct elements of national culture in some countries (such as collectivism in India for example) and religion in other areas (such as the perseverance of Islam in driving behaviours in countries such as Indonesia), as well as the specific nature of the economic and educational system in each country, means that we do not see overall convergence between the attitudes and behaviours of the younger generation across countries in Asia. That said, on the other hand, there are some contextual drivers – and, thus, attitudes and behavioural characteristics – that seem to be common across the continent.

A Strong Influence of Technological Advancement

One trend that is common to Generation Z in all of the Asian countries considered here is the influence of technology on their lives and behaviour. It is clear that the members of Generation Z in Asia are not only digital natives but have grown up in a world of both social media and mobile technology. Even more so than Millennials, this is a generation who conducts much of its business – and social life – online. Across all of the countries in this book, we see the common use of the Internet and social media for carrying out the daily activities of life, should it be interacting with friends, shopping, or collaborating with colleagues. We also see the influence of technology on the way that this generation operates. For example, we see a rise in the use of cashless transactions across many of the countries. That said, there is also evidence that this generation still values face-to-face contact and interaction and, in some cases, even prefers it to that via online social media.

Technology also affects the way that this generation makes decisions as a consumer or employee. The fact that so much information is readily available via the Internet, as well as a network of millions of people via social media, means that young people in Asia are easily able to gather evidence about which purchases are the most appropriate, which restaurants to visit and so on. Thus, we see a generation who is willing and able to research the quality of a product or experience online and to discuss this with their social network. It may be this trend that has led to an apparent reliance of the older members of Generation Z's families on their younger relatives as we see them influencing their parents in their purchase decisions. With Millennials, we have also seen the beginnings of a trend in researching employers via websites such as Glassdoor – we might expect this to become the norm with Generation Z once they enter the workforce in larger numbers.

In relation to consumerism in particular, we also see here the rise of the role of influencers in many Asian countries. Generation Z in Asia will often draw their appreciation of aspects such as fashion, entertainment, and other products and experiences from those who are famous, for example, as a musician or actor, or simply as an influencer online. The increase in the number – and impact – of online influencers – who are famous only for their online profile, is a relatively new trend that we see across the world but perhaps particularly in Asia and with this younger generation. Thus Generation Z's buying choices will also often be strongly affected by the recommendations (or otherwise) of these influencers online.

The above trends have created an environment that is more challenging for vendors and employers alike. Generation Z in Asia appears to have high expectations in relation to the quality of the products it buys, experiences it invests in, and employers it works for. In this way, they may be similar to Millennials, with the difference that they are prepared to seek the evidence for this quality online and go elsewhere if they need to.

A Generation that Cares

In many of the countries, we also here see a generation that cares about the people and environment that surrounds it. Generation Z in Asia, more so than that in Europe, is characterised by their strong respect and reliance on family – particularly their parents – for guidance and feedback. In some cases, this might be driven by religion, in others, this is simply the result of a cultural emphasis on the family unit. While the concept of 'helicopter parenting' is also apparent in the western world, in Asia, we see typically high expectations of Generation Z from their parents and the continuance of close bonds within families into adulthood.

The chapters here also suggest that Generation Z cares about its surroundings – whether that be in relation to the environment, political events or other aspects. Not only does this generation care, but it appears to be willing to stand up for its opinions. This activist tendency that has become part of the stereotype of Generation Z in Europe through publicity surrounding, for example, Greta Thunberg and her campaigning on climate change, is also apparent in Asia, in, for example, the attentiveness of Turkish members of Generation Z to politics and the role of young people in political activism in Hong Kong.

Same, Same but Different

To some degree, the above trends are similar to those that we see worldwide; however, in Asia, we see the nature of these characteristics shaped by the particular cultural and institutional context in which the younger generation have grown up. Asia is a continent of diversity across many aspects of its context. While aspects such as technological advancement might be similar, other aspects appear to be driving difference in young people's attitudes, preferences, and expectations. For example, if we take the economic environment, we can compare the economic strength and dominance of China with the growth in countries such as Indonesia and India. It is clear that religion has a strong impact in Muslim countries, where we begin to see the combination of western and Muslim attitudes in, for example, the hybridisation of fashion in Indonesia. We can also see a clear impact of changes in the educational system and of different degrees of globalisation if we compare countries such as China and the United Arab Emirates.

These differences are important in our understanding of what motivates the younger generation to buy a product, or to apply for a particular job. In sum, this book supports the notion that the characteristics of Generation Z – and probably of other generations – are not universal. It is, thus, essential that those commentators and consultants that tend to drive the practice of employers, marketers, and political parties in trying to attract and retain the younger generation, consider the intersection of both year of birth and location or nationality, rather than focussing on age alone. We see here, not only that Generation Z in Asia is different to that in Europe but also that there is heterogeneity within Generation Z in Asia, based on the individual country context.

Future Prospects for the Younger Generation

Reading the chapters within this book might suggest generally positive prospects for Generation Z in Asia. At the time of writing the chapters for this edited text, most of the countries in Asia were experiencing a time of economic buoyancy, a growth in policies to improve the quality of education and employment, and a rise in mobility and opportunities. Coupled with technological advancement, we might have predicted a sense of optimism around the future of Generation Z in Asia, despite ongoing concerns in some counties in relation to natural disasters (Indonesia) or political unrest (Hong Kong).

At the current time, however, the world, including the whole of Asia, is experiencing the COVID-19 pandemic. While many Asian countries have experienced epidemics before through SARS, H1N1, and MERS, the scale and severity of this crisis is unprecedented and will be unlike anything that this generation – or their parents – have experienced before. Thus, many of Generation Z will recently (or currently) have experienced unexpected hardship through illness, bereavement, or the restriction of their freedom. Even in this, we see differences between Asian countries in the spread and control of the virus. For example, some of Generation Z in China, as the original epicentre of the pandemic, will have spent weeks on lockdown in Hubei Province, while in South Korea, Generation Z will have experienced the effective use of test and trace to apparently control the virus quickly and effectively. It is also not yet clear whether Asia will experience the same depths of economic recession expected in Europe or whether Asian countries will experience a second peak of the virus.

It is not known as yet what influence the COVID-19 pandemic and the experiences associated with this will have on Generation Z's attitudes and expectations. Will those who have experienced the pandemic during those vital formative years develop values that are different to those who have already been through this process? It is possible perhaps that this will form an inflection point in relation to attitudes and expectations and thus we will see a new generation emerge – the 'C' (Coronavirus) Generation. Only time will tell.

References

Mannheim, K. (1952). The problem of generations. In P. Kecskemeti (Ed.), *Karl Mannheim: Essays* (pp. 276–322). New York, NY: Routledge.

Parry, E., & Urwin P. (2011). Generational differences in work values: A review of theory and evidence. *International Journal of Management Reviews*, *13*(1), 79–96.

Parry, E., & Urwin, P. (2017). The evidence base for generational differences: Where do we go from here? *Work, Aging and Retirement*, *3*(2), 140–148.

Scholtz, C., & Renning, A. (2019). *Generations Z in Europe: Inputs, insights and implications*. London: Emerald Publishing Limited.

Index

www.ingramcontent.com/pod-product-compliance
Lightning Source LLC
Chambersburg PA
CBHW050646280326
41932CB00015B/2802